JOURNAL FOR THE STUDY OF THE OLD TESTAMENT SUPPLEMENT SERIES
286

Editors
David J.A. Clines
Philip R. Davies

Executive Editor
John Jarick

Editorial Board
Robert P. Carroll, Richard J. Coggins, Alan Cooper, J. Cheryl Exum,
John Goldingay, Robert P. Gordon, Norman K. Gottwald,
Andrew D.H. Mayes, Carol Meyers, Patrick D. Miller

Sheffield Academic Press

Elisha and the End of Prophetism

Wesley J. Bergen

Journal for the Study of the Old Testament
Supplement Series 286

to my mother, who taught me to read,
to David, who taught me to read carefully,
and to Brian, who taught me to re-read

Copyright © 1999 Sheffield Academic Press

Published by
Sheffield Academic Press Ltd
Mansion House
19 Kingfield Road
Sheffield S11 9AS
England

Typeset by Sheffield Academic Press
and
Printed on acid-free paper in Great Britain
by Bookcraft Ltd
Midsomer Norton, Bath

British Library Cataloguing in Publication Data

A catalogue record for this book is available
from the British Library

ISBN 1-85075-949-9

CONTENTS

Preface	7
List of Abbreviations	8

Chapter 1
INTRODUCTION 11

Chapter 2
NARRATOLOGY 15
   Introduction 15
   Author-Oriented Readings 17
   Reader-Oriented Readings 20
   Destabilizing the Dichotomy 27
   Mieke Bal 30
   Conclusion 36

Chapter 3
THE TEXT, THE READER AND THE READING 37
   The Text 37
   The Reader 39
   The Reading: Major Narratological Terms ... 40

Chapter 4
ELISHA 42
   Introduction 42
   1 Kings 19: Enter Elisha 47
   2 Kings 2.1-18: Transition 55
   2 Kings 2.19-22: Jericho's Water 66
   2 Kings 2.23-25: The Bears 68
   2 Kings 3: War against Moab 72
   2 Kings 4.1-7: The Widow's Oil 83
   2 Kings 4.8-37: The Shunammite Woman ... 87

2 Kings 4.38-41: Stew	104
2 Kings 4.42-44: Offerings	108
2 Kings 5: Naaman	111
2 Kings 6.1-7: The Floating Axe	124
2 Kings 6.8-23: The Triumph of Prophetic Power	127
2 Kings 6.24–7.20: The Siege of Samaria	136
2 Kings 8.1-6: The Shunammite Woman Returns	148
2 Kings 8.7-15: Transition	155
2 Kings 8.16-29: Transition Continues	161
2 Kings 9–13: Elijah Returns	162
2 Kings 14–25: Prophetism after Elisha	169

Chapter 5
Conclusion 175

Bibliography 180
Index of References 193
Index of Authors 199

PREFACE

An earlier version of this manuscript was presented as a dissertation to the Department of Biblical Studies at the Toronto School of Theology, under the wise and caring guidance of Brian Peckham. Brian is a thoughtful and determined critic. I confess that I was not always as careful to listen to him as he was to me, so no fault can be attached to Brian for the shortcomings of this manuscript.

I would also like to thank the members of my examination committee, who carefully read the manuscript and offered a number of valuable suggestions toward its improvement.

Any knowledge and understanding of literary theory which this manuscript demonstrates must be attributed to the guidance of David Jobling, under whom I studied at St Andrew's College in Saskatoon, Canada. It was he who introduced me to the Bible through the perspective of post-structuralism, deconstruction, feminism and a host of other disciplines. He has read earlier drafts of this manuscript, and remains a source of new ideas and encouragement.

ABBREVIATIONS

AJP	Annual of the Japanese Bible Institute
BASOR	*Bulletin of the American Schools of Oriental Research*
BDB	Francis Brown, S.R. Driver and Charles A. Briggs, *A Hebrew and English Lexicon of the Old Testament* (Oxford: Clarendon Press, 1907)
BHS	*Biblia hebraica stuttgartensia*
Bib	*Biblica*
BJS	Brown Judaic Studies
BZ	*Biblische Zeitschrift*
BZAW	Beihefte zur *ZAW*
CBQ	*Catholic Biblical Quarterly*
ExpTim	*Expository Times*
FRLANT	Forschungen zur Religion und Literatur des Alten und Neuen Testaments
HAR	*Hebrew Annual Review*
HSM	Harvard Semitic Monographs
HTR	*Harvard Theological Review*
ICC	International Critical Commentary
Int	*Interpretation*
JAAR	*Journal of the American Academy of Religion*
JAOS	*Journal of the American Oriental Society*
JBL	*Journal of Biblical Literature*
JJS	*Journal of Jewish Studies*
JNES	*Journal of Near Eastern Studies*
JSOT	*Journal for the Study of the Old Testament*
JSOTSup	*Journal for the Study of the Old Testament*, Supplement Series
JTS	*Journal of Theological Studies*
JTSA	*Journal of Theology for South Africa*
NCB	New Century Bible
NIBC	New International Bible Commentary
OTL	Old Testament Library
PEQ	*Palestine Exploration Quarterly*
RSR	*Recherches de science religieuse*
SBLDS	SBL Dissertation Series
SR	*Studies in Religion/Sciences religieuses*
ST	*Studia theologica*

TLZ	*Theologische Literaturzeitung*
TTod	*Theology Today*
TTZ	*Trierer theologische Zeitschrift*
TZ	*Theologische Zeitschrift*
VT	*Vetus Testamentum*
WBC	Word Biblical Commentary
WMANT	Wissenschaftliche Monographien zum Alten und Neuen Testament
WTJ	*Westminster Theological Journal*
ZAW	*Zeitschrift für die alttestamentliche Wissenschaft*
ZTK	*Zeitschrift für Theologie und Kirche*

Chapter 1

INTRODUCTION

The purpose of this study is to explore the effect Elisha has on the understanding the reader of Genesis–2 Kings gains concerning the role of the 'prophet' in Israel.[1] I wish to demonstrate that the Elisha narrative provides a negative judgment on prophetism and confines prophets to a rather limited scope of action in the narrative world.

As I will show, the narrative never provides for the reader an explicit condemnation of prophets or prophetic activity. Elisha is consistently regarded as a true prophet of YHWH, and his power is never questioned. There will always be, however, fragments of doubt as to the nature of the connection between YHWH and Elisha. There will also arise questions regarding his character, and especially regarding his value to YHWH and to Israel. Finally, there will remain the question of the

---

1. Since the writing of this study, a number of new books on 2 Kings have come out, including Paul R. House, *1, 2 Kings* (Nashville: Broadman & Holman, 1995); Iain Provan, *1 and 2 Kings* (New International Biblical Commentary; Peabody, MA: Hendrickson, 1995); Ronald S. Wallace, *Readings in 2 Kings* (Edinburgh: Scottish Academic Press, 1996). While these books would have added to the body of available discussion partners, they do not anticipate my argument in sigificant ways.

More in line with my study is David Marcus, *From Balaam to Jonah: Anti-Prophetic Satire in the Hebrew Bible* (BJS, 301; Atlanta: Scholars Press, 1995). Marcus studies four stories from the Old Testament, and shows how they fit into the modern category of *satire*. One of the passages he studies is 2 Kgs 2.23-25, the story of Elisha and the bears, and he demonstrates how it contains the elements of satire (pp. 43-65). He also notes how the story never casts doubt upon the legitimacy of the prophet (p. 164), a point I will argue extensively below. Marcus makes generous use of rabbinic studies in his argument, which significantly distances his method from mine. In addition, he feels that this particular story is out of character with the other Elisha stories (p. 54), a point I would dispute.

continuation of prophetic activity, as prophetic power is lost in Israel (north) after the death of Elisha.[2]

The texts to be studied include all the references to Elisha in Genesis–2 Kings. These include 1 Kgs 19.15-21; 2 Kings 2–9; 13.14-21. Elisha will be understood as a character within the larger story of Genesis–2 Kings. I will neither make any assumptions nor reach any conclusions regarding the possibility that these texts once existed outside their present context. Rather, the character of Elisha will be studied in comparison with other characters in the larger story and in connection with the legal passages which might cause readers to judge his actions.

This study of these passages is also limited to their impact on our understanding of the role of the prophet. There are many other interesting and potentially fruitful avenues into these passages. There are also sections of the text that have no impact on our understanding of the role of the prophet. This study will limit itself to the question of the role of the prophet as presented in the narrative. Other questions will be set aside in the interests of concision.

While it may be that the Elisha material was either influenced by or had influence upon the Latter Prophets, and while it is certainly the case that readers are likely to be influenced by the larger picture of 'prophets' as it emerges in the Bible, the question regarding this influence is not dealt with. This is because I am unwilling to assume that the narrative picture of 'prophet' which might be drawn on the basis of a reading of the Latter Prophets is the same as the narrative picture arising from a reading of Genesis–2 Kings. If I cannot assume this, then a much larger study than this would be necessary to investigate the possible parallels and contrasts.

The tools I will be employing for this study can be broadly categorized as *narratological*. Since there are many reading strategies that might be included within this term, the second chapter of this book will provide a more detailed description of my method, especially as it compares with that of other people in the field. My study is intended more as a study of the biblical text than a methodological exploration, so the second chapter will explain certain choices I have made, rather than being a general methodological statement.

The biblical text, then, is understood as a narrative, with a narrator,

---

2. The lone exception, Jonah in 2 Kgs 14, will be discussed below. The prophetic activity mention in 2 Kgs 17.13, 23 may have preceded Elisha.

1. Introduction

characters, plot, action and so on. The narrative is treated as a realistic narrative, as an attempt to have readers believe that the narrative world is the 'same' world as the readers' world. Thus, disjunctions between the narrative world and the actual geography of Palestine, for example, will be treated as significant because as they threaten this identification. This does not apply, however, to the question of the miraculous. The miraculous is so important to the work of Elisha that any attempt to naturalize the miracles would demonstrate that the reader is unwilling to fully enter the world of the narrative.

While it is assumed that the text is realistic, this does not mean that I am making any statement regarding the relationship between the Elisha stories and events which took place in geographical Palestine in the ninth century BCE. I will make no judgment regarding the likelihood that the events portrayed actually took place. I do treat these texts as historical insofar as they create the history of Israel, as they create the people of Israel. Thus, the narrative is understood as an attempt to create a people who live within the society created by the text. Specifically, the role of the prophet created by the narrative is taken to be a guide for the readers' understanding of the 'correct' role for the *prophet* in the reader's society. This role is simultaneously created and delimited by the narrative.

Elisha serves to undermine the rather grandiose picture of the prophet which might otherwise be produced by the narrative. The great prophets like Moses, Samuel and Elijah are mirrored by Elisha, who crosses the Jordan on dry ground (2 Kgs 2.14), acts as adviser to kings (3.16-20), heals and restores to life (4.35; 5.14). Yet he also causes suffering (2.24; 5.27), his aid in time of battle is finally insufficient (3.27; 6.23-24), his miracles unrequested (4.28) or pointless (6.6-7). The voice of YHWH is never heard by the reader, and we have only Elisha's word that YHWH has ever spoken.[3] Thus readers are warned regarding the aggrandizement of the prophet. The prophet is powerful, but the power is not unambiguously good.

On the surface, Elisha should be ushering in a new era of peace and prosperity for Israel. Baal appears nowhere in the story to challenge the

3. While the mention of יד־יהוה in 2 Kgs 3.15 might suggest that the narrator also believes the voice of Elisha to be the true voice of YHWH, nowhere else in Genesis–2 Kings is this phrase connected to the voice of YHWH (e.g. Exod. 9.3; Num. 11.23; Deut. 2.15; Josh. 4.24; Judg. 2.15; 1 Sam. 5.6,9; 7.13; 12.15; 1 Kgs 18.46).

supremacy of YHWH. Jezebel has quietly disappeared, and the kings are portrayed in a surprisingly positive light. Elijah's victory appears complete, and Elisha remains to bask in this success. Yet these factors all reappear at the end of Elisha's mission. Thus they have not been missing; it is more that they appear to have been ignored or repressed.

The picture that finally emerges is of a prophet who fails to do precisely the things readers might expect of a prophet. Elisha has no message, at least not in the sense of proclaiming YHWH's praise or condemnation upon the acts of individuals, or of guiding them toward YHWH's goals. Elisha's actions are guided by no moral or ethical constraints. Finally, his entire existence is undercut by return to the 'real' world in 2 Kings 9, with the return of Baal, Jezebel, and the sins of the Ahab dynasty.

Chapter 2

NARRATOLOGY

Introduction

Narratology, simply put, is the study of narratives. Like the study of any other specific object, it has its particular vocabulary and rules. These derive from the difference the object of study has from any other object.

In this book, narratology will be understood as a set of descriptives or concepts rather than a method. Since the object of my study is obviously a narrative, it is logical to use narratological vocabulary in the study. The vocabulary acts as a set of tools but does not fully dictate the type of study which might be accomplished with these tools.[1]

Much of the vocabulary in this paper is common to most of narratology. That which is not is taken from Mieke Bal's *Narratology*.[2] Bal provides the most helpful introduction I have found, specifically because she proceeds from the definition of specific terms rather than from theory. This increases the intersubjectivity of the discussion.[3]

This chapter is not an attempt to outline a comprehensive theory of the study of narratives, nor even of biblical narratives. Neither will I advance a 'poetics' which would attempt to describe the inner rules governing biblical narrative. These projects have already been undertaken, with greater or lesser degrees of success. Rather, the theoretical basis of my paper will be outlined in the form of definition-through-

---

1. While any choice of tools does limit possible interpretive activity, one might use narratological tools in feminist, deconstructive, theological or ideological analysis, to name only a few.
2. Mieke Bal, *Narratology: Introduction to the Theory of Narrative* (trans. Christine van Boheemen; Toronto: University of Toronto Press, 1985).
3. I am not suggesting that Bal's work is without or beyond theory but simply that her explanation begins with definition, making the set of descriptives more readily usable.

conversation. I will not try to suggest that my method is superior to that of scholars outlined or that my scholarship has superseded theirs. Rather, I will suggest that numerous options are available to anyone doing narrative study, and I can choose only one. Thus I will defend my choice only as one viable alternative among many.

The measure used to distinguish between the various authors is to place them on a continuum between 'reader-oriented' and 'author-oriented'. This is, of course, only one possible way of describing the differences between them. It is used here because it best exemplifies the style of reading the various authors employ as it compares with my own. In each camp is a wide variety of options: author-oriented could include 'old' and 'new' New Critics, various formalists, some structuralists and so on; reader-oriented includes much of feminism, deconstruction and reader-response, as well as some liberation perspectives. I have chosen these particular examples of reading strategy because they best exemplify the various options.

As noted, this is a continuum rather than a simple distinction. Some of the authors might dispute the place I have given them. It is not my intent to criticize or praise based on my understanding of their reading practice. Neither will I be making reference to reader-response theory as the 'correct' paradigm for reading. My intent is to create an awareness of the role of readers in the production of the narrative.

The question is not one of objectivity versus subjectivity. It is more one of readers or writers taking responsibility for their own actions. Reading a text is an activity. It can be done badly, even incorrectly. Reading a text is an attempt at intersubjectivity insofar as the author has written to communicate and readers read to understand. Both parties hold a considerable degree of power in this relationship.

This is especially true in narrative, where the text attempts to create a world. In the case of biblical narrative, the stories attempt to coerce readers into believing that its world is the readers' world, that its story is the readers' story. But the creation of this narrative world is the product of both text and reader.

In reading the biblical narratives, this last fact is often obscured. This is partly due to the quality of the narrative, and partly due to its adoption as scripture by most of its readers.[4] Thus the narrative world is read as 'the world' rather than as a creation of the reading process. This

---

4. Literary critics reach a similar point by considering the Bible to be 'significant' or 'foundational' literature.

obscures the role of the reader, allowing readers to forget themselves in the production of the narrative world. This creates the illusion of the passive reader, an illusion which must be recognized as such.

Finally, reader/author-oriented must be recognized as a false dichotomy, except insofar as it describes what readers believe themselves to be doing. The only choice one has is whether to read. I cannot say that I will 'allow the text to speak for itself' and still write 'about' the text. Neither can I claim that a reading is not a 'reading of' something.[5] It is, as I said earlier, a matter of taking responsibility for my actions.

Author-Oriented Readings

Clearly the scholar who best advances the power of the author in the creation of the narrative is Robert Alter. For Alter, all power is given to the author. The purpose of reading is to understand what or how the author is trying to communicate. In making this presumption, Alter is able to bypass most of current theory, which has placed a much heavier emphasis on readers as the ones who produce a reading.[6]

Alter is all too aware of the problem this poses in biblical studies, especially as it relates to the Pentateuch and Former Prophets. The modern notion of author does not do justice to the compositional history of the ancient text, nor to the notion of writing under which these texts were produced. Nevertheless, Alter usually takes recourse in the notion of the final redactor having freedom to emend his sources. Thus he does not need to resort to the notion of textual meaning, which is outside the control of the author. Even though he acknowledges that 'there are always many feasible readings for any text',[7] in the case of the biblical story he believes it to be 'willfully, provocatively open-ended'.[8] This move allows control to be retained by the author/redactor, rather than recognizing the interested and therefore reader-directed nature of any reading.

---

5. And certainly no one would make either of these claims absolutely.
6. While 'reader-response' criticism is the most obvious example, much of feminism also belongs here due to its focus on experience, as does deconstruction, which has proclaimed the death of the author.
7. Robert Alter, *The World of Biblical Literature* (New York; Basic Books, 1992), p. 138.
8. Alter, *World*, p. 152.

Another option from the author-oriented perspective is found in the writings of Meir Sternberg. While Sternberg would likely not agree with being placed in the category of author-oriented readings, I place him here because ultimately his reader is allowed no choice in the reading process.

The Bible, according to Sternberg, is uncompromisingly ideological.[9] Nothing is allowed to override the worldview that the text attempts to establish in the reader. This ideology is also singular.[10] In practice, this means that Sternberg believes he can account for all gaps, inconsistencies and supposed divergences as functions of the narrator's art of persuasion.

Given this emphasis on the narrator and the text, readers might expect Sternberg to present himself firmly on the author-oriented end of theoretical discussion. This is, however, clearly not the case. Sternberg constantly emphasizes the role of readers in the process of reading, readers who must make judgments and fill gaps.

Nevertheless, Sternberg also operates with the notion of an ideal reader, which, not surprisingly, turns out to be himself.[11] Other readers are assigned the label of underreaders, overreaders or misreaders.[12] Thus, the reader-oriented options are quickly limited to one, the reader who is willing to place himself[13] under the authority of the omniscient narrator as presented by Sternberg.

One of the difficult aspects of this notion of a single competent reader is the number of people Sternberg must label as misreaders. While Sternberg lists only 'extreme examples', this group includes the rabbinic tradition, source critics, Christians and so on.[14] In fact, I can find few examples of readers Sternberg considers competent. In the end I am left wondering if Sternberg considers himself the only person who has ever read the Bible correctly.

---

9. I looked in vain for a clear definition of 'ideological', unfortunate given the wide variety of possible definitions. His working definition is suggested as parallel to 'worldview' and in contrast with 'didactic', suggesting both an existential and a persuasive element to the term (Meir Sternberg, *The Poetics of Biblical Narrative* [Bloomington: Indiana University Press, 1985], pp. 37-38).

10. Sternberg, *Poetics*, p. 37.

11. For this critique I am indebted to Mieke Bal, *On Storytelling* (Sonoma, CA: Polebridge Press, 1991), pp. 61-62.

12. Sternberg, *Poetics*, p. 50.

13. Sternberg's discourse uses male pronouns throughout.

14. Sternberg, *Poetics*, p. 50.

2. Narratology

Sternberg is able to maintain the idea of a single reader by claiming that the Bible is written in a style he calls 'foolproof composition'.[15] That is, all readers are drawn into the story, which establishes 'a common ground... of understanding', such that certain conclusions are inevitable.[16] The text is written in such a way that readers are drawn into its world and can easily make sense of it.

This does not mean, however, that Sternberg believes the Bible to be a piece of simplistic writing. Rather, the complex artistry of the Bible is presented in such a way that even the simplest reader can make sense of it. This style he contrasts with the elitist style of the Gospels, where the text differentiates between insiders and outsiders to its message.[17]

At first glance it would seem that Sternberg's case can be made simply by his being able to read the Bible as ideologically singular. That is, if he can do it, he must be right. There are two obvious caveats which need to be noted here.

First, the idea of foolproof composition, when combined with Sternberg's vast array of misreaders, means that he must make a distinction between foolproof and damned-foolproof. And if Sternberg's world is populated by large numbers of intelligent people he insists are damned fools, I wonder how foolproof the text can really be.[18] Second, the ability to read the text as ideologically singular is also a prime contention of Christian fundamentalists,[19] a group which certainly would not escape Sternberg's ire. Their ability to maintain this position, however, has never been convincing to the majority of biblical scholars.

Perhaps it would be helpful to take an example from Sternberg to illustrate. On pages 309-11, he cites a portion of the story of Elisha and the Shunamite (sic) woman (2 Kgs 4.12-16). As always, Sternberg uses specific passages to illustrate narratological features rather than doing detailed readings of stories as part of a narrative. In this case he is illustrating the use of surprise as a chronological gap.

---

15. Sternberg, *Poetics*, p. 50.
16. Sternberg, *Poetics*, p. 50.
17. Sternberg, *Poetics*, pp. 51, 53.
18. A similar comment is made by Daniel Boyarin, 'The Politics of Biblical Narratology', *Diacritics* 20.4 (1991), pp. 31-42 (35).
19. See the comments in D.M. Gunn, 'Reading Right: Reliable and Omniscient Narrator, Omniscient God, and Foolproof Composition in the Hebrew Bible', in D.J.A. Clines, S.E. Fowl and S.E. Porter (eds.), *The Bible in Three Dimensions* (Sheffield: JSOTSup, 87; JSOT Press, 1990), pp. 53-64 (57, 62).

20   *Elisha and the End of Prophetism*

Sternberg correctly recognizes that readers have no knowledge of the Shunammite's childlessness until it is revealed by Gehazi (v. 14). He also connects this story of childlessness to similar stories of Sarai (Gen. 11.30), Rebekah (Gen. 25.21), Rachel (Gen. 29.31), the unnamed wife of Manoah (Judg. 13.2) and Hannah (1 Sam. 1.2). Sternberg uses these possible parallels to illustrate the unusual nature of this surprise.

From there, Sternberg goes on to assume that the Shunammite's childlessness must be considered an unfortunate plight and that the Shunammite can do nothing except respond with skeptical joy. At this point, Sternberg makes an abrupt turn from description-by-comparison to an assumption that readers can only believe that all barren women in Israel have fully taken on the identity which the male world has provided for them, namely as 'childless one'.

This is how Sternberg can successfully read the text as ideologically singular. The story is open enough, is readable enough, that Sternberg's conclusion is plausible and indeed convincing to those willing to be convinced. It does not mean, however, that readers are left with no choice. The tone of the woman's reply is a gap that must be filled by the reader. Sternberg's choice of skepticism is certainly one option, but only one of many (as I will demonstrate below). Readers who chooses to read the Shunammite's tone as one of displeasure are neither misreading nor counterreading. They are simply not Sternberg-as-ideal-reader.

Reader-Oriented Readings

Given the general framework which narrative theory establishes for its practitioners, it would be difficult to imagine two more divergent descriptions of biblical narrative than those offered by Sternberg and Peter Miscall.

At first glance it is their similarities that are more in evidence. They both offer close readings of a complex and elusive text.[20] Both devote considerable space to dealing with gaps in the narrative and with parallels between stories.

The difference emerges as they deal with the questions that arise in the course of their reading. As we have seen for Sternberg, the text offers its reader a singular ideology that readers are subtly but unavoid-

20. Peter D. Miscall, *The Workings of Old Testament Narrative* (Philadelphia: Fortress Press, 1983), p. 1. For Sternberg, see pp. 18-20.

ably drawn into. For Miscall, this applies only to the clarity of description that the narrative supplies, but this clarity contrasts sharply with the 'opaqueness of significance'.[21]

One of the more helpful examples of this contrast is found in Miscall's study of Gen. 12.11-13.[22] Miscall notes the parallel between this story and a similar one in Genesis 20. He further notes the contrast between Abraham's characterization of the people of the Negeb in Gen. 20.11-13 with his recognition of the possibility of righteous people in Sodom and Gomorrah (Gen. 18.23). However, for Miscall the problem is whether to read Genesis 20 in light of Genesis 18, or vice versa. As he says, 'This would produce a quite different understanding of Abraham and his intercession with God.'[23]

Thus the text, through its use of parallel plots, themes, words and so on, forms a 'network of analogies',[24] by which 'the text itself is trying to show how it should be read'.[25] However, these parallels produce many possibilities, too many to offer definitive answers.

Further, Miscall is aware of the difficulty in trying to ascertain what the text gives and what readers supply.[26] He recognizes that there are many parallels in the text, but he also contends that it is finally readers who produce parallels.[27]

Finally, the picture of the Old Testament that emerges from Miscall is of a text that offers readers no definitive reading of itself. Even in explicit judgment statements, places where the text presumably tenders 'offers of reliable and essential knowledge',[28] Miscall demonstrates how these offers are feints, are withdrawn later, so that readers do not have a privileged site from which to perceive truth.[29]

One of the more interesting implications Miscall draws from these observations is that we need not expect our picture of God to be any clearer than are other parts of the text.[30] This is considerably different

21. Miscall, *Workings*, pp. 7, 22, 47.
22. Miscall, *Workings*, pp. 31-40.
23. Miscall, *Workings*, p. 32.
24. Miscall, *Workings*, p. 29.
25. Miscall, *Workings*, pp.13-14.
26. Miscall, *Workings*, p. 141.
27. Note, e.g., his statement, 'I establish parallels ... ', Miscall, *Workings*, p. 3.
28. Miscall, *Workings*, p. 50.
29. Miscall, *Workings*, p. 61.
30. Miscall, *Workings*, p. 37.

from Sternberg's notion of the centrality of God's consistent omniscience.[31] This difference is not easily resolved, since both authors move quickly to the biblical text to demonstrate their points. Miscall's point is certainly easier to defend, since he need only show one example of an inconsistent characterization of God, whereas Sternberg must (and claims to) be able to demonstrate consistency throughout the text.

It is not evading the issue, however, to again point out that the difference lies in the attitude of each author to the position of the reader. Sternberg's singular male reader has been discussed above, as well as by Mieke Bal.[32] But who is Miscall's reader? It comes as no surprise to find Miscall discussing deconstruction at length prior to his extended reading of 1 Samuel.[33] His work shows clear signs of the influence of deconstructive thought. Finally, however, he claims that his reading is not deconstructive, since 'the OT... is not attempting to establish or defend some clear definitive meaning for either a character or a theme.'[34] He quotes Burton Feldman as saying, 'The OT is already deconstructed: now read it!'[35]

At this point I take exception to Miscall's stance. While Miscall's Old Testament may be already deconstructed, Sternberg's certainly is not. While I recognize that Miscall has the overwhelming weight of modern biblical scholarship on his side,[36] the position for consistency still can produce numerous strong readings. Finally, Miscall's denial of deconstructive approach rings hollow. Although the inconsistency of the current text has long been noticed, the search has always continued for the consistent presentation, the source which is not at odds with itself. It is only within the confines of the postmodern agenda that the shifting text can be allowed to remain without recourse to theories of redaction or emendation. It is only a reader who is aware of decon-

31. Sternberg, *Poetics*, p. 46.
32. Bal, *On Storytelling*, p. 61.
33. Peter D. Miscall, *1 Samuel* (Bloomington: Indiana University Press, 1986), pp. xx-xxv.
34. Miscall, *1 Samuel*, p. xxiv.
35. Miscall, *1 Samuel*, p. xxiv.
36. By this I mean that scholarship has long recognized that the biblical text presents a variety of positions regarding its characters and even its God. This is the basic impetus behind the division of the text into sources, J's theology being noticeably different from E's. While traditional scholarship has not been formulated in deconstructive terms, the impact of traditional scholarship is clearly noticeable in Miscall's reading.

struction who can recognize the deconstructive elements in a text. And since deconstruction always claims that the text is always and already deconstructed,[37] one wonders if Miscall's disclaimer is in fact not precisely its opposite.[38]

I wonder also what final reason Miscall would suggest for the writing and preservation of his text where change is the only constant. In this respect Sternberg is certainly correct. The Bible is undoubtedly ideological, in the sense that it wishes to convince and cajole readers into accepting its history as their history, its reality as their reality. While the picture readers find there may not conform to their notions of coherence, Alter is helpful in suggesting that readers must not anachronistically impose modern notions of unity on an ancient text, but must instead look for the text's own unity.[39]

Nevertheless, Miscall is the biblical scholar who offers the most thorough discussion of the dialogue between reader and text, both in the reading of the biblical text in general and in his reading in particular. Like his own picture of the shifting biblical text, he does not present a singular portrayal of the reader- versus author-oriented aspects of meaning production. This is to his credit, for as a reader he wishes to remain true to the text, but as a self-conscious reader he recognizes that readings are productions of readers, that it is he who is writing his books, rather than attempting to erase his own presence in the process.

His work also stands as an important illustration of the fact that reader-oriented readings are no less textual than author-oriented ones. At no point is Miscall any more guilty of displacing his own ideology on to the biblical text than are Alter or Sternberg. Neither is his attention to the details of the text less rigorous. In this way, he exposes the reader/author-oriented dichotomy as illusory, or at best a purely heuristic device. The distinction I have been pursuing in effect only describes who it is who receives the credit or blame for what readers find in a text. It does not affect what is found or how it is found.

37. Jonathan Culler makes this point constantly in his *On Deconstruction* (Ithaca, NY: Cornell University Press, 1982).

38. While Miscall is correct that what he attempts is not strictly speaking like the work of Derrida, de Man or Johnson, it may be equated with what Stephen Moore calls 'soft deconstruction' (Miscall, *1 Samuel*, p. xxiv; Stephen D. Moore, *Literary Criticism and the Gospels* [New Haven: Yale University Press, 1989], p. 136).

39. Alter, *World*, p. 72.

Another pair of authors who have helpfully articulated the impact of the reader on the reading process is Danna Fewell and David Gunn. Jointly, Fewell and Gunn have produced numerous works, including most recently a general introduction to the study of biblical narrative,[40] and a reading of Genesis–2 Kings.[41] Both of these are works of considerable theoretical complexity, and thus their approach is not easily summarized in a few short paragraphs. Placed on the reader/author-oriented axis, they come down clearly on the reader-oriented side. They explicitly designate their work as a 'reader-oriented approach'[42] and characterize texts as 'multivalent'[43] and 'inherently unstable'.[44]

The two books differ, however, in the way they approach the biblical text. *Narrative in the Hebrew Bible* can be broadly characterized as exposition-by-expansion, where short biblical stories are expanded, gaps are filled in and details are added. The rather laconic story of Judah and Tamar in Genesis 38 is expanded into 12 pages of comment, much of which involves instructing readers as to how to construe the various actions and attitudes of the characters, informing them of things the characters 'can' or are 'expected' to do.[45] This style of reading is not as significantly reader-oriented as they claim, since readers are guided toward specific choices in decisions of interpretation, and these choices are made to sound natural or obvious.

The other main difficulty in this book is its lack of clarity regarding the interests of readers. Although Gunn and Fewell do attempt to keep the reader in mind regarding who is doing the reading, they fail to ask the question of why the reader is reading. Surely a distinction must be made between the reader reading for pleasure and one reading for spiritual guidance, between the reader with patriarchal interest and the reader with feminist interests.

In this context, *Gender, Power, and Promise* is a much more explicitly interested book, which also makes it a more interesting book. Fewell and Gunn state from the outset that 'we go looking for women

---

40. David M. Gunn and Danna Nolan Fewell, *Narrative in the Hebrew Bible* (Oxford: Oxford University Press, 1993).

41. Danna Nolan Fewell and David M. Gunn, *Gender, Power and Promise* (Nashville: Abingdon Press, 1993).

42. Gunn and Fewell, *Narrative*, p. 9.

43. Gunn and Fewell, *Narrative*, p. 9.

44. Gunn and Fewell, *Narrative*, p. 10.

45. Gunn and Fewell, *Narrative*, p. 38.

in our reading'.[46] This interest is contrasted with the interest or subject of the text, or as they put it, 'the governing conscious (or unconscious), the point of view whose interests this text expresses, or better, constructs'.[47] Thus Fewell and Gunn clearly attempt to read against the grain of the text, since they assume the biblical text to be directed toward 'adult male heads of households'.[48]

Nonetheless, *Gender* still adopts a rather open-ended, innocent stance toward the text. While open-endedness is a hallmark of any good study, it cannot be used to cover the reader's interests. Fewell and Gunn claim that 'we do not know where our own reading will take us'.[49] While that is to be expected, readers of *Gender* are also left wondering why it is they are on this journey to nowhere. Even if they assume an open-ended stance, they still might prefer to have a specific goal, while being open to the possibility of arriving elsewhere.

The discussion around the role of readers in the production of the narrative must also deal with the question of the nature of the text itself, for certainly what readers bring to their reading is dependant upon what they think they are reading. Robert Culley has brought this clearly to our attention. He describes the biblical narrative as a composite, traditional, religious text.[50] Each of these four elements receives individual attention, but finally it is the combination of the elements that separates Culley's work from most other studies. He discusses various authors who share parts of his framework. For example, he notes the emphasis historical criticism has placed on the composite nature of the Bible but claims that it has done so at the expense of its textuality.[51] Similarly, he notes various literary scholars who have written about the Bible as text but have neglected its composite and traditional nature.[52]

Finally, Culley opts for a fluid view of 'text', one which wishes to treat the narrative as a story with some sort of unity, while recognizing its composite and traditional nature. In this picture, it is readers who have a choice as to how they will read or what kind of perspective they

---

46. Fewell and Gunn, *Gender*, p. 18.
47. Fewell and Gunn, *Gender*, p. 17.
48. Fewell and Gunn, *Gender*, p. 13.
49. Fewell and Gunn, *Gender*, p. 20.
50. Robert C. Culley, *Themes and Variations* (Semeia Studies; Atlanta: Scholars Press, 1992), p. 6.
51. Culley, *Themes*, p. 13.
52. Culley, *Themes*, p. 29.

will adopt.[53] Culley considers his choice to be 'pragmatic', one which will best enable him to find the patterns in the text which he seeks.[54]

Culley's assertion of a pragmatic stance that chooses not to deal directly with the challenges of postmodern and feminist theory[55] at first strike me as superficial. This is belied, however, by the quality of his reading and the ease with which he can summarize the various theoretical options. In the end his casual approach to his own theory may be a ruse to disguise a bold claim to methodological uniqueness.

For all this, however, Culley does sidestep the whole question of why he wishes to undertake a study of theme and variation in biblical narrative. If his methodology is chosen because it will get him where he is going (my understanding of 'pragmatic'), readers are left uninformed as to why Culley wishes to go there, or even precisely where it is they are going. While he avoids a simplistic dichotomy between descriptive and interpretive reading, he leaves me wondering how his own work should function for me as reader.

A discussion of Josipovici's *The Book of God* forms a logical conclusion to this discussion on reader-oriented readings.[56] His work belongs here because he is so consciously liminal to the usual narratological discourse, yet so thorough in his reading of the text.

The reader-oriented character of this book is illustrated both by its subtitle (*A Response to the Bible*) and its choice of focus. For Josipovici, the central question for readers is not 'What is the text saying?' but, 'What is happening to me as I read?'[57] Further, reading a particular text is always, for Josipovici, a reading of part of the Bible, a response to a particular passage within the unity-without-closure that is the canon.[58]

This reader-oriented focus does not, however, exclude the possibility that the text wishes to make certain demands upon readers. Josipovici still insists that his reading is following the lead of the text, and he invites readers to 'trust the book itself and see where it will take us'.[59]

---

53. Culley, *Themes*, p. 43.
54. Culley, *Themes*, p. 43.
55. Culley, *Themes*, p. 33.
56. Gabriel Josipovici, *The Book of God: A Response to the Bible* (New Haven: Yale University Press, 1988).
57. Josipovici, *Book*, p. 93.
58. Josipovici, *Book*, p. 91.
59. Josipovici, *Book*, p. 27. In this quote, 'the book' clearly refers to the Bible,

One of the results of this 'canonical' reading is that he insists that Leviticus and Numbers are just as central to an understanding of the Bible as are Genesis and Samuel and must be approached in the same way. Thus he chides Alter and Sternberg for their failure to take these sections into account in their 'literary' readings, distinguishing here between the 'narratives *in* the Bible' and the 'narrative *of* the Bible'.[60]

It would require a major section of the book to discuss all the lessons in reading that can be found in *The Book of God*. For my purposes, one of the difficulties with this book is its broadly thematic character. *The Book of God* is so responsive, even antiphonal, in tone that it does not lend itself easily to use in a book such as this. The experience of reading the Bible is narrated in such a way that the book is as much or more about reading than it is about the Bible (insofar as the distinction is meaningful).

Nevertheless, Josipovici's central question ('What is happening to me as I read?') provides a useful place to begin my study of Elisha. For in order to demonstrate my thesis, I will need to account for the effect the text has on the readers' perception of the various characters in the story world. It is finally in presenting its own discourse as the 'natural' one (the effect of the omniscient narrator) that the text is able to convince the reader that prophetic discourse is 'unnatural'. Thus prophetic discourse 'cannot' offer a viable alternative to the discourse of the text.[61]

Destabilizing the Dichotomy

I have already suggested in my discussion of Miscall that the dichotomy between reader- and author-oriented readings is finally illusory. This idea needs further clarification before I can proceed to analyze the Elisha stories. There is no better place to begin this discussion than by noting the contribution of Cheryl Exum. Exum's work begins with a recognition of the complex interrelationship of voice, language and ideology. If Alter so helpfully focused our attention on the importance of speech in biblical narrative,[62] Exum tempers this recognition with the suggestion that the speech of women in the biblical story does not offer

---

but this is also precisely what Josipovici wishes us to do with his own writing.
   60.   Josipovici, *Book*, p. 91, emphasis his.
   61.   It 'cannot' if the text can convince us that its world is our world.
   62.   Robert Alter, *The Art of Biblical Narrative* (New York: Basic Books, 1981), pp. 65, passim.

28   *Elisha and the End of Prophetism*

a real alternative to the dominant male ideology of the text.⁶³ Thus, while they are given speech, their voices are not their own.

Yet Exum also claims that there are real women's voices in the text, however 'submerged'⁶⁴ or 'muted'⁶⁵ they may be. Her interest, then, lies in exposing and undermining the interests of the biblical narrators (sic).⁶⁶ Her strategy is to 'read these stories (in this case the stories of Jephthah's daughter and Michal) without being confined to them'.⁶⁷

This reading strategy suddenly muddies the rather clear distinction I have been making between reader- and the author-oriented readings. The narrative notions of text and reader are challenged by the psychoanalytic category of repression and the further introduction of deconstructive terminology. This challenge is not an occasion for disagreement, however, but an opportunity for clarification.

If in these examples Exum resists an easy placement along the reader/author-oriented axis, she does help sharpen what we might mean by reader-oriented. Reader-oriented reading is not free association. Neither is it the belief that any text can be used to support any position a reader might conceivably take.

Exum's reading of the Jephthah story describes the text as a clear articulation of male-centred ideology.⁶⁸ Both her deconstructive and psychoanalytic strategies, however, also assume that a text contains within itself a repressed element where it subconsciously includes in the story that which is repressed, in this case the voice of women.⁶⁹ Thus, readers who choose to read against the dominant ideology of the text, as women might be inclined to do, are not reading against the text so much as listening for the quiet voices that undermine the dominant one.

This idea still assumes, however, that there is a dominant voice that is heard by at least the majority of readers. This is what keeps me from placing Exum firmly on the reader-oriented pole. While I admit that a

---

63. J. Cheryl Exum, 'Murder They Wrote: Ideology and the Manipulation of Female Presence in Biblical Narrative', in Alice Bach (ed.), *The Pleasure of her Text* (Philadelphia: Trinity Press International, 1990), pp. 45-67 (58).
64. Exum, 'Murder', p. 46.
65. Exum, 'Murder', p. 59.
66. Exum, 'Murder', p. 46.
67. Exum, 'Murder', p. 58.
68. Exum, 'Murder', p. 49.
69. I use psychoanalytic language in the hope that it is more familiar to the reader. One should note that the theory is from Kristeva rather than directly Freudian.

2. Narratology

majority of scholars would agree with Exum that the world of the text is male-centred, this admission is balanced by the awareness that the scholarly community is too homogeneously white, Euro-American and middle-class to claim to encompass all or even most possible perspectives.

If the dichotomy I have been using between reader-oriented readings and author-oriented readings is finally false, then what remains to me is to describe the interested nature of all readings. As a white, Euro-American, middle-class reader, Exum recognizes that she is unable to transcend these limitations. Yet she does offer us a credible alternative to traditional readings, which allows us to read the text in a new way. This new way is determinedly feminist, and it is at this point that I am unsure how to proceed.

One of Exum's strengths is her presentation of a voice that is clearly 'other', other to my own and to much of biblical scholarship and narrative research. In recognizing that her work arises precisely out of her recognition that she wishes to read as a woman, I am left as permanently other. I can never read as a woman. I do not regret this, neither do I wish to hide it. I hope I have learned from Exum's work, but I must consciously continue to read as a man.

This can be further illustrated with reference to the individual work of Danna Fewell, another person who consciously reads as a woman. An example of how she reads a text can be found in her commentary on Joshua.[70] After introducing the major section of the book of Joshua, and noting the predominant theme of exclusion, Fewell continues by addressing the question of the place of women in the story. While this is certainly a common question in feminist scholarship, the focus on (largely absent) women[71] ignores the problem of how women can read a text that explicitly addresses itself to males.[72] This suggests that for Fewell readers are to look in the text for clues to its world (here a world with few women worth mentioning), rather than constructing a world in conjunction with the text (how might a woman reader deal with the

---

70. Danna Nolan Fewell, 'Joshua', in C.A. Newsom and S.H. Ringe (eds.), *The Women's Bible Commentary* (Louisville: Westminster/John Knox Press, 1992), pp. 63-77 (63-66).

71. Fewell locates them 'between the lines' ('Joshua', p. 64).

72. In Josh. 1.12-14, while the narrator assures us that Joshua is speaking to the tribes, Joshua's commands are directed towards men only ('your wives' versus 'the warriors among you', Josh. 1.14).

disjunction between her textual absence and her own physical presence?). The section on 'Women and men's history' moves in this direction but fails to focus on real women readers.[73] I must be careful not to judge too closely based on so little evidence. Still, short papers often allow us to see what the author believes to be key to the project.

Perhaps the author who has most consistently articulated the interested nature of all reading and writing is David Jobling. Jobling challenges us to recognize the political aspect of all writing, of both the biblical text and commentary. As he says:

> First, then, we do not insulate our work from political discourse; rather, we see our interpretation of the Bible as fully embedded in the political. The role of the biblical scholar, as I conceive it, is to *take responsibility* for the discourse of the Bible ... (namely) all ways ... in which the Bible works upon us and our culture, how it has entered everything from the structure of the western novel to the Gulf War.[74]

A full discussion of the impact of the above statement on biblical studies would be a dissertation in itself. In part, this thesis is written in response to the challenge of Jobling and others to integrate the political and the theological into textual studies. For the most part, however, Jobling's comments will affect my work as a guide for the goal of my reading rather than in specifically methodological ways, for much of his work is better categorized as meta-theoretical. It would be a disservice to the larger program of his work to attempt to replicate specific methodological aspects of his reading strategy.

Mieke Bal

Mieke Bal merits her own section for a number of reasons. She is the most prolific of the authors reviewed thus far. Her work is also the most diverse, ranging as will be seen from theory to metacriticism to criticism. Finally, her work is densely written, often much more challenging than the more accessible writings studied thus far. Hers are also the works that will have the most impact on my discussion of Elisha.

As I suggested, Bal's work can be seen to fall into three general

---

73. Fewell, 'Joshua', p. 65.
74. 'Hannah's Desire', *Bulletin of The Canadian Society of Biblical Studies* 53 (1994), pp. 19-32.

2. Narratology

categories. *Narratology*[75] and major sections of *On Storytelling*[76] are works of theory, providing readers with a set of descriptors by which to account for the various parts of narrative writing. They can be distinguished from works on biblical narrative in that they make no attempt to describe how or why a particular text or group of texts work. Rather, Bal's objective is to describe how one might go about doing what Sternberg or Alter claim to be doing.

Murder and Difference[77] fits the category of metacriticism in that it is a criticism of criticism. In some ways this book is almost historical-critical in orientation, except that the object of Bal's historical/semiotic analysis is works of biblical criticism. Thus, she subjects the various critics to careful scrutiny regarding the sources and *Sitz im Leben* of their work. However, this is done not via a study of the culture of the authors but through careful semiotic analysis of their work, using especially the idea of *codes*.

She begins with the premise that 'the hermeneutic approach practiced within an academic field or discipline is based on a code that defines and delineates this field or discipline'.[78] However, contra Sternberg, Bal does not dismiss or denigrate the work of other critics. Rather, she demonstrates that their work, like her own, is limited by the semiotic conventions and constraints that a particular methodology imposes.

This approach has the effect of increasing the possible conversation between disciplines, as all are taken seriously, and read carefully. This is in stark contrast to Sternberg, whose dismissive attitude does little to endear him to the bulk of the guild.

Bal's reading and subsequent deconstruction of the work of traditional scholars also provides a significant response to the charge of rampant subjectivity that is often made against literary scholars. As she so clearly demonstrates, her work is no more subjective than is any other, it is simply her choice of codes which distinguishes her reading. She also argues, however, that the choice of codes is not an innocent one. Codes are 'restrictive', 'interested' and 'institutionalized'.[79] The choice of codes results from and in a particular construction of reality

---

75. Bal, *Narratology*.
76. Bal, *On Storytelling*.
77. Mieke Bal, *Murder and Difference* (Bloomington: Indiana University Press, 1988).
78. Bal, *Murder and Difference*, p. vii.
79. Bal, *Murder and Difference*, pp. 4-5.

that arises in a particular social context. Codes are controlled by the dominant groups within specific institutions. This control extends both to type of code used and uses of a specific code.[80]

Finally she argues for the use of multiple, interdisciplinary codes in which the limits and interests of individual codes are made evident by their contrast with others.[81] This interdisciplinarity does not lead to greater objectivity but to greater honesty as each 'recognizes itself as a code, with all a code's limitations, interests, and hermeneutic power'.[82]

Both *Lethal Love*[83] and *Death and Dissymmetry*[84] are more strictly works of criticism. While Bal recognizes that issues of methodology remain central to her ability to offer convincing readings of the biblical text, these works demonstrate what Bal's theory can produce when applied to narrative texts.[85]

It would be difficult in the space of a few paragraphs or pages to summarize all I have learned from reading Bal. Much of what I have read has been absorbed in a less conscious way, so as to be apparent to readers without my being aware of my debt. This is, of course, true of much that we read. There are, however, a few aspects of her theory which will become important in our reading of the Elisha stories and which I readily acknowledge as relying upon Bal's work.

One of the key questions which has fascinated biblical scholars for centuries in relation to Genesis–2 Kings is, who speaks? This question has led to theories of Mosaic authorship for the Pentateuch, as well as to the more elaborate theories of the documentary hypotheses and the Deuteronom(ist)ic History. These, of course, are often used in conjunction with theologies of revelation since, as Sternberg notes, the narrator of the text is omniscient in a world where only God is omniscient.

In much of modern literary theory, the question of who speaks is

---

80. Bal, *Murder and Difference*, p. 7.
81. Bal, *Murder and Difference*, pp. 3, 96.
82. Bal, *Murder and Difference*, p. 3.
83. Mieke Bal, *Lethal Love* (Bloomington: Indiana University Press, 1987).
84. Mieke Bal, *Death and Dissymmetry* (Chicago: University of Chicago Press, 1988).
85. I suspect that Bal would object to my differentiation between criticism and metacriticism, for it reinstitutes the distinction between *text* and *criticism* upon which much of biblical scholarship depends, and which she critiques. I maintain the distinction from the perspective of narratology, *criticism* not usually being written in a narrative style.

often addressed by discussions of *point of view*.[86] Bal, however, prefers to borrow the term 'focalization' from Genette, while altering his definition.[87] Using this term, she can distinguish between the focalizer (the one who sees) and the focalized (that which is seen), while distinguishing focalizer from both narrator and character.

Bal equates focalization with both 'center of interest' and 'orientation'.[88] It includes the concepts of '*selection*, from among all possible materials, the content of the narrative', '*vision*' both in the concrete sense of *seeing* as well as the abstract sense of 'considering something from a certain angle', and '*presentation*'.[89]

One of the key uses Bal makes of focalization is the production of 'a non-coincidence between technical speaker, or voice, and ideological "speaker", or focalizer'.[90] That is, she alerts us to the possibility that the one who speaks, whether this is the narrator or a character, may be presenting the views of another, albeit unintentionally. The unintentional aspect of this process allows for a unified presentation of a character, while recognizing the intrusion of an ideological perspective which we recognize from other parts of the narrative.

Thus focalization, rather than being a typology of narratives as in Genette, becomes a means to clarify the attempt made by aspects of the narrative to impose meaning on the whole. This attempt is what Bal calls 'force'. Force is defined as a 'combination of interest and urgency'.[91] It is at the level of force that the ideological aspect of narratives comes to the fore, as the speaker (whether narrator or character) attempts to move beyond the mimetic to impose meaning upon a text. Thus, force is the foundation of meaning.[92]

For my purposes, force becomes important as I attempt to delineate the closure of meaning which the text might wish to enforce on the reading. This, as Bal points out, should be most noticeable where it

---

86. See the helpful discussion in Adele Berlin, 'Point of View in Biblical Narrative', in Stephen Geller (ed.), *A Sense of Text* (Winona Lake, IN: Eisenbrauns, 1983), pp. 71-113.

87. Gerard Genette, *Narrative Discourse: An Essay in Method* (trans. Jane E. Lewin; Ithaca, NY: Cornell University Press, 1980), p. 189. The reasons for Bal's preference are clearly articulated in *Narratology*, pp. 100-102.

88. Bal, *On Storytelling*, p. 92.
89. Bal, *On Storytelling*, p. 92.
90. Bal, *On Storytelling*, p. 1.
91. Bal, *Death and Dissymmetry*, p. 130.
92. Bal, *Death and Dissymmetry*, p. 134.

fails, where the excess of force causes fissures in the surface of the narrative.[93] It is at these points, which I suspect other scholars have also noticed but have assigned to other causes, that both force and its failure will become evident. If I am right that the text wishes to present the reader with an anti-prophetic meaning, then this should be most noticeable precisely where the force needed to impose coherence cannot be contained without the voices used sounding shrill or stressed.

My study of Elisha will not, however, be a reading based solely or even largely upon Bal's theory. This is due to a number of factors. First, the ease with which Bal handles theory occasionally leads to neologistic excess, a charge to which she admits.[94] While I will strive for methodological clarity at all points, terms like 'extradiegetic' would require more explanation than their own explanatory power is worth.

Second, while Bal is not an inconsistent critic, she is quite clear that for her narratological precision is a means to various types of criticism, rather than a type of criticism itself. Thus, there is no single Balian theory which I can follow. Her work moves from speech-act to psychoanalytic theory, or even a combination of both.[95] It is always feminist and undeniably ideological, but each of these terms have enough variation within them to provide only the barest outline of a generalized methodology.[96]

Nevertheless, Bal will remain my key exemplar as I work through the Elisha stories. No one else has combined theory and criticism in such a helpful way. Especially helpful will be the delineation of terms that is found in *Narratology*, since narratological terms are often used by different authors in different ways.

One final note from Bal. One of the difficulties she addresses in *Narratology* is the definition of the term *narrator*.[97] For Bal, the narrator is 'that agent which utters the linguistic signs which constitute the text'.[98] While this is a usable definition, she allows me no way to distinguish

---

93. Bal, *Death and Dissymmetry*, p. 134.
94. She calls it 'terminological exuberance' (Bal, *On Storytelling*, p. 95).
95. As seen in her statement, 'psychoanalysis *is* a speech-act theory' (Bal, *Death and Dissymmetry*, p. 135).
96. Note the variety of approaches taken in *Ideological Criticism of Biblical Texts* (Semeia, 59; Atlanta: Scholars Press, 1992).
97. Bal, *Narratology*, pp. 120-26.
98. Bal, *Narratology*, p. 120.

between this agent and the specific agent whose 'I' utters the parts of the story normally called narration.

For example, in the following sentence it would be helpful to distinguish three 'speakers':

> Then the prophet Elisha called a member of the company of prophets and said to him, 'Gird up your loins; take this flask of oil in your hand, and go to Ramoth-Gilead' (2 Kgs 9.1).

The first 'speaker' is responsible for the words from 'Then the prophet' to 'said to him'. The second 'speaker' is Elisha, as is indicated in the English by quotation marks. The third 'speaker' is the one uttering all of these linguistic signs, whom Bal calls the *narrator*. But if this third speaker is the narrator, what am I to call the first speaker?

One possible answer is to employ *implied author* in place of Bal's narrator, thus leaving *narrator* for the parts that are strictly narration. The difficulty with *implied author* has been discussed by numerous authors. For Bal, *implied author* 'is the *result* of the investigation of the meaning of a text, and not the *source* of that meaning'.[99] Thus, if I recognize the participation of the reader in the production of textual meaning, *implied author* is more than I wish to say.

Given the impasse I find myself in, I will employ *narrator* to speak of the 'voice' of those parts of the text that are not direct discourse. I will contrast this with the term *narrative* to speak of the impact of the whole, the direct and indirect discourse together. The term is deliberately non-anthropomorphizing, for the 'voice' of the whole does not exist outside the act of reading, outside the consciousness of the reader. Since the 'result' of a reading is an abstraction of the reader, I cannot pretend that I am examining the work of another. *Narrative* should be thought of as a heuristic device only and says nothing about the possible intention of the storytelling or the storyteller. *Narrative*, the whole-as-it-is-read, is further distinguished from the *text,* the marks on paper which the reader reads.

This distinction between *narrator* and *narrative* also allows me to avoid the problematic *implied author*, whose 'voice' is always also a production of the reader. This will become important as I examine the many parallels between the Elisha corpus and other stories in Genesis– 2 Kings. Since parallels are produced by the reader, I can argue that

---

99. Bal, *Narratology*, p. 120.

they exist in the narrative, without deciding if they are either a deliberate production of the author or an unavoidable feature of the text.[100]

Conclusion

The authors above form a broad spectrum of options for the reader approaching the text with narratological tools. This is especially true as I read an ancient text whose authors are largely unknown and unknowable to me, and whose poetics are discernible based solely on a study of this text.

The choices I will make in the use of these tools will be based on my question. My question is finally one that attempts to grasp the construction of a particular part of the story world. I want to understand Elisha as part of the textual creation of the category 'prophet', and what impact these stories have on our (re)construction of the role and function of the prophet in the text's world.

This necessitates careful distinctions between *narrator, narrative* and *character*, in order to account for the effect of the text on our constructed world. It means attention must be paid both to the intricacies of biblical narrative and to the possible parallels between this story and others in the text, between these characters and both earlier and later characters.

These and many other details will be worked out as I read and write. The lack of narratological study of my passage provides both opportunity and challenge. The success of this venture will depend on a balance between methodological precision and simple reading competence, between attention to detail and recognition of the bigger picture. I intend to read Elisha as a somewhat comic figure, while keeping a close eye out for bears.

---

100. See the comments on 'Cross-References' in Peter D. Miscall, *Isaiah* (Readings:A New Biblical Commentary; Sheffield: JSOT Press, 1993), p. 20.

Chapter 3

THE TEXT, THE READER AND THE READING

The Text

The question that this section attempts to answer is how I as a modern reader conceive of the conditions of the production and initial consumption of this ancient text. While this question may at first appear out of place in a 'narratological' study, it becomes important as my reader (you) attempts to understand particular moves that the reader in the analysis makes.

This statement regarding the production and consumption of this text is a working hypothesis. It is both a presupposition of my work, and a conclusion arising from it. That is, I cannot understand the text apart from some understanding of when and why it was produced, and I also cannot understand when and why it was produced apart from a reading of the text, since the text itself is my major piece of evidence. As the text is my main piece of evidence, a reading of the text must always take priority over any assumptions regarding the conditions of production of the text. The working hypothesis below is one that has already taken into account my particular reading of the Elisha stories.

I will be reading the text (both the Elisha stories and the whole of Genesis–2 Kings) as a product of Israel under Persian rule. This context informs my reading in that it supposes that the role of 'king' is no longer one present in the society of the author, while the role of 'prophet' likely is. I am assuming that prophetism in some form is still practiced in Persian Israel, and that the author is dealing with ancient prophets in a way that affirms his understanding of the 'correct' role of prophets in his own society. The question as to the role of the 'prophet' is one with direct consequences for the author's understanding of his own world.

The relationship between the text and the social world of its production is crucial, insofar as I understand the central question of history-writing[1] to be 'Who are we?' J. Huizinga has defined 'history' as 'the intellectual form in which a civilization renders account to itself of its past'.[2] Aside from the problems of any work being carried out by a 'civilization' for 'itself', the process of the writing and dissemination of 'history' is clearly aimed at a reader, who, in the context of the writing of Israel's 'history', is likely thought of as someone inside the civilization being described. Thus, for readers the question 'What happened to us in the past?' is linked to the question 'Who is this "us" who is being described?' In this way, an account of the past is always also an account of the present. This connection between past and present is true for both the ancient and modern reader. This is a (hi)story which clearly wishes to become 'my (hi)story' for its reader.

Within this definition of history-writing, I understand the 'we' of its ancient producers and consumers to be those who consider themselves to be the ruling class in Israel, its 'natural' leaders. These people might include descendants of the kings, as well as those of the households of current or former high-ranking officials. It is difficult if not impossible to ascertain the amount of real political power this group holds at the time of this writing.

This rather limited view of 'we', however, needs also to be broadened to include in some fashion those whom the ruling class also considers to be 'Israel'. The legal material is written so as to be binding upon all of Israel, rather than as rules specific to the ruling class. Further, there are significant sections that place limitations on the division of 'Israel' into class categories (e.g. Lev. 25.23-38). Thus, while the text is written by and for the elite, it claims to include within its audience 'all Israel' (Deut. 1.1; 31.1 and passim).

The text is a product of a group that does not include 'prophets' among its members. Nor would it include those who would have comprised groups that resemble the 'sons of the prophets' as portrayed in the text. Yet the text also would claim to include these groups, insofar as it defines their 'proper' role in 'Israelite society'.

---

1. I use 'history-writing' here to distinguish the act of writing from the events which the writing describes.

2. J. Huizinga, 'A Definition of the Concept of History', in R. Klibansky (ed.), *Philosophy and History: Essays Presented to Ernst Cassirer* (New York: Harper & Row, 1963), p. 9, as quoted in John Van Seters, *In Search of History: Historiography in the Ancient World and the Origins of Biblical History* (New Haven: Yale University Press, 1983), p. 1.

3. *The Text, the Reader and the Reading* 39

If I would attempt a reading that seeks to address its society 'from below', I believe that I would need to read against the grain of the text. My particular reading might form the preliminary study to such a reading, but makes no claim to be doing this kind of analysis.

The above statement is meant to provide a general introduction to my reading. This is what my reader believes the text to be. The reading below will not attempt to discuss any of these points individually, nor to provide substantiation for them. Hopefully the reasons for these beliefs will become clear as you read my reading.

The Reader

In the context of this study, the question posed is how 'readers' understand the prophets, and their role in society. While this question may not be the direct question addressed by the ancient author, it is possible to study a text and ask regarding the effect this text may have upon the readers as they attempt to understand the question 'Who are we?'. The difficulty in studying this question is compounded by the fact that the ancient text is read by modern readers. The modern reader, however, is not analyzing the story, but is drawn into it, as the story wants to become the reader's story. This is not an analysis of a hypothetical ancient reading, but a modern reading of an ancient story, with a reader who wishes to resonate as much as possible with the narrative themes. For the modern reader, the question remains 'Who/what are prophets?' rather than 'Who were prophets?'.

I use the term *reader* to denote one possible creator of a narrative. My reader is in most ways myself, but I find the term *reader* helpful as I try to present a reading that is one of many valid readings. I will try to present readings that are possible conclusions based upon certain evidence and presuppositions, but which are not necessary or unavoidable conclusions. I will also demonstrate the plausibility of my reading based upon the actual readings of others.

My reader will also assume the position of one who is naively credulous. This will be most noticeable as I continue to attempt to understand the story through a straightforward, chronological reading. My reader will desire to make sense of the story in its current form, rather than rearranging incidents or details to better suit his or her sense of 'good history'. My reader will also continue to read Elijah and Elisha as two separate characters, rather than choosing to read them as one character in two forms, despite the fact that this conclusion might follow logically from the analysis. This credulity is not a necessary part of a narrative reading, but is merely the strategy adopted by my reader.

The Reading: Major Narratological Terms

In self-consciously doing a reading of a text, it is helpful to distinguish as much as possible between conclusions based upon simple observation, and those based upon less verifiable criteria. In order to facilitate this, I will be distinguishing between *text* and *narrative*. In this study, *text* will be used to designate the words on the page. Thus, two texts can be compared to one another by comparing word usage, syntax, and other aspects of words on a page that are subject to simple verification.

When text is read, it becomes a *narrative*, a story that is the creation of readers when they read. When I compare two narratives, my observations will be built upon comparisons of plot, theme, character development, or more general impressions based upon my understanding of the narrative world.

The *narrator* is the voice who utters all words that are not the direct speech of one of the characters. The delineation of the narrator's voice can be done on the basis of *text*, but an understanding of the voice of the narrator can only be done on the basis of *narrative*. Similarly, the voice of the whole, narrator and direct speech, can be described either as *text* or *narrative*, depending on whether one is talking on the level of grammar or the level of understanding. The voice of the whole does not need a separate term, for its voice *is* the narrative, always a creation of the encounter between reader and text.

As readers read, they create a *narrative world*, an internal picture of the geography, politics, economics, religion and general society of his encounter with a text. This world is constructed from a whole host of material, including the society and personality of the reader, the reader's general understanding of the historical time and place in which the narrative is set, the reader's understanding of the time and place of the text's composition, and of course the text itself. The various materials are not separable from one another, insofar as each is transformed by proximity to the other. For example, the readers' personality will both transform and be transformed by their understanding of the time and place of the story. For this reason, the goal in describing a narrative world is not to finally construct the 'correct' world (for this, too, is a

3. *The Text, the Reader and the Reading*

text to be read), but to construct as much as possible a world that is useful to my reader in further refining his or her own narrative world.

Each narrative world that is constructed operates by a system of rules and expectations. Included in this are the *roles* that the various actors in the narrative play, the systems of power that govern the interaction between characters, and various other aspects that are necessary for any reader to make sense of a particular narrative world. In this world, the various characters are assigned roles, sometimes by the text (e.g. king, prophet), and sometimes by the reader (e.g. antagonist, simple farmer). Each role contains certain expectations, which the character either fulfills or thwarts.

The rules and expectations of the narrative world need not coincide with the rules and expectations of the reader's society, nor in this case with the rules and expectations of the actual society that the narrative claims to describe. The actions of a particular character within the narrative world are subject to the rules and expectations of that world (although they may violate the norms which the narrative world sets forth), but they are not necessarily subject to the rules and expectations that the historian may claim for that society.[3] For example, the reader's evaluation of Elisha as a prophet is subject to the role expectations for 'prophet' which the reader has deduced from the narrative, and also the reader's general expectation of what a 'prophet' should or should not do; however, independent historical reconstructions of eighth-century Israel only enter the picture as part of a 'reader's general expectation', and then only for the reader who believes a particular reconstruction.

In this study, the expectation for the role of *prophet* will be highlighted. Since a reader's general expectations are impossible to account for in a comprehensive way, this reading will confine itself to expectations that may have been created by the larger narrative (i.e. the expectations of *prophet* as created by the reading of other prophets such as Moses and Samuel).

---

3. Bal calls this expectation the *frame of reference* for the character. See *Narratology*, pp. 80-85.

Chapter 4

ELISHA

Introduction

This study will read the presentation of the character of Elisha as a belittling portrayal of the prophet and prophetism in general. This is a somewhat unique approach to this text, and one for which there is little support in the secondary literature. I do not claim to be reading against the grain of the text. The discernment of the grain of the text is precisely the question which this study addresses. Finally, however, grain is more a characteristic of *narrative* than of *text*, more a product of the reading process than of marks on paper. This study limits itself to the initial exploration of the effect of the text upon a reader.

This study will focus on the role of the prophet that is presented in the stories of Elisha. There are many other possible avenues into this text. I will limit my observations to the parts of the text that impact on this question. I do, however, believe that a negative assessment of prophetism is one of the central effects that this text is likely to have on the reader.

The world of the prophet Elisha is presented as being distinct from the larger world of the narrative. It is as if we are entering a different reality, which operates with different rules from the reality of the rest of Genesis–2 Kings. This is shown by the transition passages both into (2 Kgs 2) and out of (2 Kgs 8) the world of Elisha, where the normal concerns of the narrative (Baalism, Jezebel, the evil of the kings) are suspended in favor of new relationships between the king and the prophet. This is also seen in the appearance and the subsequent disappearance of the sons of the prophets,[1] a group that has virtually no narrative existence outside the Elisha stories.

---

1. The lone appearance of the sons of the prophets outside the stories of Elisha is in 1 Kgs 20.35.

4. *Elisha*

Inside this new world, two distinct scenarios are explored as possible roles for the prophet. Within the distinct world of Elisha these scenarios can be explored safely, as ideas that are options only within this slightly unreal world.

The first scenario that is raised is of the prophets as an alternative to monarchy. This idea is never specifically stated as such, but often Elisha acts in such a way as to present a possible threat to the power of the king. As quickly as this scenario arises, it is rejected, and power is swiftly restored to the king.

A similar scenario is also raised in other contexts in Genesis–2 Kings, as seen most clearly with Samuel and his confrontation with Saul (1 Sam. 15). It is also explored in the confrontations between Nathan and David (2 Sam. 12), and Elijah and Ahab (1 Kgs 17–18). This scenario is not a new one, but is a part of the continuing definition of the role of the prophet in the narrative.

The second scenario that is raised is of prophetism presenting an alternative to the normal structure of Israelite society. This possibility is raised by the presence of the sons of the prophets, who appear to form a *sub-culture* within the larger societal context. This scenario is also rejected as a viable alternative, as the sons of the prophets are shown to be inept, foolish and simply unable to provide for their own needs, at least without the continued assistance of the miracles of Elisha.

The narrative does not present these two scenarios as real options for the reader, but only raises them in order to dismiss them. Rather, it limits the prophet to two possible roles. These roles are ones that might be enacted within the larger narrative world. One of these roles is continually presented in a subtly negative way, while the other is shown in a largely positive light.

The questionable role for the prophet is that of wonder-worker. The power of Elisha is never in doubt. While the text has no word for *miracle*, it is clear that Elisha is able to accomplish things that other characters are unable to perform. What he predicts comes about, and he single-handedly defeats armies, cures and causes leprosy, and creates military victory for both Israel and Aram. The questions that arise, however, are in connection with the *source*, the *usefulness* and the *continuation* of prophetic miracles.

The *source* of Elisha's power is never in doubt, at least on the surface of the text. YHWH is the only deity in the Elisha stories, at least the only one who is granted the status of actor.[2] This would almost necessitate the conclusion that YHWH is the source of Elisha's power. The difficulty arises when we study the details of the prophetic word that accompanies the miracles. There are three problems here. The first is that where I might expect the usual phrase which records the fulfilment of the words of YHWH, כדבר יהוה ('according to the word of YHWH'), I often find the phrase כדבר אלישע ('according to the word of Elisha'). While the case is not clear cut, it may raise in the mind of the reader a certain doubt regarding the relationship between Elisha's word and YHWH's.

The second problem regarding the source of Elisha's power is the transference of the messenger role from Elisha to Gehazi. In much of Genesis–2 Kings, the prophet acts as a messenger to bring the word of YHWH to its final recipient. Messages travel from God through prophet to target. Thus, for example, in the story of Naaman, the reader might expect the word of healing to come from YHWH through Elisha to Naaman. In the Elisha stories, however, the messenger role is taken up by Gehazi or others. If Gehazi takes the role of messenger/prophet, this leaves for Elisha the role of God. The transference of role is never stated explicitly. It exists as an option for the reader, one which is likely to make the reader uncomfortable with displays of prophetic power.

The third problem regarding the source of Elisha's power is the lack of divine initiative in the story. YHWH has no direct speech in any of the stories; neither is there any sense of larger divine purpose to Elisha's actions. The prophet appears as a loose cannon, wandering around Israel firing off miracles at random. This is most striking given the explicit directions of YHWH that initiate his prophetic ministry.

The *usefulness* of prophetic power is questioned in two ways: by the non-fulfillment of expectation, and in relation to the sons of the prophets. The reader's expectation centres around three characters, Baal, Jezebel and the king of Israel. Elisha is explicitly given the task of eradicating Baal worship from Israel. Further, Jezebel is still alive, and is presumably living in Samaria, having an influence upon both her sons as kings of Israel, and sons-in-law as kings of Judah. Given the history of conflicts between Jezebel, Baal and Elijah, the reader is likely to

---

2. Baal is completely absent, Chemosh is not mentioned in connection with the Moabites (2 Kgs 3), and Rimmon is only mentioned as one to whom the king of Aram bows, but does not act in the story (2 Kgs 5).

expect these conflicts to continue in the Elisha stories. Neither of these characters appears in the Elisha stories.

Another expectation created by the larger narrative is prophet as opposition to the evil kings of Israel. The continuing evil of the kings is noted in the succession passages (1 Kgs 21.52-53; 2 Kgs 3.2,3), and the house of Ahab continues on the throne in Samaria. Yet Elisha is often shown in surprisingly good relationship with the kings of Israel. Hints of a positive, or at least ambivalent relationship appear throughout the stories. Most often, Elisha is shown to be useful not in challenging the kings of Israel, but in aiding them.

In his relationship to the sons of the prophets, Elisha is surely useful in providing food, healing and looking out for their general welfare. A careful reading of the stories, however, highlights not the wonderful deeds of Elisha but the hopelessness and helplessness of the sons of the prophets. If these are truly the prophets' sons, then the prophets are capable of engendering only the most pitiful offspring.

The *continuation* of miraculous prophetic power is raised as a question by the succession of Elijah by Elisha. This sets up the possibility of a succession of prophets, an on-going line of wonder workers and heroes for YHWH. In the Elisha stories, the candidates to succeed Elisha are Gehazi or the sons of the prophets. Yet these are continuously shown in a negative light, and do not occupy the role of heir to the prophetic mantle.

The possibility of succession is also dealt with in another way. Given the largely negative or at least ambivalent portrayal of Elisha in these stories, the reader is unlikely to view him as someone worth following. This is especially true as I recognize my Elisha does not fulfill our expectations of his role as defender of Yahweh worship in an evil kingdom.

Given that the Elisha stories provide little positive comment on the prophet as wonder worker, there remains one role that Elisha does fill, and one upon which the story pronounces positive judgment. That is the role of royal oracle. In every case where the prophet encounters the king of Israel, he aids the king by performing specific tasks. While he may perform this task grudgingly or only under threat, he works at all times to aid the king when the king needs him. This is the positive role that the stories allow the prophet.

The idea of prophet as royal oracle remains the only option for the rest of the story of Genesis–2 Kings. The narrative records no further prophetic activity in Israel before the fall of Samaria, with the exception of Jonah in 2 Kgs 14.25. In this instance, Jonah is placed clearly in the role of oracle to King Jeroboam of Israel regarding the restoration of border of Israel. The two prophets in Judah will be Hulda and Isaiah, and it is precisely the role of royal oracle which both take up. Hulda's words of prophecy are in response to a direct inquiry from King Josiah to God (2 Kgs 22.13), and she fills the role by speaking the words of YHWH as if directly to the king (22.15). Further, the non-fulfillment of Hulda's prophecy concerning Josiah's death (22.29//23.29) would increase any skepticism the reader may have concerning the importance of prophecy.

Isaiah acts in response to a request from Hezekiah (19.2-7), and sends messages to Hezekiah regarding future events (19.20; 20.1-11) and the judgment of YHWH (20.16-18). While he briefly acts in the role of healer (20.7), it is only in response to an earlier message from YHWH, and the healing is reported in very naturalistic terms.

Insofar as I have helpfully summarized the role of the prophet that is affirmed by the narrative, it is important to recognize that the narrative makes the point with considerable subtlety. The narrator never provides explicit negative comment on the miracles of Elisha, nor does he explicitly condemn the sons of the prophets. The Elisha character has often been read by others in a highly positive way, and this continues to remain an option for the reader who wishes to do so. The difficulty with reading Elisha as an exemplary prophet arises in the details and intricacies of the text, and the mental gymnastics that are required to uphold his status.

It is also important to remember that this picture emerges as part of the continued flow of the narrative. The text never provides a handy summary for the reader regarding its intended effect. The narrator does not provide morals at the end of each story. This study will follow the text as a narrative text, and observe how the above picture emerges in the narrative world. I might have chosen to proceed by fitting the narrative into the above outline, but this would be an injustice to the reading process. My choice arises out of a particular reading strategy, one which attempts to enter the narrative world as much as possible, and to observe the effect this world has on the reader.

The narrative that emerges as I read will be subtly negative in its judgment of Elisha. It raises for the reader the possibility of a world under prophetic control. It then casts this world in a negative light, and

1 Kings 19: Enter Elisha

1 Kings 19 introduces the reader to the character Elisha. Not only is he introduced, but the program of his life is set out even before we meet him. This program will follow Elisha all through the rest of the stories, and form a major criterion by which the reader can assess the results of Elisha's work. Further, Elisha is introduced in the context of YHWH speaking directly to Elijah. Both of these elements (Elijah and the direct speech of YHWH) will also haunt the stories of Elisha, as the reader constantly compares him to his predecessor.

The first introduction to the character Elisha is found in the voice of God in 1 Kgs 19.16. Elisha's appointment is the third of a three-part instruction that YHWH gives to Elijah, namely to anoint Hazael as king of Aram, Jehu as king of Israel and Elisha as prophet 'in your place' (תחתיך, v. 16).

Others have noted that this is the only place in Genesis–2 Kings where a prophet is to be anointed (משח).[3] This, however, is readily explained if I understand that the focus of the verb משח is on its subject rather than its object, on the one performing the action rather than the one who is anointed. Anointing is an action done *by* Moses (Exod. 28.41; 29.7, 36) or Samuel (1 Sam. 9.16; 15.1; 16.3), rather than an action done specifically *to* priests or kings. Thus, Elisha is anointed because this is something that prophets do to confer authority. Elisha is the only prophet ever anointed because he is the only prophet whose authority rests upon his being the legitimate successor of another prophet.

The command is accompanied by an explanation, namely that the three persons anointed are responsible for killing. Elisha is to be the third party, the final one responsible for killing those not killed by the other two. This explanation needs further elaboration, since the identity of those to be killed and the reason for the killing follows (v. 18). As in v. 17, a waw-consecutive links the verses, as Elijah is told of the

---

3. Gwilym H. Jones, *1 and 2 Kings* (2 vols.; NCBC; Grand Rapids: Eerdmans, 1984), II, p. 334; John Gray, *I and II Kings* (OTL; Philadelphia: Westminster Press, 2nd edn 1970 [1965]), p. 366.

magnitude of the killing, as deducible from the number remaining (seven thousand), and is informed that only those Israelites who have not bowed their knees to Baal or kissed him are to be spared.

The rather backhanded way YHWH gets to the problem is striking. The reader reasonably might expect the oracle to be delivered in reverse order: problem, solution, means. One reconstructs the mini-story as follows: the people of Israel are worshiping Baal, except for 7000 who do not; those who worship Baal must be killed; Hazael, Jehu and Elisha will do the killing.

This reconstruction causes difficulty as the reader follows the events of the larger story. To the best of the reader's knowledge, the priests of Baal have recently been killed by Elijah (18.40), and the people of Israel have turned from their Baal worship to return to YHWH (note 'all Israel' is assembled at Mt Carmel in 18.19, and 'all the people' proclaim their faith in 18.39).[4]

Further, the oracle connects Elisha's task directly to the eradication of Baal worship, although in an oblique manner. It is only as readers reconstruct the story that they find that Elisha is finally responsible for killing all Baal worshipers in Israel. This will become important as I continue, since Baalism is conspicuous only by its absence in the Elisha stories, until it reappears with the rise of Jehu in 2 Kings 10, and his eradication of Baal worship in 10.28. Parzen goes so far as to speak of the 'abolition of Baalism' during the time of Elisha.[5]

This oracle is in keeping with the description of the situation in Israel which Elijah has just given Yahweh (19.14). It seems that YHWH has accepted Elijah's reading of the situation, and is willing to act upon it. Part of YHWH's action as carried out by Elijah is the anointing of Elisha as his successor. Thus, Elisha's whole textual life falls under the shadow of the commands of YHWH, the God of Horeb. The reader's reactions to him are strongly determined by the perceived correspondence between his actions and this injunction.

The association the reader is likely to make with Horeb is with

---

4. Flanagan considers this and other occurrences of 'all Israel' in these stories (9.14) to be late glosses (Deuteronomistic), but this does not affect the readers' judgment concerning the effect this phrase has on the story (James W. Flanagan, 'The Deuteronomic Meaning of the phrase "kol yisra'el"', *SR* 6.2 [1976–77], pp. 159-68 [160]).

5. Herbert Parzen, 'The Prophets and the Omri Dynasty', *HTR* 30 (1940), pp. 69-96 (77).

Moses, thus connecting Elijah with the ideals of Mosaic prophetism. The associative text is Deut. 18.15-22, where Moses speaks of a prophet 'like me' (v. 15), and quotes the request made by the people at Horeb (v. 16). The role of the prophet is briefly spelled out here (v. 18), as is the means by which the people can tell which prophet has the true word of YHWH (vv. 21-22). This latter declaration places Elijah, and consequently Elisha, under the rule of prophetic validity, namely that all things the prophet speaks will take place or prove true (v. 22).

The context of Elisha's introduction into the narrative influences the readers' perception of Elisha before they have met him. But they do not have long to wait. Immediately Elijah sets out from Horeb, where Elisha is plowing in a field (v. 19). The order of the instructions in the command of YHWH might have caused the readers to expect Elisha to be the third one anointed, rather than the first. Their surprise is sustained as they continue reading, since Elijah never directly carries out the other two commands (19.15-16).

From Horeb, Elijah immediately goes to find Elisha, who is plowing in a field with 12 yoke of oxen (19.19). The description of Elisha's plowing is pregnant with allusions and possible associations. Agriculturally, 12 yoke of oxen is 'an indication of fantastic wealth'.[6] Further, Elisha's position at the end of the line of oxen indicates that he is likely the one in charge, since this is the best vantage point to keep an eye on the other workers. The symbolism of the number 12 is also not likely to be lost on the reader, with possible associations with the 12 tribes.

This is where Miscall's notion of 'clarity of description' versus 'opaqueness of significance' is important.[7] The reader is in no way directed to connect the 12 oxen with 12 tribes, nor is the text able to control what this connection might signify for the individual reader. Elisha may be the one in charge of the plowing, as I suggest, or he may just be another hired hand. These decisions affect how Elisha will be seen in the rest of the narrative, but are beyond the control of the text.

Elijah interrupts the sweaty scene by crossing over (עבר) to Elisha and throwing his mantle over him. The use of עבר anticipates 2 Kgs 2.11, 14, the crossing of the Jordan, a story that more clearly symbolizes the passing of authority from one prophet to another. It is also reminiscent of 1 Kgs 19.11, where YHWH announces his intention to

---

6. Richard D. Nelson, *First and Second Kings* (Interpretation; Atlanta: John Knox Press, 1987), p. 122.
7. Miscall, *Workings*, p. 7.

pass by Elijah. While Elijah's act thus parallels YHWH's, the impact of the action is certainly less significant; Elijah receives not only a message but a special contact with YHWH, Elisha receives his message second hand from Elijah.

Schaefer-Lichtenberger has suggested that this story serves as a call of Elisha to the service of Elijah, while 2 Kings 2 represents the real call to prophecy.[8] This makes little narrative sense, since the same symbol of prophetic authority (אדרתו, 'his mantle', 1 Kgs 19.19; 2 Kgs 2.8, 13, 14) is used in both instances. If the mantle serves as a sign of prophetic authority and power in 2 Kgs 2.14-15, where the mantle is used to part the waters of the Jordan, it cannot serve here merely as a sign of servanthood.[9]

I must not make too much of the mantle, however, as Coulot does. He insists that the mantle is a symbol of the personality and prerogatives of its owner.[10] He uses 1 Samuel 24 as the basis for this conclusion, which is dubious since there is no mention of a mantle in this passage. Nonetheless, there is a definite sense of call in the story, a call to a specific mission. This sets up for the reader an anticipation by which Elisha's actions will continue to be judged.

Elisha's response to the throwing of the mantle is to abandon (עזב, 19.20) his oxen and run after Elijah. He then returns to his oxen, and slaughters them, and, using the plowing equipment for fuel, shares the meat with those around (v. 21). The movement of the story is ambiguous insofar as the movement toward following is simultaneously a movement away from producing.

Initially the slaughter of the oxen can be read as an action that involves the sharing of goods. The difficulty with this movement is that, economically, sharing must be accompanied by producing. Yet in these stories Elisha continually shares without being productive. Commentators have made the same assertion regarding the sons of the prophets. In this way, the story presents a scenario that is economically unviable. One might understand the implications of this by noting that some of

---

8. Christa Schaefer-Lichtenberger, 'Joshua und Elischa: Ideal-Typen von Führerschaft in Israel', in M. Augustin (ed.), *Wünschet Jerusalem Frieden* (New York: Peter Lang, 1988), p. 278.

9. Note also 1 Sam. 15.27-28; 24.4, 21 and 1 Kgs 4.29-31 where clothing is connected to the loss or transfer of power.

10. Claude Coulot, 'L'investiture d'Elisee par Elie (1 R 19.19-21)', *RSR* 57 (1983), pp. 87-92 (88).

the disciples in the Gospels left their nets to follow Jesus, but they did not burn their boats.

This movement from producing to not producing at first might appear rather unimportant, but as will be shown below, both not producing and sharing become major factors in the presentation of the sons of the prophets. Often in those stories, the sons of the prophets are implicitly non-producing, and Elisha, himself a non-producer in the usual agricultural sense, is called upon to share.

However we understand the throwing of the mantle, Elisha gives us his interpretation of the event immediately (v. 20). For Elisha, the call is clearly one that requires him to leave his parents and follow Elijah. Elijah's reply (לך שוב כי מה־עשׂיתי לך, 'Go back again, for what have I done to you', v. 20), however, might cause the reader to doubt whether Elisha's understanding of the situation is the correct one.

Elijah's reply is sufficiently ambiguous to have been given various interpretations.[11] Coulot helpfully parallels this statement with 1 Sam. 26.18, where David informs Abner that David has just held himself back from killing Saul by using a similar question, and 1 Sam. 29.8, where David proclaims his innocence with a rhetorical question. Using these parallels, he understands the statement to be Elijah's denial of any responsibility for the action.[12] This is in keeping with the narrative logic of the story. While the choice of specific action is Elijah's, the command to anoint Elisha comes from YHWH. Further, Elisha's response to this action is dictated neither by YHWH nor by Elijah. It is possible to understand the first two words of Elijah's response (לך שוב, 'Go back again') to mean that Elijah does not want to be followed so much as replaced.[13] This is similar to the repeated request of Elijah in 2 Kings 2 for Elisha to remain behind.

In any case, Elisha follows the command of Elijah and returns (וישׁב, v. 21). The language of his actions at this point clearly parallels the usual language of sacrifice, although as Coulot notes, the motivation for the sacrifice is omitted.[14] This action of Elisha recalls the recent contest of Elijah on Mt Carmel.

---

11. See the summary and interpretation in Coulot, 'L'investiture', p. 90.
12. Coulot, 'L'investiture', p. 90.
13. Robert L. Cohn notes the parallel wording in 1 Kgs 19.15, where the command is direct and straightforward ('The Literary Logic of 1 Kings 17-19', *JBL* 101 [1982], pp. 333-50 [349]).
14. Coulot, 'L'investiture', p. 91.

There are two elements missing from this account if it is to be understood as a sacrifice. The first is the building of an altar, the second is a reference to YHWH. There are, however, four words that directly parallel the instructions given for the passover in Deut. 16.1-8, namely אכל ('eat'), בקר ('oxen'), בשל ('boil'), and זבח ('slaughter'), which is certainly suggestive of a formal sacrificial act. BDB includes this reference under the heading 'slaughter for eating', with the note '(connected also with sacrifice, as all eating of flesh among ancient Hebrews was sacrificial)'.[15]

After the meal, Elisha goes after Elijah, and becomes his servant (וישרתהו, v. 21). The reader is left to decide what the connection is between this action and the intention of YHWH (v. 16). While one might think of the idea of a time of preparation for the task of prophecy, there are no parallel accounts of prophetic preparation in Genesis–2 Kings to reach a firm conclusion. The following stories of Gehazi and the sons of the prophets may provide the reader with some clues, but as will be shown, they are notable more for their differences to this relationship than their similarities.

The above attention to the semantic details of the text should not blind me to the more general associations that the story might have for the reader. The introduction of Elisha as a successor to Elijah may call to mind the earlier succession of Moses by Joshua. Thus, while I have noted no direct verbal links between the passage under discussion and Num. 27.18-23 (the call of Joshua), the larger movement of the plot points toward a thematic connection. This is especially true in the narrative where prophetic succession is the exception rather than the rule.

While neither unique nor original in making explicit this association,[16] Schaefer-Lichtenberger provides the most detailed exploration of

---

15. BDB, p. 257. Note, however, the strict instruction against sacrifice in just any place in Deut. 12.14.

16. See Coulot, 'L'investiture', pp. 85-87; R.P. Carroll, 'The Elijah-Elisha Sagas: Some Remarks on Prophetic Succession in Ancient Israel', *VT* 19 (1969), pp. 400-15 (409-13); Gunkel pushes the parallel further, including Elisha-Gehazi in his discussion of succession (*Geschichten von Elisa* [Meisterwerke hebräischen Erzählungskunst, 1; Berlin: Karl Curtius, 1925], p. 5); see also J. Roy Porter, 'The Succession of Joshua', in J.I. Durham and J.R. Porter (eds), *Proclamation and Presence* (Atlanta: John Knox Press, 1970), pp. 102-32 (120), who also notes the numerous monarchical aspects of the Elijah-Elisha succession, such as anointing, the mantle and the ascension.

the parallels involved.[17] Her studies focus helpfully on a possible reconstruction of problems such a pair of associated stories may have addressed for their early readers.[18] She does not, however, appear to recognize her own position as reader of readers, the latter of which are hypothetical constructs of the former. Thus, she focuses on both stories in their relationship to Deuteronomy 16–18, rather than on their relationship to each other.

One of the difficulties in making an association between two figures or events in a larger story is being able to describe how this might affect the reading of either story. Thus, a description of similarity of theme does not fully answer the question of how Joshua intrudes into the construction of the character Elisha.

If I understand 1 Kings 19 as the legitimation of Elisha as the successor to Elijah, then Num. 27.18-23 serves as the legitimation of the practice itself. Since Moses serves as the prototype for leadership in Israel,[19] then a YHWH-directed successor to Moses would serve as a prototype for all future leadership succession. The central difference between 1 Kings 19 and Numbers 27 is the role of the priest. YHWH commands Moses to have Joshua stand before Eleazar the priest (v. 21, fulfilled v. 22), presumably both for legitimation and as a mediator, through the Urim, between Joshua and YHWH.

It is in this light that the sacrifice in 1 Kgs 19.21 takes on additional significance. Here Elisha creates a situation wherein he takes on the role of the priest, thus simultaneously replicating and dismissing the importance of the priestly function. This is not the only point in the story where Elisha will take on priestly or priest-like functions (see on 2 Kgs 4.42-44 below).

I should not place too much, emphasis, however, on the importance of priest in sacrifice. Clearly the prerogative of sacrifice that the priests enjoy is often exercised by great leaders in Israel's history. The most immediate parallel for the story is the sacrifice by Elijah on Mt Carmel.

---

17. Schaefer-Lichtenberger, 'Ideal-Typen'; *idem*, '"Joshua" und "Elischa": Eine biblische Argumentation zur Begründung der Authorität und Legitimatät des Nachfolgers', *ZAW* 101 (1989), pp. 198-222.

18. Schaefer-Lichtenberger, 'Argumentation', pp. 200-201.

19. Contra Schaefer-Lichtenberger, who sees Moses as the prototype for the political ruler and Elijah as the prototypical prophet ('Ideal-Typen', p. 273). Clearly Moses' role as prophet is central to his character as it is now found in Genesis–2 Kings.

Here there is no mention of priests, nor any suggestion that Elijah has exceeded his authority.

It is in places like this that the narrative gives me little clue as to how I am to judge such an incident. There is no command of YHWH that precedes this conflation of roles. Neither is there an explicit response from YHWH. The only clue might be the general portrayal of Elisha in the larger narrative, and this, as I will show, is also highly ambiguous. At this early point in the story, one needs to note the question of Elisha's function as priest, and be attentive for further comments on this question.

The other question that arises immediately is the relationship between the oracle of Yahweh (19.16-18) and its eventual fulfillment or non-fulfillment in the rest of the story. Miscall has helpfully demonstrated how the simple point-for-point relationship between prophecy and fulfillment only works if the study is limited to a few select texts; however, 'once we take other texts into account, the simple pattern explodes'.[20]

While Miscall's argument cautions us regarding the assumption of simple schema, it does not remove the general place of expectation in our reading. Thus, while readers may not be surprised that the oracle is not fulfilled in every detail, they will certainly continue to read the story as some sort of response to the oracle.

The readers' introduction to Elisha begins with Elisha as a functionary in someone else's story. He is brought into the narrative in the speech of YHWH, and appointed to the task of killing. Later he is introduced as a character, and is given both action and speech. Given the direct movement of the story between YHWH's word and Elisha's call, the reader is likely to expect that the rest of YHWH's commands will be obeyed with similar dispatch. The reader is also likely to expect Elisha to be a prophet like Elijah. The reader is thus set up to expect specific things from the new character, and will judge the actions of this character by this yardstick.

The reader is also led to expect the story to revolve around Elisha in conflict with Baal. The non-fulfillment of this expectation will place in question the usefulness of Elisha to YHWH. The theme of prophetic continuity is raised by the succession of Elijah by Elisha. Will someone arise to follow Elisha as well? These are themes that readers are likely to keep in mind as they enter the stories of Elisha.

20. Peter D. Miscall, 'Elijah, Ahab and Jehu: A Prophecy Fulfilled', *Prooftexts* 9 (1989), pp. 73-83 (75).

4. *Elisha*

2 Kings 2.1-18: Transition

The initial introduction to the character Elisha is found in the middle of stories that centre around other characters, most notably Elijah. 2 Kings 2 serves as a transition between the Elijah and Elisha stories, setting the stage for stories that focus on Elisha.[21]

2 Kings 2 is set within a period of transition between monarchs in Israel. The record of the death of one king is usually followed by the announcement of the rule of the next king (e.g., 1 Kgs 16.5-10, 25-30, and so on). Here the death of Ahaziah is recorded in 1.17-18, along with an abbreviated mention of Jehoram's accession, but the formal record of Jehoram's rule is not found until 3.1. Nelson notes this chronological anomaly, and suggests that 'this event takes place on another plane of action'.[22]

This chronological deviation is consistent with the lack of explicit chronology in the following Elisha stories. As will be seen, the stories not only lack chronological markers, but often undermine any attempt by the reader to reconstruct a chronology. While chronological order is not necessarily part of literature, it is certainly part of Genesis–2 Kings.

This chronological confusion is paralleled within the story by geographical uncertainty, which begins in the first verse. The first verse begins with a description of what will certainly be one of the major events in the story, the going up (עלה) of Elijah into heaven in a storm. This form of introduction, where a major event in the story is detailed in advance, is unique in Genesis–2 Kings. Critics are divided as to whether this introduction in fact highlights the climax of the story or proves that this event cannot be the climax.[23]

---

21. The distinction here is not one concerned with sources, only with central characters. Thus, the extended discussion as to whether 2 Kgs 2 properly belongs to the Elijah or Elisha cycles is not relevant here.
22. Nelson, *Kings*, p. 158.
23. Those who see this as the climax include Burke O. Long, *2 Kings* (FOTL, 10; Grand Rapids: Eerdmans, 1991), pp. 24-26; T.R. Hobbs, *2 Kings* (WBC; Waco, TX: Word Books, 1985), p. 17. Contrary position are taken by Gunkel, 'Elisha: The Successor to Elijah (2 Kings ii.1-18)', *ExpTim* 41 (1929), pp. 182-86 (182); E. Haag, 'Die Himmelfahrt des Elias nach 2 Kg.2, 1-15', *TTZ* 78 (1969), pp. 18-32 (19). Long attempts to resolve the dispute by appealing to Gen. 18.1 and 22.1. Both of these are instances where some of the plot of the ensuing story is revealed in the

The verse continues with the beginning of a journey. The journey of Elijah and Elisha 'from Gilgal' is incongruous, since readers have no notice of their having been at Gilgal, nor do readers know what they were doing there. Further, this is the first indication of Elisha's presence with Elijah since 1 Kings 19. In this way, anomalies in chronology, geography and personnel are combined to place the story outside its immediate context. These anomalies detract from the impression of verisimilitude, as the journey takes place outside of normal geographical and chronological movement.

The mention of Gilgal also places readers within the semantic context of Joshua and Samuel.[24] Twenty-six of the 33 instances where Gilgal is mentioned in Genesis–2 Kings occur in relation to Joshua or Samuel. The appearance of Elisha and Gilgal in the same verse reasserts the Elisha-Joshua parallel I noted earlier, and might cause one to be on the lookout for more Samuel connections.

A Samuel connection would be helpful for my thesis since Samuel is the last judge in Israel.[25] The failure of judgeship in dealing adequately with Israel's needs forms a thematic background to the failure of prophetism to provide an adequate alternative to the narrative's 'natural' social organization. Further, the problem of succession for the judges (1 Sam. 8.5) parallels the question of prophetic succession, and the establishment of continuity in leadership.

Many attempts have been made to make 2 Kings 2 into a geographical chiasm. The most common feature they all share is their near success. Near success is certainly a sign that something is happening, but perhaps not what readers were hoping to find. As Alter noted, unsuc-

---

opening verse. Thus he reads 2 Kgs 2.1 as a 'typical anticipatory device' which directs readers toward one particular reading of the narrative (*Kings*, pp. 25-26). I find these parallels unconvincing, since the verses from Genesis do not provide the detail found in this text. Further, the closest parallel, Gen. 22.1, provides readers not with a description of events but an interpretive framework. This verse reads more as an introduction to an oral tale than a guide for inquiring readers.

24. The suggestion that Gilgal is to be identified with Jiljilia rather than Gilgal near the Jordan does not affect my reading. The semantic association of place names would be made whether or not the same Gilgal is meant. See Mordechai Cogan and Hayim Tadmor, *II Kings* (AB, 11; Garden City, NY: Doubleday, 1988), p. 31; Gray, *Kings*, p. 424.

25. Note David Jobling, *The Sense of Biblical Narrative II: Structural Analysis in the Hebrew Bible* (JSOTSup, 39; Sheffield: JSOT Press, 1986), pp. 49-51.

4. *Elisha*

cessful repetition is a key element in biblical narrative,[26] and unsuccessful chiasms would easily fit in the same mold.

In this instance, the geographical movement is as follows:

```
              Jordan (vv. 6-14)
           Jericho (v. 4)- - -Jericho (v. 15)
        Bethel (v. 2) - - - - - - - - - - - - - - - Bethel (v. 23)
     Gilgal (v. 1) - - - - - - - - - - - - - - - - - - - - -- ?? Mt Carmel (v. 25)
                                                    Samaria (v. 25)
```

It is precisely the failure of the neat chiasm that indicates the failure of the story to resolve itself. While this is not a major indication of the frustration of expectation, it does provide another clue as to the general tone of the story.

The story continues with Elijah instructing Elisha to remain in Gilgal, for, he says, YHWH has sent him 'as far as Bethel' (עד־בית־אל, 2.2). Once there, the sons of the prophets come out to meet Elisha.

It is important to note the connection between actors that the narrative makes here. Elijah speaks only to Elisha. The sons of the prophets speak only to Elisha, and they call Elijah 'your master' (אדניך). There is no indication of any direct contact between Elijah and the sons of the prophets in this story.

One of the unique features of the Elisha stories is the recurring presence of the sons of the prophets. Certainly Genesis–2 Kings has documented other groups of prophets in relation to other characters (especially Saul and Samuel—see 1 Samuel 10.5-13; 19-20), but the repeated use of the phrase בני־הנביאים ('sons of the prophets') in these stories distinguishes this group from the others within the semantic world of the text.

The specific designation בני־הנביאים ('sons of the prophets') first occurs in 1 Kgs 20.35. Curiously, at least for the modern reader, the term is given no semantic context, that is, there are no remarks to indicate what or who this group is, and how they fit into the social world of the text. This designation then disappears until 2 Kings 2. The rest of the story in 1 Kings 20 is about the actions of an individual prophet, who is labeled as such (הנביא, 'prophet', v. 38; הוא מהנבאים, 'one of the prophets', v. 41), and there is nothing to distinguish this prophet from the others in surrounding stories. The designation also disappears after

---

26. Alter, *Art*, pp. 97-105.

the Elisha stories, and the reader is given no hint of their demise or possible continuing presence.

There is disagreement as to whether the phrase בן־נביא ('son of a prophet') in Amos 7.14 refers to the same group.[27] For the purpose of historical reconstruction, however, Amos provides little additional information. Further, for the purposes of this study, I will leave open the question of whether the prophetic writings constitute the 'same' semantic world as Genesis–2 Kings. It may be that a narrative reconstruction of the role of the prophets in their society as found in the latter prophets is similar to the picture we form from Genesis–2 Kings, but this remains to be proven, and cannot simply be assumed. Thus, any description of prophetism in the latter prophets will be unavailable for my use, pending further analysis of this question.

Commentators have provided rather diverse descriptions of this group, all based on the same textual evidence. The differences lie in the reconstructions of Israelite society that the various authors are working with, and the theories regarding the collection of the Elisha stories and the reason for their inclusion in their present textual context.

It is almost universally assumed that the sons of the prophets were responsible for the collection of at least some of the Elisha stories.[28] It is also generally agreed that the picture of the sons of the prophets that the text provides is generally negative. Ruprecht speaks of them as the '*sozial Deklassierten*' (social underclass).[29] Petersen speaks of a group depicted as dependant upon alms and minimal food gathering and upper-class support for their existence.[30] Gray depicts a group with low moral standards, where 'credulity flourished',[31] and suggests that the sons of the prophets stories impair the reputation of Elisha.[32] Nelson

---

27. Compare James G. Williams, 'The Prophetic Father', *JBL* 85 (1966), pp. 344-48 (348); Hobbs, *2 Kings*, p. 26.

28. Hans-C. Schmitt is the lone exception I found. His argument is based on the complexity of the literary arrangement of the Elisha stories (*Elisa: Traditionsgeschichtliche Untersuchung zur vorklassischen nordisräelitischen Prophetie* [Gütersloh: Gerd Mohn, 1972], p. 17).

29. Eberhard Ruprecht, 'Entstehung und zeitgeschichtlicher Bezug der Erzählung von der Designation Hasaels durch Elisa', *VT* 29 (1979), pp. 73-82 (73).

30. David L. Petersen, *The Roles of Israel's Prophets* (JSOTSup, 17; Sheffield: JSOT Press, 1981), p. 49.

31. Gray, *Kings*, p. 428.

32. Gray, *Kings*, p. 416.

talks about the group 'gathering like hobos around stewpots'.[33] Würthwein notes the poverty of the group, and also how the stories show the problems that existed in the groups.[34] Yet despite these analyses, none of these authors are willing to throw doubt upon the prevailing assumption that the Elisha stories originate within the circle of the sons of the prophets. One wonders, at this point, why it is that a group that collects, and presumably originally composed such stories, would consistently portray itself in such a negative light.

Rofé is the clearest example of the difficulty of this argument. He has dismissed the suggestion that Gehazi may have been a source for the Elisha stories, since Gehazi is portrayed in a consistently negative fashion.[35] He also recognizes that 'in general [the sons of the prophets] are portrayed as impoverished, defenseless, simple people, in need of the man of God to provide protection and the basic necessities'.[36] Later he speaks of them as 'provincial followers—admirers from the outlands and border towns'.[37] Yet he sees no discrepancy between his dismissal of Gehazi as likely source and his acceptance of the sons of the prophets as origin[38] despite the similarities in the way the two are portrayed.

There is, however, another group of scholars who provide a much more positive picture of the sons of the prophets. Wifall speaks of the sons of the prophets as worship leaders beside the priests in the major religious centres.[39] Porter suggests that they gained a high and influential status in Israelite society under Elisha as instruments of opposition to the 'religious policies of the house of Omri, and especially Jezebel'.[40] Morton Smith parallels them to a party organization, perhaps involved in terrorist activities.[41] Gunkel speaks of these groups as being found in every city throughout Israel,[42] and even Gray, who attaches them to the

---

33. Nelson, *Kings*, p. 175.
34. Ernst Würthwein, *Die Bücher der Könige* (Das Alte Testament Deutsch, 11.2; Göttingen: Vandenhoeck & Ruprecht, 1984), p. 288.
35. A. Rofé, *The Prophetical Stories* (Jerusalem: Magnes Press, 1982), p. 22.
36. Rofé, *The Prophetical Stories*, p. 45.
37. Rofé, *The Prophetical Stories*, p. 56.
38. Rofé, *The Prophetical Stories*, p. 22.
39. W. Wifall, *The Court History of Israel* (St Louis: Clayton, 1975), p. 100.
40. Joshua R. Porter, 'Bene-hanabi'im', *JTS* 32 (1981), pp. 423-29 (427-28).
41. Morton Smith, *Palestinian Parties and Politics that Shaped the Old Testament* (New York: Columbia University Press, 1971), p. 34.
42. Gunkel, 'Elisha', p. 183.

shrines in Israel, considers the community at Bethel to be 'numerous and influential'.[43]

Both the positive and negative depictions of the sons of the prophets have their connection to the Elisha stories. If I were to characterize the two, I might say that the former group were dependant upon the specific narrative descriptions of the group in the stories themselves, while the latter are more dependant upon historical reconstructions of the place such a group might have had in 'historical' Israel.[44] This can be seen most clearly with Nelson's 'hobos around stewpots',[45] which is clearly taken from 2 Kgs 4.38-41, as compared to Smith's notion of terrorist prophets,[46] which has no specific textual basis whatsoever.

The other avenue which might bring us to a better understanding of the sons of the prophets may be characterized as sociological. Here the social place and function of the sons of the prophets is examined, possibly in parallel with similar groups in other societies. Williams is the commentator who best fits this description.[47] He focuses on the importance of the term בן ('son'), which he suggests designates those who separate themselves from society and devote themselves to אב ('father'), the prophetic father.

For the purposes of this study, I will continue to look at the sons of the prophets with regard to their function within the unfolding drama of the narrative. It is not my intention to probe the characteristics of a group of people who may have been the archetype for this narrative. Rather, as a reader, I want to explore the ways these actors contribute to the creation of my (re)construction of the textual world, and explore the function they perform within this world.

The speech of the sons of the prophets (they are not accorded individual voices) acts as the first test of Elisha: Do you know (הידעת, 2.3)? Elisha responds that he does know and the speakers should be silent. This serves both to pass the test and to establish the relationship that he believes to be the correct one between himself and the sons of the prophets, namely that he is the one in charge. The latter he accom-

43. Gray, *Kings*, p. 424.
44. I recognize here that there is little data that separates 'historical' from 'narrative' Israel, the former being a scholarly construction built on the foundation of the latter.
45. Nelson, *Kings*, p. 175.
46. Smith, *Parties*, p. 34.
47. Williams, 'The Prophetic Father', p. 344.

4. *Elisha*

plishes by issuing a command. The command indicates to the reader that Elisha issues commands to the sons of the prophets, rather than being a passive recipient of their verbal initiatives.

The scene is repeated almost verbatim in vv. 4-5, this time in connection with Jericho, and is begun but not finished in v. 6, as the dialogue between Elijah and Elisha takes place, but the subsequent question by the sons of the prophets is not found. The main deviation between the first two parallel incidents is in v. 5, where the sons of the prophets 'drew near' (ויגשו) to Elisha. This verb often implies close contact between the subject and object, including even sexual contact (Exod. 19.15). Thus, the text draws the relationship between sons and Elisha tighter, which further loosens the possible connection between sons and Elijah.

Verse 7 breaks the chain of waw-consecutive verbs by beginning with a noun (וחמשים, 'fifty'). This disjunction informs the reader that a new episode of the story is to begin. This is evidenced also by the new role which the sons of the prophets play in the story. Whereas before they served to heighten expectation and focus readers' attention upon Elisha, here they serve as witnesses to the events that are about to unfold.

The enormity of the miracle in v. 8 is contrasted by the simplicity of presentation. The action is presented through a series of five verbs, the first three of which describe Elijah's actions, the fourth details the division of the water, and the final verb informs us of the passage of the two men. Much of this verse is repeated in v. 14. As in most cases of repetition in these stories, it is the second incident that should draw the readers' attention.[48]

It is at the far edge of the Jordan that Elijah offers Elisha a favor (מה אעשה־לך, 'what may I do for you', 2.9). Elisha responds by asking for a share of *Elijah's* spirit (ברוחך, v. 9). It is here that readers first see the ambiguity of power that will be found throughout the Elisha stories. There is certainly no indication of the working of any other deity besides YHWH, and there are sufficient indications of YHWH's presence for the reader to assume that all miraculous power emanates from YHWH. Readers must also be careful not to expect the text to provide them with formulaic sayings at every possible location. These stories

---

48. See R.A. Carlson, 'Elisee: Le successeur d'Elie', *VT* 20 (1970), pp. 385-405 (385).

evidence a high degree of literary skill, which militates against simple verbatim formulas.

However, just as slight divergence in repetition can point me to subtle shifts in meaning or emphasis, so lack of formal features can serve as markers for textual ambiguity. In the case of vv. 9-10, what is lacking is explicit reference to YHWH. The spirit that Elisha wants a part of is that of Elijah. While this request reinforces the connection between the two individuals, it simultaneously diminishes the connection between Elisha and YHWH. This connection will also need attention as we continue reading.

The ambiguity of the request is highlighted by the absence of previous references to Elijah's spirit. The Elijah stories contain references both to YHWH's spirit (1 Kgs 18.12, in the mouth of Obadiah), and also to a spirit (wind) which does not contain YHWH's presence (19.11). There is no indication, however, that YHWH's spirit is either possessing or possessed by Elijah.[49] While this question will receive some clarification in 2.14, at this point the question is raised in the mind of the reader, the easier to return when the ambiguity again arises.

The absence of YHWH from this text is also notable due to the parallels in the account of the succession of Joshua in Num. 27.18. Here there is a mention of Joshua having (already) a spirit in him (אִישׁ־רוּחַ בּוֹ), but the words are those of YHWH, and thus the connection between YHWH and the power of Joshua is made explicit. While YHWH will continue to be invoked (albeit irregularly) when Elisha uses his power, the voice of YHWH disappears from the text, and the security which that voice engenders is removed.

The translation of פִּי־שְׁנַיִם ('double share') has received considerable attention. There are basically two arguments. The first one recognizes the connection back to Deut. 21.17, where the eldest son is accorded פִּי שְׁנַיִם of the estate of his father. Thus it is translated 'double portion', since we cannot know how many other sons there may be.[50] The second translates it as 'two thirds', a more specific ratio of available power.[51]

---

49. Note the divergence on this point between Cogan and Tadmor, and Z. Weisman, as cited in Cogan and Tadmor, *Kings*, p. 32.

50. Haag, 'Himmelfahrt', p. 22; F. Deist, 'Two Miracle Stories in the Elijah and Elisha Cycles and the Function of Legend in Literature', in W. Wyk (ed.), *Studies in Isaiah* (Pretoria: University of Pretoria Press, 1979), pp. 79-90 (80); etc.

51. Raymond Brown, citing L. Ginzberg's *Legends of the Jews* IV (7 vols.; Philadelphia: JPSA, 1913), p. 239, notes that Jewish tradition translates 'two-

While the inter-Biblical reference has appeal, there is no indication of another heir. The Deuteronomy law only applies to cases with multiple heirs. Further, as will be seen below, Elisha is not always shown to work with the same ease with which Elijah performed great deeds. Thus, the phrase as it stands in this sentence is ambiguous, but clearly indicates that Elisha is likely to be less powerful than Elijah.

Elijah responds to Elisha's request by placing a condition upon its fulfillment. Elisha will receive the power *if he sees* (אם־תראה, v. 10) Elijah being taken from him. There is no reason given for the condition placed upon the fulfillment of the request, except possibly because it is a 'hard thing' (הקשית לשאול, v. 10).

As they continue walking and talking, a chariot of fire and horses of fire (רכב־אש וסוסי אש, 'a chariot of fire and horses of fire', v. 11) separate them. This image parallels a similar one in 6.17, where סוסים ורכב אש ('horses and chariots of fire') surround the hills of Dothan. Seeing is also part of the parallel between 2.11-12 and 6.17, where the chariots and horses of fire are only visible after YHWH opens the servant's eyes. Thus, again readers will need to wait until the second or possibly third (13.14) member of the pair before discerning the first.

The sudden appearance of the military images of horses and chariots[52] reminds readers that this is not only a story about prophets and their relationship to each other. Elijah was and Elisha is expected to be a major player in the political and military life of Israel.

Elisha *sees* Elijah being taken up (ואלישע ראה, v. 12), which indicates that he has clearly fulfilled the condition of Elijah's promise.

---

thirds'('Jesus and Elisha', *Perspective* 12 [1971], pp. 85-104 [90]). See also Carlson, 'Elisee', p. 402; Gunkel, *Elisa*, p. 10; *idem*, 'Elisha', p. 84; Wurthwein, *Könige*, p. 275.

52. Whether פרש (v. 12) is to be translated 'horses' or 'horsemen' is unimportant for my argument, except insofar as Elisha's exclamation is not a direct parallel to the narrator's description. On the translation, see Martinus A. Beek, 'The Meaning of the Expression "the chariots and the horsemen of Israel" (2 Kings ii 12)', in *idem* (ed.), *The Witness of Tradition* (Leiden: E.J. Brill, 1972), p. 2 n. 1; Kurt Galling, 'Der Ehrename Elisas und die Entrueckung Elias', *ZTK* 53 (1956), pp. 129-48 (135); Haag, 'Himmelfahrt', p. 25.

Lundbom's suggestion that the chariots and horses of Israel should be understood literally as the king abducts Elijah is clearly anachronistic (J.R. Lundbom, 'Elijah's Chariot Ride', *JJS* 24 [1973], pp. 39-50 [48]). While Elisha's call is certainly to be interpreted 'literally', the literal reading from within the world of the story indicates a heavenly force.

Thus, presumably he should now be in possession of some part of Elijah's spirit.

The question of Elisha's power is cleared up in vv. 13-14 as Elisha, now in possession of Elijah's mantle, parts the Jordan and crosses over. At least this would be the case if not for the difficult wording in v. 14. This verse poses two problems.

The first is the awkward אף־הוא.⁵³ The LXX transliterates *aphpho* (אפפו), which translates 'indeed' and is moved up in the sentence.⁵⁴ Since I wish to follow the MT wherever possible, I will read the text as it stands, and understand this phrase as a challenge to YHWH ('Where is YHWH, the God of Elijah, even he?'), the emphatic אף ('how much more') changing a possible cry of the devout into a challenge of the impatient.

This reading reinforces the shift in emphasis in the relationship between the prophet and his power. While Elijah is portrayed as the servant of YHWH, Elisha is given a much greater control over power. He is the inheritor of Elijah's spirit, Elijah's mantle, and now demands a demonstration of power from YHWH. While this change in emphasis may serve to highlight the power of the prophet (or the mantle), it simultaneously distances the prophet from the desires of YHWH. The possibility that YHWH does the prophet's bidding is not one which would sit comfortably with the reader firmly enmeshed in the world of the text.⁵⁵

Thus, the choice of translation, while being a technical one, may have theological motivation, and certainly has theological implications. A narrative that portrays YHWH acceding to the demands of an impatient prophet does little credit to either prophet or god. The reader of most English versions is relieved of this difficult possibility by the sensitive translator, who chooses the theologically easier path.

---

53. Cogan and Tadmor provide a helpful summary of the difficulty, but do not reach a firm conclusion (*Kings*, p. 33), although they do translate as 'indeed' (= אפפו).

54. 'Where, indeed, is YHWH, God of Elijah' (Cogan and Tadmor, *Kings*, p. 33)

55. Even Moses must implore (ויחל) YHWH when requesting that YHWH do a specific action (Exod. 32.11). The request of Joshua is followed by a word from YHWH, not merely by silent obedience (Josh. 7.6-15). Thus, while YHWH may do the bidding of his prophets, the narrative includes words from YHWH so that YHWH's action can be seen as purposeful.

4. *Elisha*

The last part of v. 14 confirms the fulfillment of the promise that Elijah has made to Elisha with the parting of the Jordan. The succession theme, which until this point has been awaiting verification, is now complete. The exact parallel between the two accounts of the parting of the water (ויחצו הנה והנה, 'parted to the one side and to the other', vv. 8,14) allows no room for doubt.

The reader's confirmation is given expression in the response of the sons of the prophets (נחה רוח אליהו על־אלישע, 'the spirit of Elijah rests on Elisha', v. 15). Further, the identification of the spirit with Elijah rather than YHWH is continued. While this is certainly a continuation of the strong theme of succession, it also serves to distance Elisha from YHWH. Elisha has Elijah's spirit, and YHWH is Elijah's god. In this way the text allows for an unfavorable judgment of the prophet. If the text continued its close identification between prophets and YHWH, the reader would be unlikely to come to a negative conclusion regarding the activity of a prophet. Here the possibility is raised of a prophet whose connection to YHWH is not as clear, and thus the reader is given more freedom to judge his actions.

The narrative continues with the search of the sons of the prophets for Elijah. The reader already knows that Elijah has been taken up into heaven (2.1,11). Further, we know that the sons of the prophets knew in advance that this would happen (2.5). But the knowledge of the sons of the prophets is not directly parallel to the knowledge of the reader. The sons of the prophets knew that Elijah would be taken away (לקח), but they do not indicate that they know where he will be taken to. Further, the reader is not told how much Elisha knows in advance, nor exactly what Elisha understood when Elijah was taken away. Elijah himself when describing the event uses לקח ('taken away'), and the description השמים ('into heaven') is found only in the voice of the narrator (vv. 1, 11).

In these terms, vv. 16-18 demonstrate to the reader that Elisha is more knowledgeable concerning the event than the sons of the prophets. He is aware of the futility of a search, while they are insistent.

I should also note here further indications of the relationship between Elisha and the sons of the prophets. He is clearly portrayed as their leader (they bow down to him, v. 15, and note the use of repeated signs of subordination in v. 16, נא, 'please' [2×], עבדיך, 'your servant'), yet is subject to their pleading if pressed עד־בּשׁ ('until ashamed', v. 17).⁵⁶

Thus the narrative begins with initial indications of the major relationships in the life of Elisha. He is connected back to the work and person of Elijah, and connected also to the enigmatic sons of the prophets. He is also connected in some manner to YHWH, and the text has raised sufficient disquiet in my mind that the source of Elisha's power remains an issue that I will keep track of.

The narrative also begins the transition from the world of Elijah to that of Elisha. Elijah now disappears from the story until readers are returned to the world of Elijah, with the return transition beginning in 8.7.

The reader is shown a smooth transition of power, a succession story, and thus expects Elisha to be a prophet like Elijah. This succession will act to highlight either the similarities or differences between them, depending on whether readers' expectations are confirmed or thwarted.

2 Kings 2.19-22: Jericho's Water

The succession story is followed by the story of the healing of the waters of Jericho. While vv. 19-22 clearly constitute a self-contained episode in the larger story, it is linked to what precedes it by a waw-consecutive. This removes any ambiguity regarding the identification of 'the city'(v. 19), which is unnamed in the story itself. The identification of the city as Jericho is further upheld by the continuation of the chronological chiasm in v. 23 (Bethel), and the narrative insertion[57] in v. 18 which firmly places Elisha in Jericho.

This episode is also the beginning of a pattern that continues through much of the following narrative, in which shorter episodes are interspersed between longer ones.[58] In this case the connection between the longer and shorter units is clearly chronological, which will not always be the case. The continued juxtaposition of longer and shorter units is at the same time a variation in the presentation of Elisha. I shall discuss this aspect further as I continue to read through the narrative.

---

56. See below on 8.11, pp. 157-58.

57. By 'narrative insertion' I mean that the phrase והוא ישׁב בירחו ('he had remained at Jericho') (v. 18) disrupts the flow of the sentence, offering a comment to clarify for the reader a possible point of confusion.

58. 3.1-27 followed by 4.1-7; 4.8-37 followed by 38-41 and 42-44; 5.1-27 followed by 6.1-7.

4. Elisha

As with many of the other short episodes, this one focuses on a particular miracle. This is perhaps the most straightforward of the short miracle stories, and thus serves as a paradigm for our understanding of the others. This is similar to Judg. 3.7-11, where the story of Othniel serves as paradigm for the rest of the judge stories. Here, as there, readers can choose to focus on either similarities or differences.

The paradigm is set out with the following elements. There are some characters, a problem and a solution. These are the basic elements of a plot. There is a specific means by which the solution is brought about (new bowl, salt, throwing), and reference to the word of YHWH (vv. 20-21). Then the resolution of the problem is announced, as well as a recognition that all has come about according to the word of Elisha (v. 22).

This final element introduces a disquieting component into the story. While Elisha offers the correct form of prophecy (כה־אמר יהוה, 'thus says YHWH', v. 21), the fulfillment is credited to the word of Elisha (כדבר אלישע, 'according to Elisha', v. 22). This is in stark contrast to the use of כדבר ('according to') in the Elijah narratives, and the rest of Genesis–2 Kings. The usual formula for the fulfillment of prophecy is כדבר יהוה ('according to YHWH'), as found in Josh. 8.8, 27; 1 Kgs 12.24; 13.26; 14.18; 15.29; 16.12,34; 17.5,16; 22.38; 2 Kgs 1.17; 4.44; 7.16; 9.26; 10.17; 14.25; 23.16; 24.2.[59]

The case for a general change in language is not clear, since כדבר יהוה is also found in the Elisha corpus. There is, however, a definite change in formulation in this particular instance, especially given the number of occurrences of the standard formula. Further, the formula כדבר אלישע is repeated in 6.18, although there the clause refers directly to the actions of YHWH, as a response to the request of Elisha (6.18).

The readers, as those who read sentences and stories rather than individual words, are not likely to pause long over a small semantic shift such as this. It is precisely this type of small shift, especially in combination with numerous other irregularities, which causes the readers' perception to change in ways of which they may not be aware. The result is not a prophet who is directly discredited in the minds of readers, but one which makes readers uncomfortable with this prophet in particular, and prophetism in general. The narrator has already estab-

---

59. Note, for example, the contrast between 1 Kgs 17.15 and v. 16. The woman acts כדבר אליהו, but the meal and oil act כדבר יהוה. While human beings can obey the word of other humans, the miraculous is ascribed to the word of God.

lished in readers a suspicion of any character or event that takes away from the centrality of YHWH. Here the readers' suspicion is subtly turned toward the prophet, specifically in regards to the source of his power, without a direct assault being launched against this venerable institution.

The text of this short episode also contains a small discrepancy between problem and solution. The men of the city complain about both the water and the earth (v. 19), while Elisha's solution deals only with the water (vv. 21-22), although he takes in the difficulty of the earth in his healing of the water (משכלת, 'unfruitful', vv. 19, 21), and adds his own interpretation (מות, 'death') to the problem the water is causing.[60]

Small discrepancies in a text are easily overlooked by readers, who can certainly make sense of the story without resorting to formal textual emendation. What is challenged by these small shifts is the level of comfort that readers experience in the movement from problem to solution. A reader expects that the problem solved is the same as the one expressed. As readerly expectations are thwarted, readers become less comfortable with the heroic aspects of the main character.[61] Thus, the readers' admiration for Elisha may be diminished precisely at the same time as it is being enhanced.

2 Kings 2.23-25: The Bears

The final episode in the initial journey of Elisha has caused readers a great deal of difficulty. It is the story of Elisha and the boys from Bethel, where Elisha's curse causes the death of 42 of the boys. Gray says the story is 'in every respect a puerile tale',[62] and goes on to heap derision on the sons of the prophets who presumably are responsible for it. Jones feels similarly, saying that the story 'cannot have a serious point, and it does no credit to the prophet'.[63]

---

60. Burney suggests taking ארצ as 'inhabitants of the land' (C.F. Burney, *Notes on the Hebrew Text of the Book of Kings* [Oxford: Clarendon Press, 1920], p. 267). While this is possible, it does not significantly alter the difference between the complaint of the inhabitants and the words of healing offered by Elisha.

61. For example, if Poirot would go to solve a *murder* only to 'resolve' the case by catching a *thief*, readers would become uncomfortable with their confidence in 'the little grey cells'.

62. Gray, *Kings*, p. 428.

63. Jones, *Kings*, p. 389.

4. *Elisha*

This is the first place where I notice the obvious difficulty in harmonizing two major assumptions of many of the commentators. It is usually assumed that the group the text calls the sons of the prophets is the community responsible for collecting many of the Elisha stories. They did this supposedly for the purpose of enhancing the reputation of Elisha,[64] and subsequently to legitimate the communities themselves.[65] Yet as will be seen, the stories leave the reader with a largely negative opinion of the sons of the prophets, which suggests that the stories are not likely to function as the commentaries assume they were intended to.

In general I agree with Nelson that the difficulty with the death of 42 children is largely a modern problem,[66] although Rofé notes that even the Rabbis had difficulty with the brutality of this incident.[67] Narratologically, I am reading as a modern reader of an ancient text. As best I can, I try to enter the world of this text, and therefore need to ask regarding the text's own judgment on this incident. If I detect a negative textual portrayal of what I see as a negative incident, I can more easily allow the narrative world to become my own world.

Unfortunately in this narrative, as in most narratives in the Bible, I look in vain for explicit narratorial judgments on the action depicted. There are various components in the story that may lead to positive or negative impressions of the incident, but I am is largely left to my own resources in making explicit judgment.

The first possible indication of the tone of the story is found in the mention of Bethel as the place where the incident occurs (v. 23). As Conroy notes, the story has a definite anti-Bethel tone, especially when read in the light of 1 Kings 13 and 2 Kings 23.[68] It is questionable, however, whether readers would make this association. The mention of Bethel is clearly part of the geographical chiasm of the story, and the first mention of Bethel (2.2-3) speaks of the sons of the prophets who were in Bethel, which for readers is likely to be a positive association, or at worst an ambiguous one. Thus the mention of Bethel has a more

---

64. Deist, 'Two Miracle Stories', p. 80; Rofé, *Stories*, p. 22.
65. Richard D. Nelson, 'God and the Heroic Prophet', *Quarterly Review* 9 (1989), pp. 93-105 (95).
66. Nelson, *Kings*, p. 161.
67. *b. Soṭ.* 46b; Rofé, *Stories*, p. 15; Cogan and Tadmor, *Kings*, p. 39.
68. Charles Conroy, *1–2 Samuel, 1–2 Kings* (Wilmington, DE: Michael Glazier, 1983), p. 199.

immediate antecedent as a 'home to the sons of the prophets' rather than a 'place with the evil golden calves'.

Part of the ambiguity in the story rests with the picture readers have of the actual threat a group of boys poses to Elisha. The boys are alternately called נערים קטנים ('small boys', v. 23) and ילדים ('youths', v. 24). At whatever age I wish to place these boys, the seriousness with which stone-throwing Palestinian children are treated by Israeli troops might cause me to take their actions more seriously.

The pace of the narrative slows considerably for the actions of Elisha in v. 24. The movement of Elisha from Jericho to Bethel, and the jeering of the boys, is described in v. 23. Then the action slows and describes in detail an action which would have taken only seconds (ויפן אחריו ויראם ויקללם בשם יהוה, 'when he turned around and saw them, he cursed them in the name of YHWH', v. 24). The detail included here places a great deal of emphasis on the actions of Elisha. The physical action of turning is followed by the mental action of seeing, which is followed by the curse.

Würthwein best describes another problem that the text poses for the reader when he suggests בשם יהוה ('in the name of YHWH') as a later insertion.[69] As he often does, Würthwein deals with this narrative difficulty by excising the offending words from the story he reads. In this case, he focuses my attention on the central cause of my discomfort by deleting the problematic words.

The difficulty with בשם יהוה is not that curses should not be offered in the name of YHWH. Rather, the difficulty is evident when I compare this curse to that in 2 Kgs 1.10,12. In the latter verses, there are two aspects that lessen possible reader discomfort with the offhand manner in which Elijah causes the death of 100 men. First, the power exercised is related to the status of Elijah as איש אלהים ('man of God') rather than being directly attributed to YHWH. Second, the choice of punishment is made by Elijah. In these two ways, the prophet carries the blame for the death of these men, and prophets are notorious for fiery tempers anyway.

In the Elisha story, YHWH is invoked directly, and it is YHWH who chooses the manner in which the incident is dealt with. The wording of Elisha's curse is not given, and the reader is left in the uncomfortable

---

69. Würthwein, *Könige*, p. 278.

position of blaming YHWH for the death of a rather large number of small boys.

The reader is left with two directions in which to go with this discomfort. The first is to question the propriety of the action of YHWH. While this is not the only place where the reader is allowed this option (see 2 Sam. 6.6-8), it is certainly not the usual narrative position.[70] The other option is to again question the propriety of Elisha. If, as I suggested earlier, the attention to the detail of Elisha's action in v. 24 allows readers to transfer this blame to Elisha, it does so only at the expense of giving control over the actions of YHWH to the prophet. Further, there is little in Elisha's specific action that calls for condemnation, and so readers condemn redactors (Würthwein) or collectors (Gray, Jones), and becomes less comfortable with these stories of the great deeds of prophetism.

The larger story ends with the breaking of the chiastic movement. It is broken with the addition of two geographical references in place of the final element that would have completed the chiasm, a return to Gilgal. The two added elements provide the reader with further connection to the stories of Elijah (Mt Carmel) and another indication that something new is happening ('return', שׁוב, to Samaria).

There is a strong element of symbolism in all the geographic references in 2 Kings 2. The symbolic aspects are highlighted by the ease with which the characters move around the countryside. The final verse underscores the symbolism, with a journey both long and without explicit purpose.

The final element of the geographical movement provides a transition to the following story. Until the mention of Samaria, the story has dealt only with locations significant to the reader in more religious terms. Gilgal, Bethel, Jericho and the Jordan are all sites sacred to Israel's past, and Mt Carmel is immediately associated with the recent defeat of Baalism. 'Samaria' returns me to the present political context of the Omride dynasty. The narrative will continue to move between these two worlds, between the realm of the king and the realm of the prophet, often moving between them in the same story. This chapter has set Elisha up as the clear inheritor of the role of Elijah, both of his mantle and his power. It has also begun the process of casting a shadow on my

---

70. See Sternberg, who views God's omniscience as the singular message of Biblical narrative (*Poetics*, passim). I presume that a God who knows everything would not act improperly.

perception of the relationship between Elisha and YHWH, and of discrediting Elisha as a character who is worth following. It has also caused me to question the usefulness of Elisha's miraculous power, and thus to question the entire role of prophet as wonder worker.

2 Kings 3: War against Moab

The mention of Samaria in 2.25 connects the world of the prophet to the world of the kings. Now 3.1-3 firmly re-establishes the narrative within the sphere of monarchical influence. Once again there is a king firmly on the throne in Samaria, and readers are assured that normal royal chronology is in effect.[71] The stories that follow often do not name the king of Israel.[72] This has led to speculation regarding the possible chronological dislocation of certain stories.[73] While this may be historically defensible, the present story clearly indicates that Jehoram is king in Samaria (3.6).

The condemnation which by now readers expect against any king in Samaria (see 1 Kgs 16.25-27, 29-30; 22.51-53; and so on) is repeated against Jehoram, with a divergence that separates him from the evils of his father and mother (רק לא כאביו וכאמו, 'only not like his father or his mother'), namely that 'he removed the pillar of Baal that his father had made' (v. 2).

The unusual mention of his mother reminds me of the continuing presence of Jezebel, who is still alive in the world of the text, despite being ignored until Jehu is first introduced as her proper nemesis (9.7). However, the presence of the pillar of Baal, presumably in Samaria, is attributed to the work of Ahab. This places readers safely back in the world of male control, although the possibility of female control may be lingering in the back of their minds.

The final note concerning the ascension of Jehoram also contains the standard reference to 'the sins of Jeroboam son of Nebat' (v. 3). While

---

71. On the superficiality of the chronological framework in the Elisha narratives, see my 'The Prophetic Alternative: Elisha and the Israelite Monarchy', in R.B. Coote (ed.), *Elijah and Elisha in Socioliterary Perspective* (Semeia Studies; Atlanta: Scholars Press, 1992), pp. 127-38 (133-35).

72. Jehoram is mentioned in 3.6, and then not again until 8.16.

73. See, e.g., J. Maxwell Miller, 'The Elisha Cycle and the Accounts of the Omride Wars', *JBL* 85 (1966), pp. 441-54 (466), who sees ch. 3 as the third victory predicted in 2 Kgs 13.14-19.

4. *Elisha*

this is certainly part of a now expected formula, it is strangely out of place in the midst of stories that make no mention of what in particular this sin constitutes. The stories of Elijah and Elisha make no mention of Dan, and the references to Bethel are without explicit negative comment. If readers have already experienced a vague sense of dislocation moving between the world of the kings and the world of the prophets, this sense is now focused more sharply.

Usual narrative time is restored with the introduction of the actions of Mesha of Moab in 3.4. The previous verses constitute a chronological aside wherein a large section of time is commented upon, but not given narrative life. Verses 3.4–9.24 constitutes the action that was prejudged in 3.2-3.

The story continues, and reads much like a straightforward battle report. The kings are duly mentioned, the reason for the battle, the allies and the plan are all laid out for the reader. Readers may be puzzled by the total commitment of Judah to this battle, but the similarity with 1 Kgs 22.4 suggests that this is not unusual. In fact, the historical logic is more obvious in this story, since a stronger Moab constitutes a possible threat to Judah as well.

This rather clear parallel with 1 Kings 22 might also create a definite expectation in the mind of the reader. Thus, when Jehoram alone dictates the plan for the battle, readers may be expecting YHWH to be consulted (2 Kgs 3.8//1 Kgs 22.5-28). This deviation is made more noticeable by the unusual direction for the march.

Historians have noted the logic of Jehoram's plan, since the Moabite stone suggests a kingdom that has fortified its northern cities, the more natural path for an invasion from Israel.[74] Readers, however, do not have the information that makes this choice logical, and so within the world of the narrative it appears a bad plan. Thus, the eventual lack of water can be blamed directly on Jehoram's ill-advised planning, and hence the lack of initial consultation with a prophet.

At this point a complication is introduced into the story. Würthwein has helpfully divided the story into its three constituent plot lines, showing us the complexity of the present story.[75] Verse 9 changes the

---

74. Note, however, that Liver cautions that the stone 'contains no reference to Mesha having met and defeated the Israelite king in battle, or of having engaged the Israelite forces in battle' (J. Liver, 'The Wars of Mesha, King of Moab', *PEQ* 99 [1967], pp. 14-31 [22]).

75. Although he prefers to read the stories separately, for he allows no complex

narrative from a simple war account by raising a logistical concern, namely a lack of water, which requires outside intervention to resolve.

The comment of the king of Israel in v. 10 (אהה כי־קרא יהוה לשלשת המלכים האלה לתת אותם ביד־מואב, 'alas, YHWH has summoned the three kings, only to be handed over to Moab'), and its near repetition in v. 13 (אל כי־קרא יהוה לשלשת המלכים האלה לתת אותם ביד־מואב, 'no, for YHWH has summoned these three kings to be handed over to Moab'), sets the scene for readers with the introduction of YHWH as an actor in the story. The king of Israel makes a firm statement regarding the accessibility of YHWH's plan, which he himself knows. This is countered by a less sure Jehoshaphat, who wishes for the intermediation of a prophet to inquire (נדרשה) of YHWH for them (v. 11). Given the prior impression the narrator has provided readers concerning Jehoram (3.2-3), it is likely that the king of Israel's initial pronouncement regarding the will of YHWH will sound hollow.

In the context of the plot, the pronouncement also parallels the prophecy of the 400 prophets in 1 Kgs 22.6, who also proclaim YHWH's intention of securing victory for Israel. The shift in speakers from 400 prophets to one king is easily accounted for within the story line itself, as this number of prophets would be unavailable in the wilderness of Edom. There is also an indirect reference to this group of prophets in 3.13 (לך אל־נביאי אביך ואל־נביאי אמך, 'go to your father's prophets or to your mother's'). Thus, the parallel in elements of the plot cause me to make parallels that are undisturbed by the change in speaker.

Jehoshaphat's question regarding the availability of a prophet of YHWH (האין פה נביא ליהוה ונדרשה את־יהוה מאותו, 'is there not here a prophet of YHWH, through whom we may inquire of YHWH', v. 11) directly parallels the movement of the story in 1 Kgs 22.7, where Jehoshaphat asks האין פה נביא ליהוה עוד ונדרשה מאותו ('is there not here another prophet of YHWH, through whom we may inquire'), and so I should not be surprised that a prophet, in this case Elisha, is introduced as a further possible avenue to YHWH's designs. Readers are, however, consistently surprised by his presence,[76] which suggests that the parallel movement of two plots is not sufficient to overcome the anomaly of Elisha being present with the army as it moves through the wilderness of Edom.

The text gives me no relief for my discomfort with Elisha's sudden

plots in his reconstructed narratives (Würthwein, *Könige*, p. 281).
    76. See, e.g., Cogan and Tadmor, *Kings*, p. 49; Jones, *Kings*, p. 392; and so on.

4. *Elisha* 75

presence. No reasons are given. In fact, my discomfort is increased by his seeming unwillingness to inquire of YHWH for the king of Israel.[77] If he is not there expressly for that purpose, then why, I must ask, is he there at all?

Texts are filled with gaps, places where the questions of the reader are not answered by the narrative. This particular gap is a creation of the existence of a remarkably parallel story, and the expectation raised by Elisha's designation as successor to Elijah. These two expectations make the question almost impossible to ignore.

A reader might also notice here the irony of Elisha's being introduced as someone who pours water, in the context of water shortage. Or perhaps the introduction expresses within itself the reason why Elisha should be consulted, that is, his noted skill with water. While the phrase is likely a metaphor for a disciple/master relationship, the choice of metaphor shows the comic aspects of an otherwise serious narrative.

My puzzlement is further increased both by the means Elisha employs to inquire of YHWH, and the seeming variety of messages this consultation produces. The use of music may recall for readers 1 Sam. 10.5, the story of the ecstatic prophetic orchestra.[78] In this parallel, while the narrative does not clearly present a negative picture of these prophets, the narrator also does not provide readers with any explanation for their presence, nor indicate that this activity is in any way beneficial to Saul or the larger community. Thus this is at best an ambiguous presentation of the usefulness of prophetic activity.

It is the narrator who suggests that Elisha's words are a direct result of the hand of YHWH (v. 15). As I noted earlier, however, this is the only place in Genesis–2 Kings where the phrase יד־יהוה ('hand of

---

77. There is a possible parallel with Micaiah's lying prophecy in 1 Kgs 22.15b, but readers are likely to make a strong distinction between the honest refusal to prophesy and the dishonest provision of an incorrect prophecy. Micaiah clearly takes on the role of the prophet who speaks בזדון (Deut. 18.22), while Elisha does not. Elisha continues to play the role of the true prophet of YHWH. This role is never in doubt on the surface of the text. It is the failure of the many other expectations that frustrates the readers' attempt to think positively of this prophet, or to think positively of prophetism in general.

78. Gray, *Kings*, p. 432. Note also 1 Sam. 10.12, 'and who is their father', which Williams explores in his study of prophetic fathers (Williams, 'The Prophetic Father', pp. 347-48). This rather disconnected question strengthens the connection between the two stories, since it foreshadows the idea of a band of prophets needing a leader such as Elisha.

YHWH') is directly connected to a prophetic word. Thus, readers are more likely to expect an action of YHWH through Elisha than a word of Elisha.

The use of the phrase יד־יהוה in this context allows the presentation of two separate messages (distinguished by the formula כה אמר יהוה, 'thus says YHWH', vv. 16, 17), with numerous foci. The messages move from poetic puzzle to explanation to foretelling of victory to explicit instruction for the waging of the campaign.

The double use of כה אמר יהוה (vv. 16, 17), while not unique in Genesis–2 Kings, is unusual. YHWH uses a double introductory formula in 2 Sam. 7.5, 8, in regards to the message Nathan is to bring to David. The first part of the message specifically deals with the request by David to be allowed to build a temple for YHWH. The second part changes focus from YHWH's house to David's.

In 2 Samuel, the two messages are separated by the prophetic formula ועתה כה־תאמר לעבדי לדוד ('now thus you will say to my servant David', 7.8). This lengthy formula suggests that there are two distinct messages being delivered, which are linked thematically but not logically. That is, while both messages speak about the matter of houses, the second message is not predicated upon the first. The building of David's house is not causally linked to the not-building of YHWH's. Further, the two messages are distinguished by the addition of צבאות ('of hosts') to the second introductory formula.

The second instance of a double introductory formula more closely parallels the text under discussion. In 2 Sam. 12.7,11, Nathan again delivers a message with two such formulas. Here there is no intermediate prophetic formula that separates the two messages; the second continues right on from the previous one. Further, the two messages are logically linked, as the evil (רעה) which YHWH intends to raise within David's house is to be understood as further punishment for the killing of Uriah. The lack of separation, however, causes a rather abrupt break in the flow of the text. The link between the two messages exists both thematically and logically, but is not made syntactically.[79]

Thus, in comparison to these two instances of double introductory

---

79. There is a third case of double introductory formulas, in 2 Kgs 22.15, 16. In this case, however, the first formula simply makes explicit that not only the message but the command to deliver the message comes from YHWH. I suspect that it exists to ease (and simultaneously reinforce) the readers' potential discomfort with a woman commanding the delivery of a message.

4. *Elisha*

formulas, this text reads rather smoothly (ויאמר כה אמר יהוה ... כי כה אמר יהוה, 'and he said, "Thus says YHWH ... for thus says YHWH"', vv. 16-17). The connection between the first and second messages is made on all fronts. The thematic connection of the provision of water is provided by the repetition of נחל ('wadi'). The logical connection is created by the possibility of reading the second message as an explanation for the rather cryptic initial message. The syntactic connection is provided by the conjunction כי ('for'). Given the triple nature of the connection between the first two parts of the message, and the existence of similar yet less thorough parallel instances of double introductory formulae, why are some commentators so insistent that this passage is a problem that needs to be solved?[80] I suspect that the answer lies both in the cryptic nature of the first message and in the changes in theme over the course of the longer message.

The first part of the message (עשה הנחל הזה גבים גבים, 'make this wadi full of pools', so NRSV, v. 16) poses a minor translation problem.[81] Even when translated, however, I am uncertain as to the connection between the prophecy and the problem it is supposed to address. עשה (make) can be understood as an imperative ('Make this valley full of pools') or as a first-person singular future ('I will make this valley full of pools'), but in either case the prophetic word is insufficient either to ease the concern of the kings or to fulfill the expectation of the reader. The kings want water, not גבים ('pool', 'cistern'). I want a solution that addresses the problem. If the problem is simply one of digging to find existing ground water,[82] this is hardly a difficulty that necessitates the word of YHWH. Further, if גבים are to be understood as natural depressions,[83] then the message is indecipherable without further explanation. Even Burney's, 'I will make this torrent-bed nothing but cisterns', requires v. 17a as an explanation, as he himself notes.[84] Indeed, v. 16 adds nothing to the reader's construction of the narrative, for it is unclear without v. 17, and adds nothing to it. Thus, the first 'word of YHWH' is more cryptic than helpful, providing neither king nor reader

---

80. See, e.g., Werner Reiser, 'Eschatologische Gottessprüche in den Elisa-Legenden', *TZ* 9 (1953), pp. 321-38 (323); B.O. Long, '2 Kings 3 and the Genres of Prophetic Narrative', *VT* 23 (1973). pp. 337-38 (339-40).
81. See the helpful discussion in Cogan and Tadmor, *Kings*, p. 45.
82. Jones, *Kings*, pp. 396-97.
83. Burney, *Notes*, pp. 269-70; Cogan and Tadmor, *Kings*, p. 45.
84. Burney, *Notes*, pp. 269-70.

with useful information regarding YHWH's intention.

The numerous changes in theme within the extended message pose the more pressing problem for me, as does the content of the message. Readers who are familiar with the other miracles of the prophets would not be surprised by Elisha's ability to bring YHWH's message of both salvation to kings and victory in battle. Within the context of a story concerning Elijah's successor and Ahab's son however, readers are likely to be surprised not so much by the provision of water as by the sudden assistance that YHWH is apparently rendering to Israel's military campaign. Here the contrast between 2 Kings 3 and 1 Kings 22 becomes all the more obvious.

There is, however, a possible thematic connection that allows the reader to understand YHWH's action. YHWH's assurance of victory over Moab is introduced by the phrase ונקל זאת בעיני יהוה ('this is a small thing in the eyes of YHWH', v. 18). The contrast is between 'small thing' (נקל, presumably the water) and the great actions of YHWH that are to follow. The focus on YHWH's greatness reminds the reader of Elijah's contest on Mt Carmel, and thus acts as further demonstration for the king of Israel (and readers) of YHWH's power. It is precisely this focus that precipitates the great thematic anti-climax of v. 27.

The fulfillment of this complex prophecy combines a number of perspectives, themes and foci. The various parts need to be separated on the basis of narratological style in order to be fully appreciated. The actual provision of water (v. 20) is recounted from the perspective of someone on the ground, as water flows from the direction of Edom. The drama comes from the והנה ('suddenly') which is used to allow me to view the event from the perspective of a human observer, rather than a detached narrator. This accounts for the lack of specific formula for fulfillment, which would need to come from the narrator.

The focus shifts quickly, as the scene changes both in location and time. Verse 21 begins some time in the past when the Moabites first hear of the approaching army, and recounts the mustering of the Moabite army. Verse 22 returns readers to the narrative present, as they see the miraculously supplied water (בבקר, 'in the morning', bringing us back to the same term in v. 20, and המים, the water, connecting the events that follow to the prior difficulty of the Israelite army [vv. 9, 11, 17, 20]). The wording of the description of the water (אדמים כדם, 'red as blood', v. 22) also reminds me of the choice which the king of Israel made in the strategy of the attack (מדבר אדום, 'the wilderness of

Edom', v. 8), which may suggest that the choice was either fortuitous or already part of YHWH's plan. I then see what the Moabites see, and listen in on their conversation (ויאמרו דם זה, 'and they said, "this is blood"', v. 23).

The entire account of the initial battle itself requires only a single verse (v. 24), and the story moves quickly to recount the fulfillment of Elisha's prophecy (v. 25). The enormity of this action, both in terms of its actual performance and its impact on Moab's economy, is passed over. There is here, however, a rather different relationship between prophecy and fulfillment being played out.

In v. 20, something happens as it has been predicted (v. 17). While this must be interpreted as an action of YHWH, Elisha's role is ambiguous. Is he merely a messenger, or does his inquiry prompt YHWH to act?

In vv. 21-24, this initial action of YHWH precipitates an overly eager attack by the Moabites, which causes their defeat. Thus, readers view a scene where the fulfillment of YHWH's word (here Elisha is simply passive messenger, and the Israelites passive recipients) is given a naturalistic explanation (sun shining on water).

In v. 25, the Israelite army is explicitly obeying instructions. This means that they must believe that Elisha's word is actually YHWH's word before the prophecy can be fulfilled. The other two fulfillments required no such belief on their part (there is no suggestion that the army ever dug trenches). This suggests a significantly different role for the prophet, and also role for YHWH, in the battle plans of the Israelite king. Both the trickery involved in the victory and the explicit instructions regarding the actions of the army after defeating the enemy are reminiscent of the battle accounts in Judges. Readers may recall Gideon and his trumpets, jars and torches (Judg. 7.15-22), or Ehud and his hidden sword (Judg. 3.15-30).

With this parallel, it is Elisha who takes on the role of the judge. The kings of Israel and Judah disappear from the story, except for a brief mention in the words of the Moabites (v. 23). I should note in this context, however, that Elisha also disappears as an actor, as does YHWH. The remaining actors are the Israelites, the Moabites and their king and the king of Edom. The presence that binds the story together is the Word, the Word of Elisha/YHWH, the final fulfillment of which is conspicuously absent in vv. 21-27.

Thus, within the context of my study, the question arises as to the relationship of Elisha to this Word. If the story ended with v. 26, I could safely construct a picture of Elisha the messenger/judge, who delivers Israel from drought and commands them in the conquest of their enemies. Further, there would be a clear connection made between word and action, between prophecy and fulfillment. Elisha predicts and it comes about, Elisha commands and it is done. Surely the word of Elisha is the word of YHWH.[85]

The smooth movement from prophecy to fulfillment that readers might hope for, however, is not reflected in the smooth movement of the narrative. There are numerous disjunctions in the narrative flow in vv. 21-26. Verse 20 has supplied me with a clear, chronological explanation regarding the supply of water to the troops, but v. 21 returns me to the initial muster of Moabite troops, before v. 22 returns me to the narrative present. Further, while v. 20 is also a description of the events from the perspective of the Israelites (note the והנה, 'suddenly'), v. 21 is clearly from the perspective of the narrator, for the information regarding the muster cannot be known by the Israelite troops. Then v. 22 is told from the perspective of the Moabites, while v. 23 is again the narrator, who claims to know the conversation of the Moabite troops.

Verse 24 effects a strange reversal in the movement of the troops. Moab begins by attacking Israel, then Israel is portrayed as attacking the Moabites. There is no explanation given for this reversal of initiative. Israel continues on the attack through v. 25, and pauses at Kir-hareseth with an ambiguous reference to the 'slingers' (הקלעים). The narrative then abruptly changes focus to the king of Moab, who notices that he is not doing very well (v. 26), and who responds by first attempting to break through opposite Edom (v. 26), and then sacrifices his son on the wall (v. 27).

This lack of smooth narrative flow, in chronology, point of view and focus, affects the readers' perception of the movement from prophecy to fulfillment. Readers are forced to work very hard to construct a continuous narrative from the disjunctive details, and thus are forced to work hard to see the connection between Elisha's word and the events that follow.

Even should I succeed in constructing a smooth narrative of prophecy and fulfillment from the text, the entire structure collapses with v. 27.

---

85. I am assuming here that readers assume that YHWH's word will always be fulfilled. The problem for both character and readers is how to discern YHWH's word.

4. *Elisha*

Long points this out most clearly when calls 2 Kings 3 an 'oracle actualization narrative', but must leave out vv. 26, 27 to make this case.[86] Suddenly the actions of the king of Moab cause[87] a 'great wrath' (קֶצֶף־גָּדוֹל) upon Israel. Victory becomes defeat, or at least withdrawal. I am left in the awkward position of needing to fill an almost unfillable gap in the narrative, namely the question of the relationship between this event and the earlier word of Elisha/YHWH.

Commentaries are divided as to the source of the wrath. Gray is unequivocal that the wrath is that of Chemosh, the god of Moab[88], as is Jones.[89] Nelson leaves open the question of whether the wrath is from YHWH or Chemosh.[90] Rehm notes that the narrative is monotheistic, and therefore the wrath must be YHWH's, but also separates the wrath from the sacrifice of the king's son.[91] Studies on the use of the word קֶצֶף (wrath) also prove inconclusive. Montgomery notes that, with two exceptions, the term is used entirely of deity.[92] Yet Würthwein, dating this text to the postexilic era, says that wrath is not connected to God in postexilic literature, but 'um eine selbständige numinose Grosse handle' (proceeds from an independent spiritual dimension).[93] Hobbs takes another tack, and connects Israel's defeat to Joram's (sic) presence, as the story denies Joram victory.[94]

This ambiguity is a creation of the size of the gap in the narrative. The question of why Israel was defeated will not easily go away. Nelson chooses to leave the gap unfilled, responding that the undecidability of the story highlights the undecidability of God.[95] Cogan and Tadmor

---

86. Long, '2 Kings 3', p. 347. Note that Long believes v. 27 is original to the story, but that tradents sought to bring the story in line with the form despite this.

87. וַיְהִי ('and there was') is often used to begin a new action, but the narrative connection is unavoidable.

88. Gray, *Kings*, p. 439.

89. Jones, *Kings*, p. 400.

90. Nelson, *Kings*, p. 168.

91. Martin Rehm, *Das zweite Buch der Könige* (Würtzburg: Echter Verlag, 1982), p. 79.

92. J.A. Montgomery, *A Critical and Exegetical Commentary on the Books of Kings* (ICC; Edinburgh: T. & T. Clark, 1951), p. 364.

93. Würthwein, *Könige*, p. 284.

94. Hobbs, *Kings*, p. 34. Hobbs consistently refuses to allow any possible negative inferences about Elisha in the text. See also the note by D.N. Freeman in Cogan and Tadmor, *Kings*, p. 52 n. 8.

95. Nelson, *Kings*, p. 170.

note the awkwardness of the ending, calling it 'an embarrassment to all (the ancient editor's) readers'.[96] Characteristically, they choose to note the contradiction, but do not offer the reader an effective way to fill the gap.

The problem is not merely the size of the gap. I am frustrated in that the usual explanations for such an event (wrath against Israel) are disallowed by the text.[97] Rehm is correct in noting that Chemosh is nowhere mentioned in the text, is not considered an actor in the story, and is therefore not available as a possible cause.[98] Wrath may be connected to Israel's sin (here the Judges parallel provides explanatory power, although only thematically, since Judges does not use this term), but my text portrays an obedient Israel. The textual connection between the wrath and the sacrifice of the Moabite king's son is equally frustrating, for are readers likely to believe that YHWH's actions can be so influenced by the detestable actions of a foreign king (see Deut. 18.10)? Thus, more than simply cryptic, this simple phrase frustrates both the readers' expectations and their attempts to explain this frustration.

Given the frustrating nature of v. 27, it is possible that readers may simply dismiss this verse from the general impression that is formed of Elisha in the rest of the story. Indeed, many modern scholars have taken this approach, which clearly demonstrates that this is a possible option for the reader. Most readers, however, do not work with convenient solutions such as editorial tampering, which allow scholars to overlook verses not to their liking.

Verse 27 acts as a wrecking ball, knocking down the image of Elisha that I have carefully constructed from the words of the story. Whatever discomfort I may have felt with Elisha's presence with the army in the wilderness, the text offers me the opportunity to characterize Elisha as a true messenger of YHWH, a messenger whose word is not only predictive but also obeyed by kings and armies. The shattering of an important image is a significant event in a story, for I lose faith not only in the particular character, but also in the class of characters of which this image is a representative. Next time I may be much more hesitant about building a strong positive image of the wonder working prophet. Never-

---

96. Cogan and Tadmor, *Kings*, p. 52.
97. Here Cogan and Tadmor provide a useful summary, *Kings*, p. 51.
98. See the summary of Y. Kaufmann in Cogan and Tadmor, *Kings*, p. 51. Unfortunately they fail to provide a footnote detailing where this suggestion might be found.

theless, the prophet has proven useful in aiding the king of Israel in his distress. Insofar as he responds to the initial request by the king, his positive place in the world of the narrative is upheld.

This is accomplished without any direct reference to Elisha, or any suggestion that he has failed to communicate properly the word of YHWH. The prophet performs his duty 'correctly'. I cannot dismiss Elisha as a false prophet, or a lying prophet. It is as a true prophet that I must judge the consequences of his word, and the defeat of Israel is still part of the outworking of his initial prophecy. His role as true prophet of YHWH remains intact. Since his actions occurred within the role, my judgment of him must also affix to my judgment of the role.

2 Kings 4.1-7: The Widow's Oil

This short story provides for the reader the first significant glimpse into the lives of the group called the sons of the prophets, at least as it is viewed by one of their widows. The story also proves an abrupt transition from ch. 3, as Elisha takes on an entirely different role in Israelite society.

The abruptness of this transition is highlighted by Rofé. He uses 1 Kgs 17.8-24 as a parallel, noting that the Elijah story is incorporated into the larger narrative, that is, we know why Elijah is with the widow in Zarephath. Here, however, I am parachuted into an entirely different setting without any context, either geographical or chronological.[99]

The story begins with an אשה אחת ('one woman'), identified by the narrator as מנשי בני־הנביאים ('from the wives of sons of the prophets'). This identifier suggests that the story is told from within the male perspective, since the woman is provided with a place within male society. Thus, as Exum notes, I should not expect the story to present us with an alternative to the dominant ideology.[100] As will be shown, it is precisely her submissive character that presents the opportunity for the miraculous deed of Elisha.

Nonetheless, readers should not assume that women in the Bible are always accorded the same role as housewives in 1950s television. Thus, she begins the drama by 'calling out' (צעקה) to Elisha, suggesting a certain urgency, but also providing readers an opportunity to allow her

---

99. Rofé, *Stories*, p. 132.
100. 'The women occupy narratives that, like husband and father, seek to subordinate and finally control them.' Exum, 'Murder', p. 58.

a degree of power in the narrative. This is due to the possibility that her status as widow gives her the right to demand aid from Elisha.[101] Readers may also note the reversal of roles from 1 Kgs 17.10-11, where it is Elijah who calls (here קרא) to the widow.

Readers are given a variety of possibly contradictory signals regarding the place of this woman in the story. The story begins with her, rather than with Elisha (contrast 4.8), yet she remains unnamed. She is a lowly widow of an unnamed man, yet cries out to Elisha for aid. This ambiguity allows readers a good deal of latitude in constructing her character. Admittedly, the brevity of the story gives me little opportunity to consider her a significant figure, but the narrative certainly begins by placing a good deal of emphasis on her.

Speaking to Elisha, the woman characterizes her late husband as עבדך ('your servant'). While this is a possible indicator of the relationship between Elisha and the sons of the prophets, it is more likely that the word suggests a general difference in social status (see, e.g., 1 Sam. 20.7-8). As rhetoric, the term also places Elisha in a position of obligation, as one responsible for the well-being of this individual.[102]

The woman's statement (עבדך אישי מת ואתה ידעת כי עבדך היה ירא את־יהוה, 'your servant my husband is dead; and you know that your servant feared YHWH', v. 1) is a clever piece of rhetoric in other ways. Elisha, as man of God (v. 7), is further placed in a position of obligation both by the late husband's fear of YHWH and by his knowledge of this fact. Statements such as ידעתי כי ('you know that', v. 2) not only emphasize the factual nature of the statement, but heighten the possibility of the listener's consent to the statement, since the listener, who in this case is addressed as master/patron, is unlikely to confess ignorance of so important a claim.

It is entirely likely that the taking of children in payment of debt was a common occurrence in ancient Israel. Indeed, the law acknowledges this as a possibility (Exod. 21.2-6). Yet Genesis–2 Kings shows little of the life of the ordinary Israelite, preferring to speak of leaders, kings and the wealthy.[103] Thus readers, accustomed to reading of people with

---

101. Readers are likely to assume that Elisha is bound by the law in regards to widows, e.g., Deut. 10.18; 26.12-15. Note the use of צעק ('call out') in Exod. 22.22 in regards to the 'calling out' of widows.

102. See the chapter on 'Slave and Patron' in John Dominic Crossan, *The Historical Jesus* (San Francisco: HarperCollins, 1992), pp. 43-71, especially pp. 59-65.

103. Even the Elisha stories portray the lives of wealthy farmers (Elisha himself,

4. Elisha

few financial constraints, are likely to be emotionally moved by the possible loss of two sons, especially to the widow of a righteous man. In this way any potential the story may have for highlighting the greatness of Elisha is diminished by the strong bonds of obligation that are placed on Elisha's actions.

In fact, readers may question why it is that this event has come about at all. Why is a widow of a servant of Elisha allowed to arrive at this point? Is the prophetic אב ('father') not providing sufficiently for his בנים ('sons')? Given that the narrative draws me to sympathize with the woman's plight, I can choose to blame either the sons of the prophets or the prophet directly. Neither choice allows for a positive perception of prophetism as a way of organizing human society.[104]

The first part of Elisha's response highlights his obligation to her. This is shown by the two parallel uses of the phrase מה אעשה־לך ('what shall I do for you?') in 2 Sam. 21.3 and Gen. 27.37. In the former parallel, David is addressing the Gibeonites. The story clearly indicates that David is obligated in some manner to the Gibeonites, and wishes to release himself from this obligation through expiation (כפר). The latter is in the story of the blessing of Isaac upon Jacob and Esau. Jacob has stolen the blessing, and now Isaac, realizing that he owes something to Esau as the firstborn, attempts to redeem himself. While these two parallels do not offer a definitive understanding of Elisha's statement, they do provide suggestive testimony for the conclusion that Elisha is acting under formal social obligation.

There is another close parallel to follow in 2 Kgs 4.13 (מה לעשות לך, 'what can be done for you?'). There the obligation is more obvious, as Elisha makes direct reference to the חרד (anxious care) which the woman has performed, and to which he is responding. In this case Elisha ties his actions directly to his social obligation to his host.

The rest of the story focuses upon the miraculous provision of oil. The story emphasizes the miraculous nature of the deed by contrasting many large vessels with one small jar, repeating the closing of the door, which emphasizes the absence of Elisha,[105] and providing the detail of

---

1 Kgs 19), kings, powerful foreigners (Naaman, Hazael) and powerful women (2 Kgs 4.8-37).

104. Fohrer notes that this story indicates that the sons of the prophets are not released from their financial obligations by the group. Georg Fohrer, *Die Propheten des Alten Testaments* (Gütersloh: Gerd Mohn, 1977), p. 86.

105. Gray, *Kings*, p. 441.

how the oil stopped flowing exactly when the last vessel was full.

The story also connects Elisha to the event not only in his instructions regarding the miracle itself, but also in having the widow return to Elisha for instructions regarding the disposal of the oil. The story has clearly moved its focus away from the woman. While initially she is given an opportunity to voice concerns that may be attributable to a character acting in her own best interest, v. 7 not only allows her no direct speech, but uses reporting speech to refocus attention on Elisha. The woman's voice is silent, and we hear only Elisha's command (לכי מכרי, 'go, sell'). His command states the obvious use for such a large quantity of oil. Thus, her report is not 'real', in the sense that it serves narratively not as a report of the actions of a specific character, but as a setup for Elisha, allowing him to take credit for this incident.

The miracle itself is reported without reference to its source. Readers are given no indication that YHWH is involved in any way. While the narrative does not explicitly allow for other sources for such events, the story does not give credit where (presumably) credit is due. The parallel Elijah story allows me to see an alternative. 1 Kings 17 makes numerous references to YHWH, including direct speech (v. 8), a כה אמר יהוה statement by Elijah (v. 14), and credit given to YHWH for the miracle (כדבר יהוה, v. 16). The only parallel is found in the mouth of the two widows (1 Kgs 17.12//2 Kgs 4.1).

The 1 Kings 17 parallel is also interesting in another way. In the Elijah story, the oil and meal are for food, and only to the point of sufficiency. 2 Kings 4 stresses not only the superabundant quantity of oil, but also its overabundance (בנותר, v. 7). Elisha's miracle requires the widow to act within the market economy of her time, since she must sell the oil. The widow of Zarephath can operate outside of the market, within an alternative economy set up within the miraculous provision of YHWH, a provision of sufficiency.

Thus, the movement here is from YHWH's provision outside the marketplace to YHWH's participation in the 'usual' strategies of the sale of surplus. Readers are not given the opportunity to imagine an alternative to the economic structure of the larger Israelite society.

This passage represents our first close look at the world of the sons of the prophets. The narrative allows me to glimpse a world not dominated by kings and priests, a possible alternative to the larger societal structure. As quickly as this world is opened to me, it is closed as a possibility for my serious consideration. This world is dominated by economic need, and by the inability of the group to care for its own. It is only the intercession of the great man of God that allows for salvation from economic and familial ruin. This world cannot survive without the miraculous, and even the miraculous can only save by providing a surplus of saleable goods. The movement observed in 1 Kgs 19.21 from producing to not-producing continues. The prophetic way can supply basic needs only through supernatural intervention. It is not an alternative available for ordinary people.

2 Kings 4.8-37: The Shunammite Woman

The story of Elisha and the Shunammite woman can be read in numerous ways. Readers are presented with a character who is wealthy, powerful, forthright and female, in extended dialogue with a prophet whose relationship to the above factors is unknown, except that he is clearly male. This latter factor is thoroughly explored by Mary Shields in a recent article, where she consistently emphasizes the presentation of the Shunammite's femaleness in relationship to Elisha the male prophet.[106]

Even here, however, the simple male/female relationship is clouded by the fact that Elisha is both male and prophet. Thus, in attempting to (re)construct the scene in our minds, do I view their dialogue as one characteristic of female/male relations, or female/prophet interaction? I am further confounded by the continued stress on the Shunammite's wealth, which is contrasted by the economic vacuum in which Elisha is usually presented.[107]

For my purposes, the question that is most pressing is precisely the status of Elisha within the world of the text. Up to this point, I have seen Elisha as a servant to Elijah, and as inheritor of Elijah's mantle, some part of his power and presumably his mission. He has demonstrated his power, although with some degree of failure (3.27). His actions are governed by the request of others, and he has shown no positive initiative until this point. While the narrator has provided no explicit condemnation for any of his actions, I have been given no strong reason to like him as a character.

---

106. Mary E. Shields, 'Subverting a Man of God', *JSOT* 58 (1993), pp. 59-69, passim.

107. E.g. from where does he get his food and shelter, how does he support his servant. Again, the contrast with Elijah is clear, as Elijah experiences hunger and thirst.

While the story must be read against other indications of the place of both prophets and women in that society, the story also plays an important part in my construction of this society. Thus, questions of the 'usual' or 'unusual' nature of this interaction need to be left open as much as possible.

This story is also the first one in the Elisha corpus that presents a character other than Elisha who is portrayed with definite complexity. While the Shunammite woman remains unnamed, readers can certainly piece together a rather complex picture of this person based on her various interactions with Elisha, Gehazi and her husband.

The question of whether the Shunammite woman constitutes a full character as opposed to a type or an agent need not concern me here.[108] While the reader is certainly advised to recognize the depth to which characters are portrayed in the narrative, it is equally important to recognize that ancient literature, and indeed ancient societies, did not have the same concept of the individual as we do, as inheritors of the Freudian tradition.

Indeed, Fred Burnett argues that in ancient Greek literature, all characters are types rather than individuals, and are consistently 'typical, static and immutable'.[109] While there is little parallel narrative for Genesis–2 Kings, van Seters's argument that biblical historiography can be paralleled with the Greek historians suggests that the same might be said about the characters in this story.[110]

The question of the individuality of the characters in this story also has two other aspects to it. First, David McCracken helpfully points out that biblical characters are never *in*dividuals, but are rather *inter*dividuals. Interdividuality is where characters are formed in relation to others and their reaction.[111] Thus, using Gideon as an example, McCracken states that 'this character will change... it will never be fixed, because it dwells in the between of assertion, response and anticipated next response, conducted in words that have histories from other voices'.[112]

This is an excellent description also of the Elisha character as I have

---

108. See Berlin, *Poetics*, p. 23.
109. Fred W. Burnett, 'Characterization and Reader Construction of Characters in the Gospels', *Semeia* 63 (1993), pp. 1-28 (6).
110. Van Seters, *Search*, p. 6, passim.
111. David McCracken, 'Character in the Boundary: Bakhtin's Interdividuality in Biblical Narratives', *Semeia* 63 (1993), pp. 29-42 (31).
112. McCracken, 'Character', p. 31.

been (re)constructing it. Each story transforms the picture of him, not merely adding more information, but changing my existing construction. While one may argue that this does not apply to many minor biblical characters, it applies in a special way to Elisha, since the role he is given (that of *prophet* and *man of God*) lacks sufficient prior social location for the reader to feel certain what is expected of him, except perhaps in a very general way.

At this point modern readers also need to be especially careful not to allow the modern concept of the individual to control the (re)construction of the ancient world of the text. The modern notion of the individual as 'an isolated and self-contained entity'[113] should not cloud my ability to appreciate the idea of personhood that may be found in ancient literature. Luckily, modern readers also have access to other concepts of personhood, such as those pioneered by H.S. Sullivan, as early as the 1930s,[114] as well as the death of the individual as proclaimed by postmodern writers and critics.

Unlike the previous story, this story begins with Elisha, who, for reasons unknown, is walking past Shunem. While the geography of Elisha's journey remains a mystery, readers may already have a certain picture of the village through its presence in an earlier story concerning David. In 1 Kgs 1.3-4, Abishag the Shunammite is brought to the aging David to keep him warm. Her qualification for that job is her great beauty (יפה עד־מאד). Slotki notes that according to Jewish tradition, the Shunammite woman is a sister of Abishag.[115]

The geographical mystery detracts from the positive identification between readers and the characters in the story. While the woman 'belongs' in Shunem, Elisha's unnamed journey does not allow readers to identify with the larger mission of his prophetic activity. Does he merely wander for the sake of wandering? Given the specific sense of mission that accompanies Elijah's movements (1 Kgs 17.2-3, 8-9; 18.1, 17-19, 46; 19.3, 7-8, 15), readers would certainly expect a similar sense of direction from his successor. The failure of the text to provide this

---

113. Patric Mullahy, 'A Theory of Interpersonal Relations and the Evolution of Personality', in Harry S. Sullivan, *Conceptions in Modern Psychiatry* (New York: W.W. Norton & Co., 1940), pp. 439-94 (445).

114. '*a personality* can never be isolated from the complex of interpersonal relations in which the person lives and has his (sic) being' (Sullivan, *Conceptions*, p. 10).

115. I.W. Slotki, *Kings* (Surrey: Soncino, 1950), p. 183.

information detracts from the readers' connection between Elisha and a mission from YHWH.

In one short verse, readers are introduced to the two main characters, the geographical location of the story and the social relationship between the characters. The narrator wastes no words describing the persons involved, for all will presumably become clear as the story unfolds, and as characters come alive in their interdividuality.

This is not to say that he provides no information at all. Identifying the Shunammite as a 'great woman' (אשה גדולה, v. 8) gives her a very specific place in her society. There is a place for great women, within boundaries, even in misogynist societies, for example, Queen Victoria, Nancy Reagan. In fact, their greatness might be seen in the way they test the limits of these boundaries without endangering the structure of society. Indeed, גדולה ('great'), is followed by חזק ('compel'), both of which are words related to the exercising of authority. In employing these terms, the story confounds an easy attempt to typify her behavior. When she acts, is she acting as a woman should, or as a great person should? We as readers have few prior contacts with powerful women, and thus should have few certain expectations of her behavior.

The importance of her greatness is demonstrated by looking at other instances where גדול ('great') is used to describe a person in Genesis–2 Kings.[116] All of them focus attention on the positive status of persons mentioned, whether in terms of economic (2 Sam. 19.33) or political (2 Sam. 3.38) status. גדול can even highlight the status of someone named *Nabal* (1 Sam. 25.2, 3). It indicates a person of high standing in society. As a reader I am made aware that this is a woman to be respected, and my desire also to be respected heightens the positive association I have with this woman.[117]

Nonetheless this is the only instance of the adjectival use of גדל in reference to a woman. Having few textual resources as to the role of great women in that society, and perhaps feeling uncomfortable with the possibility of powerful women in general, I can easily choose to ignore this adjective, and attribute later demonstrations of strength of

---

116. Exod. 11.3; Lev. 19.15; 21.10 (the high priest, +20t.); 1 Sam. 25.2; 2 Sam. 3.38; 5.10; 7.9; 10.5; 19.33; 2 Kgs 5.1; 10.6, 11; 18.19, 28.

117. Contrast Binns, whose paraphrase of the story denies the woman all power (L.E. Binns, *From Moses to Elisha* [Oxford: Clarendon Press, 1929], p. 229).

4. *Elisha*

character to maternal urges[118] or simple lack of manners.[119]

One of the decisions readers must make in a situation such as this is whether to allow previous legal descriptions of how the society 'should' work to cloud their judgment on how that society 'actually' may have functioned (as demonstrated in the narratives). My approach will be to allow the possibility that the description of societal roles, in this case of a particular woman, may not correspond to the assigned legal status. Thus, for example, the question of her status within her community need not be immediately resolved by reference to legal inheritance material, but should be left open to its working out in the rest of the narrative.

Verse 8 can be read as a story-in-miniature. All narrative needs three elements: actor(s), conflict and resolution.[120] All are present in five clauses of v. 8:

(1) once upon a time;
(2) first actor and action: Elisha is going past Shunem;
(3) second actor, a powerful woman, and a potential for conflict due to the presence of two powerful characters;
(4) actual conflict: the woman attempts to exercise power over Elisha. Characteristically חזק ('compel') is used of actions involving control over such things as kingdoms (2 Sam. 3.1) or hair (2 Sam. 18.9). It also suggests that the one performing the action is more powerful than the one upon whom the action is performed (2 Sam. 15.5). Gray translates חזק as 'constrained', an action that requires Elisha's acceptance in accordance with the ancient Semitic convention of hospitality.[121] The question remains open, however, as to how bound Elisha feels by normal societal conventions;
(5) he accedes, not only once, but habitually. Round one of the conflict goes to woman.

---

118. Gray, *Kings*, p. 446.
119. Long, *Kings*, p. 56. Alter skirts the issue by translating *gedolah* as 'large' ('Conventions', p. 125).
120. See Claus Westermann, 'Die Arten der Erzählung in der Genesis' in his *Forschung am alten Testament* (Munich: Chr. Kaiser Verlag, 1964), passim.
121. Gray, *Kings*, p. 443. Fuchs uses 'seize', an even stronger term (Esther Fuchs, 'The Literary Characterization of Mothers and Sexual Politics in the Hebrew Bible', in A.Y. Collins [ed.], *Feminist Perspectives on Biblical Scholarship* [Chico, CA: Scholars Press, 1985], pp. 117-36 [127]).

The reason I read this as a conflict is that it is precisely the social status of Elisha that is so often at issue in his stories.[122] Usually the story examines his status in relation to that of the king or the sons of the prophets. Here the story presents Elisha in the presence of the respectable class in Israel. Thus, while most commentators assume that Elisha's status is superior to the woman's, I believe it is precisely this question that is at issue in the story. This is a farmer/prophet, prophet of the wild God of the desert,[123] relating directly to polite society.

In vv. 9-10, her care for Elisha with food and shelter and her description of his status add to our identification with her. Her explicit description of Elisha's holiness follows rather than precedes her hospitality. It should not be read as the 'recognition' by the woman of the status normally accorded a prophet[124]—this is the only place in Genesis–2 Kings where a prophet is referred to as 'holy'.[125]

Note how the wording of her speech continues to focus the readers' attention on the woman. 'I know that the man of God is holy' (v. 9). What is shown is not a description of Elisha ('the man of God is holy') but a description of the woman's knowledge ('I know'). Readers may make a parallel with the stories of Rahab in Joshua 2 and 6, whose knowledge is one of the foci of that story.[126] I could even say that she confers holiness on Elisha—she sets him apart by making a separate room for him—which again elevates her status in the text, just as earlier the anointing of kings elevated Samuel's status.[127]

The description of the making and furnishing of the room continues in the direct speech of the woman. These things are not descriptive of a space, but of the social status and generosity of this particular woman.[128] It is her character as a woman of substance and hospitality that is highlighted. This enhances my opinion of her, and also my

---

122. The open-ended social status of prophets makes it difficult for readers to find a comfortable place for them in 'normal' society. People who do not 'fit' are relegated to marginal status, and are unnecessary to the functioning of that society.

123. Petersen, *Role*, p. 49.

124. Nelson, *Kings*, p. 173.

125. Cogan and Tadmor, *Kings*, p. 57.

126. Note the repetition of ידעתי ('I know') in Josh. 2.4, 5, 9.

127. Note the accompanying prophecy in 1 Sam. 10, which was later fulfilled in every detail.

128. Commentators differ on the social status implied by the furnishings. Montgomery regards this as 'essential furniture' (*Kings*, p. 366). I am more inclined to agree with Würthwein, who views the furniture as luxurious (*Könige*, p. 291).

identification with her. This action also establishes that Elisha is in considerable social debt to the woman.

Commentators are divided as to the motivation for the woman's hospitality. Gray suggests that the woman has the room prepared 'so that the menage of the family...would be completely safeguarded against the consequences of contact with the "holy" man of God'.[129] This suggestion is interesting as it implies the contamination of the profane by the holy. Robinson offers a similar explanation, stating that 'close proximity to the prophet on the part of a sinner would have been regarded as dangerous',[130] although he offers no supporting references. Jones rightly notes that Gray provides no parallels for his argument, and thus offers the alternative explanation that the woman believes Elisha will bring a blessing to her home.[131] Fohrer, too, suggests self-serving motivation on the part of the woman.[132]

My search for motivation on the part of the woman is itself motivated by Elisha's concern to repay her hospitality (v. 13). Without Elisha's inquiry to Gehazi, I may have easily accepted the woman's generosity as Elisha's due (although Elijah pays for his bread and board with meal and oil in 1 Kgs 17.14). Thus, this interaction and its dynamics need to be studied before passing judgment on the characters themselves.

In v. 11, the second ויהי היום (cf. v. 8) indicates a shift in point of view from the woman to Elisha. Readers walks with Elisha up the stairs and into his room. They are in Elisha's space. They watch through his eyes as he lies on the bed and dispatches Gehazi to summarily summon his host (v. 12).

The switch in point of view does not blind readers to the verbal parallel between the woman's words and Elisha's actions. The text repeats בא ('come'), סור ('turn in') and שמה ('there') (v. 10 בבאו אלינו יסור שמה, 'when he came to her he would turn in there'; v. 11 ויבא שמה ויסר, 'and he came there and turned in'). The parallel is such as to make the woman's words prophetic. Elisha does what the woman says he will do.

The disruption in point of view also does not negate the social realities of privilege. Most commentators assume that Elisha has the

---

129. Gray, *Kings*, p. 444.
130. J. Robinson, *The Second Book of Kings* (Cambridge: Cambridge University Press, 1976), pp. 42-43.
131. Jones, *Kings*, p. 404-405.
132. Fohrer, *Propheten*, p. 87.

authority to summon and speak indirectly to the woman.¹³³ However, while the woman might be thought to accede to Elisha's summons due to her respect for his holiness, I regard Elisha the farmhand (1 Kgs 19.19) summoning a great woman as a possible social misdemeanor. Again, Elisha's status in the text is open-ended, while that of the woman is given (גדולה, 'great one') and repeatedly affirmed by her words and action.

The woman comes and stands לפניו ('before him', v. 12). The question of 'before whom?' is important as it provides a clue to the social relationship between the three characters. If the woman stands before Gehazi, this would indicate that she accepts his place as intermediary between herself and Elisha. If she stands before Elisha, this would heighten my puzzlement as to why Elisha speaks to Gehazi with the woman standing directly in front of him.

In a fascinating study, Yannai suggests a homeoteleuton, in which the לפניו ('before him') of v. 12 was at one time (possibly on purpose) interchanged with the בפתח ('at the door') of v. 15.¹³⁴ He argues this based on the similarity of the words surrounding these terms (ויקרא־לה ותעמד לפניו ויאמר, 'and he called her, and she stood before him and he said', vv. 12-13; ויקרא־לה ותעמד בפתח ויאמר, 'and he called to her, and she stood in the door and he said', vv. 15-16). While I would agree with him that returning these words to their 'rightful' place would make better sense of the entire story, I do not believe this option is open to a narrative reading in a case where the text is grammatically correct. At least I would first like to try to make sense of the text as it stands, before resorting to emendations of convenience.¹³⁵

The question also arises here of the reason why Elisha would speak to the woman through his servant. Long expresses the common

---

133. Especially Burke O. Long, 'The Shunammite Woman in the Shadow of the Prophet', *BR* 7 (1991), pp. 12-19 (14).

134. Y. Yannai, 'Elisha and the Shunammite: (II Kings 4:8-37). A Case of Homoeoteleuton, or a Text Emendation by Ancient Masoretes?', in E. Fernandez Tejero (ed.), *Estudios Masoreticos* (Madrid: Instituto 'Arias Montano', 1983), pp. 125-35 (127-31). Yannai suggests that the emendation is very early, and is not corrected so that the woman is not near Elisha during the conversation regarding the birth of the child, which is a divine promise (p. 131).

135. Baumgartner also would prefer to emend the text, to remove the difficulty of the need to call back the woman even though there is no record of her having left (W. Baumgartner, *Eucharisterion* [Göttingen: Vandenhoeck & Ruprecht, 1923], p. 156).

conviction that Elisha's speech clearly shows his pre-eminence,[136] and clearly the use of messengers in Genesis–2 Kings indicates that the one who sends the messenger is more powerful than the one who receives the message. Nonetheless, this case is clearly unusual in that the messenger continues to be employed when both parties are present. In this way the usual messenger style is used beyond its usual limits, namely the sending of a message to someone not present. The position of power granted to Elisha in the use of a messenger is removed by his transgression of the boundaries of the form.

One possible parallel that may be helpful here is the story of Naaman. In 5.10, Elisha again sends out a servant to bring a message to Naaman regarding his healing. Naaman is angered by this, for he had expected certain behavior from the prophet (5.11), which included personal attention. Here again, however, I cannot reach easy conclusions regarding the use of intermediaries in conversation. Naaman's status is conflicted because he is both foreigner and great man (גדל, v. 1), and his anger may be caused by either Elisha's use of an intermediary or Elisha's non-use of expected activity associated with magical healing or both. Thus, Elisha's use of an intermediary can be interpreted as haughty and/or anti-magical. Nonetheless the woman's direct response to Elisha heightens our awareness of the oddness of the use of Gehazi in the conversation, causing us to identify with the woman in the directness of her speech.

Readers could choose to emphasize the awe-filled service of the woman (הנה חרדת אלינו את־כל־החרדה, 'since you have taken such anxious care of us', v. 13) rather than the strength of her response (בתוך עמי אנכי ישבת, 'I dwell among my own people', v. 13).[137] It must be recognized, however, that חרד is Elisha's interpretation of her actions, which the reader can choose to believe or disbelieve.[138] I have chosen to emphasize the strength of her character and her speech, which belie Elisha's reading of their comparative status.

The dynamics of power need attention as well. Elisha's first offer is to mediate human political power to her (v. 13); reliance on the

---

136. B.O. Long, 'A Figure at the Gate: Readers, Readings and Biblical Theologians', in G. Tucker, *et al.* (eds.), *Canon, Theology and Old Testament* (Philadelphia: Fortress Press, 1988), pp. 166-86 (170).

137. See, e.g., Gray, *Kings*, p. 445.

138. Sternberg reminds us that while the narrator is always reliable in his presentation of events, the characters may not be (*Poetics*, pp. 112-13, passim).

miraculous is secondary. This suggests that the text is operating in a semantic world where the power of king and military is seen to be of primary importance.[139] In this case her reply can be read as her recognition of her own superior status to Elisha. As one who lives in the area, she claims access to any influence that she needs. These are her people (עמי), not his. She can get what she wants without him.[140]

This is intensified if I read into this story Mieke Bal's recognition of possible patrilocal societal structures.[141] It is possible that she is in fact telling the truth, that these are her people, not her husband's. This is a possibility that underscores her social status. In any case, her reply is a curt[142] dismissal of Elisha's usefulness to her in this regard. She has no need for help from this prophet, holy or otherwise.

Elisha's second question in v. 14 continues to be indirect, through Gehazi. Readers are still looking through the eyes of Elisha, although we are becoming uncomfortable with the world that appears through these eyes.

Note that it is upon Gehazi's reminder of her lack of children (אבל בן אין־לה, v. 14) that Elisha concludes that what she really wants is a child (v. 16). Until this point there is no indication of any lack in her world. While it may be possible to assume that the text's world would have no room for a contented childless woman,[143] the fact that she does not

---

139. Ahlström uses 4.13 as a descriptor of Elisha's actual role in his society (G.W. Ahlström, 'King Jehu, A Prophet's Mistake', in A.L. Merrill [ed.], *Scripture in History and Theology* [Pittsburgh: Pickwick Press, 1977], pp. 47-69 [57]). Würthwein contends that vv. 12-15 are added to the story to elevate Elisha in the eyes of the authorities, and also to demonstrate that the Shunammite has no false motives (*Könige*, p. 292). In this way, both commentators underscore the importance of human political authority in the narrative.

140. Fuchs characterizes her response as 'proud' ('Literary Characterizations', p. 127). Shields suggests that in the woman's response, she 'maintains equal footing with the man of God' ('Subverting the Man of God', p. 62).

141. Bal, *Death*, p. 85.

142. She responds in four words to Elisha's 18-word question.

143. Montgomery states that Gehazi 'reports to his master her heart's desire', (*Kings*, p. 368). See also Rofé, 'Classification', p. 433; Slotki, *Kings*, p. 184. Renteria assumes that the woman must want a son, but also notes that she resists (Tamis Hoover Renteria, 'The Elijah/Elisha Stories: A Socio-Cultural Analysis of Prophets and People in Ninth-Century B.C.E. Israel', in R.B. Coote [ed.], *Elijah and Elisha in Socioliterary Perspective* [Semeia Studies; Atlanta: Scholars Press, 1992], pp. 75-126 [105]). Rofé in his *Prophetical Stories* also notes that Elisha acts 'without any regard or understanding for the Shunammite's feelings' (p. 30).

express this wish, and that her response is certainly ambiguous (אל־אדני איש האלהים אל־תכזב בשפחתך, 'no, my lord, man of God, do not lie to your servant', v. 16), suggests that this question must be left open.[144] The reader who identifies with the woman thus shares her ambiguous and ambivalent response to the pronouncement.

One might also note here the similarity between this story and the annunciation stories in Gen. 18.9-15 (Sarah), Gen. 25.19-25 (Rebekah), Judges 13 (Samson's mother) and 1 Samuel 1 (Hannah). Alter helpfully notes the variations in this story, the most salient of which he believes to be the fact that the boy (they are always boys) turns out to be an anonymous peasant rather than a hero. He uses this anomaly to suggest that this 'enables the writer to convey without explicit commentary a rather complicated attitude toward Elisha which includes both awe of his powers and satiric judgment of the all-too-human way he exercises them'.[145]

Similarly, Shields calls this story 'a parody of the annunciation type-scene'.[146] Fuchs notes that the annunciation theme is only one of many themes in the story, in contrast to the singular focus of the other type-scenes.[147] In general, readers are fully in control of the parallels they wish to make, but this one has much to recommend it. If I note this parallel, I am left with a rather twisted type-scene, the parodic aspects of which again diminish my impression of the man of God.

Elisha's prophecy regarding her pregnancy (v. 16) is also devoid of references to YHWH.[148] This minimizes the association between the prophet and YHWH, placing the power directly in the hands of the prophet. The narrator's summary of the fulfillment of the prophecy ascribes the words of power to Elisha, rather than YHWH (אשר־דבר אליה אלישע, 'as Elisha had said to her', v. 17). Nelson calls this a text

---

144. Shields notes that the structure of the woman's second response parallels Judg. 19.23 and 2 Sam. 13.12, both of which are rape scenes ('Subverting the Man of God', p. 62).

145. Robert Alter, 'How Convention Helps Us Read', *Prooftexts* 3 (1983), pp. 115-30 (126).

146. Shields, 'Subverting the Man of God', p. 63.

147. Fuchs, 'Literary Characterizations', p. 127. In contrast, Robinson uses the parallel stories of Sarah and Hannah to show the reproach that barrenness would bring to a woman (*Kings*, pp. 43-44).

148. Shields, 'Subverting the Man of God', p. 63. Würthwein rewrites the story leaving out all references to God (*Könige*, p. 294).

'decorated with some theological frosting'.[149] The focus on prophet rather than YHWH suggests that prophetic power is unavailable in the absence of a prophet.

The woman's reply to Elisha is ambiguous at best (v. 16). Reading aloud, readers can inflect the words to express delight, disbelief, sarcasm or even horror. Her words are clearly deferential (אדני ... בשפצתך, 'my lord... your servant') yet they express disbelief (אל־תכזב, 'do not lie'). But ambiguity need not detract from the class interest of the story. Rather, it maintains the illusion that these are positive stories about the prophet, for they can be read as welcome miracles, while undermining through ambiguity the hope for salvation that comes via the prophets.[150]

The deferential tone of the woman's remark (אדני ... בופחתך, 'my lord ... your servant' v. 16) does not necessarily undermine the reading that the woman claims social status superior to that of Elisha. Rather, the force of the oracle in v. 16 has created a shift in the relationship. Readers are no longer in the day-to-day world of farmers and childless widows, but have entered the prophetic world of oracle and divine power. This can be seen clearly in the transition from an offer of political aid (היש לדבר־לך אל־המלך, 'can I speak to the king for you', v. 13) to an oracle concerning the future (v. 16). This transition initiates a transformation in their relative status; the prophet is now lord, and the woman is maidservant. Within the prophetic world, Elisha has no rivals.

In v. 17 the narrator dutifully records the fulfillment of Elisha's prophecy. Whether or not it was a welcome event, Elisha's power prevails. Elisha may be characterized as weaker than Elijah in general,[151] but there is no doubt as to his power. The question is rather of the source of the power, the use to which it is put and its dispersal after his death.

Note here the parallel in Gen. 21.2. There Sarah gives birth to Isaac למועד אשר־דבר אתו אלהים ('at the time of which God had spoken to him'). In our passage, the Shunammite gives birth כעת חיה אשר־דבר אליה אלישע ('in due time, as Elisha had spoken to her', v. 17). Just as in

---

149. Nelson, *Kings*, p. 171.

150. It is not my contention that the text is unambiguously negative toward prophetic groups. Rather, the praise for the prophet on the surface of the text continues the illusion that these stories present a positive picture of prophetism. Finally, however, the text undermines this hope, presenting the prophetic alternative as unworkable as a social structure.

151. Deist, 'Two Miracle Stories', p. 82.

the preceding parallel with Genesis 18, Elisha takes the place of God in the story. The transfer of power from God to Elisha alters the readers' perception of the power, for once it has lost its connection to the divine it loses credibility.

In vv. 18-25a, the action moves quickly through the boy's early life, but slows dramatically to allow the reader to witness the moment of his death, seated on his mother's lap. Here again my sympathy is directed firmly in the direction of the woman, as we watch that most heart-rending of scenes, the death of a child.

Readers are not, however, allowed to pause and mourn. The action resumes immediately with the woman placing the child symbolically on the bed of the one responsible, then leaving him to take action. Her conversations with her husband and with the servant place her clearly in charge of the situation.[152]

The husband's reply to the woman's request (vv. 22-23) places Elisha in an entirely new role. The husband is of the opinion that Elisha's role is limited to חדש ('new moon') or שבת ('sabbath', v. 23). The first term reminds me of the feast at Saul's table in 1 Samuel 20. This is presented as a customary event, without specific references to cultic connection. The cultic connection is much more clear in Num. 10.10 and 28.11, where sacrifice is clearly indicated (זבחי שלמיכם, 'sacrifices of well being', עלתיכם..., 'burnt offerings', 10.10; עלה, 'burnt offerings', 28.11). While neither חדו nor שבת require the presence of a priest, the connection is cultic rather than prophetic. This notion of Elisha as cultic functionary is in marked contrast to the more usual role of Elisha as wonder worker, and creates further role confusion as readers attempt to construct a coherent picture of Elisha.

Verse 25b switches focus to Elisha. But the exclamatory tone of his speech suggests that it is continuing in the heightened emotional world of the woman. The trivial details of Gehazi's walk to the woman and repetition of the questions are brushed aside (cf. 4.3), just as she brushes the questions themselves aside as she has that of her husband, with an understated שלום 'peace'.

Her strong, controlling grip on the feet of Elisha is fully in keeping with the picture readers have of her so far.[153] The combination of

---

152. Contra Robinson, who suggests that she acts to save Elisha's credibility as a prophet (*Kings*, p. 44).

153. Long, 'A Figure at the Gate', p. 180. Contra Jones, who views it only as a sign of obeisance or respect (*Kings*, p. 408).

petitionary pose (ברגליו, 'at his feet') with controlling force (again חזק) signal a woman not to be trifled with, even in distress. The petitionary pose also reminds me of the dual relationship of the two characters. In the world of the everyday, the woman has superior social status, but when miraculous power is needed, Elisha is fully in charge. Here her petition confirms for me that I have re-entered the latter world, and I can expect further miracles.

Elisha's response to the woman's gesture (ויהוה העלים ממני, 'YHWH has hidden it from me', v. 27) can be contrasted with Samuel's prior divine revelation in 1 Sam. 9.15 and Ahijah's divine revelation in 1 Kgs 14.5.[154] These parallels predispose us to inflect Elisha's speech with a tone of surprise. Readers, however, are not automatically similarly inclined toward surprise.[155] Given the lack of communication between Elisha and YHWH in the text (the Elisha stories never record *any* direct speech from YHWH to Elisha), and growing scepticism of prophetism as embodied in Elisha, readers might be more surprised by Elisha fulfilling our expectations than not.

In vv. 28-30, the woman again deals directly with Elisha, even though he continues to speak to Gehazi rather than to her. Elisha's refusal to speak directly to the woman may suggest a dismissive attitude on his part, an attitude that could be shared by readers. But I must consider that even as a male reader, I am constantly drawn to identify with her. This identification could be that of a parent or adult sympathizing with the loss of a child. But this does not account for my identification with her before she became a mother. Further, the wording of her challenge to Elisha in v. 28 (השאלתי בן מאת אדני, 'did I ask my lord for a son?') reminds me that this is not merely a grieving mother, but a powerful woman who demands that wrongs be righted.[156] This is emphasized further in v. 30, when the woman refuses to allow Elisha to assign this task to his servant and his staff.[157]

---

154. Cogan and Tadmor, *Kings*, p. 58.

155. Readers are able to believe that Elisha was surprised, yet this does not mean that they need to be surprised by his lack of knowledge.

156. Hobbs goes so far as to state that 'her actions are characterized by a degree of cold, effective control' (*Kings*, p. 47).

157. Both Fohrer ('Die Elisa Uberlieferung', p. 89) and Gray (*Kings*, p. 447) note the parallels between Elisha's use of his staff and similar uses of Moses' staff in Exod. 4.1-4 and 17.8-13. Despite this, Gray does not believe the staff is meant to be effectual in healing the boy (*Kings*, p. 446).

4. *Elisha*

The inclusion of שאל ('ask') in v. 28 is also reminiscent of 1 Sam. 1.20, 27, where Hannah recognizes that Samuel is born as a result of her asking (כי מיהוה שאלתיו, 'for I asked YHWH for him', v. 20). The contrast can be made between YHWH as legitimate receptor of petitions and Elisha, who responds to petitions he does not receive. Elisha, then, takes on the role of God, a role he is unable to fill.

The woman's oath (v. 30) is one of only three oaths (of the type חי־יהוה, 'as YHWH lives') by women in Genesis–2 Kings. The first is by the widow of Zarephath in the parallel Elijah story (1 Kgs 17.12), and the second by Abigail to David in 1 Sam. 25.26. The Abigail parallel is particularly instructive, for there we have another instance of a woman of intelligence, power and action speaking in a superficially deferential manner to direct the actions of a male power figure.[158]

Further, the woman's phrase (חי־יהוה וחי־נפשך אם־אעזבך, 'as YHWH lives, I will not leave you', v. 30) is identical to the one used by Elisha in 2.4. If the oath by Elisha in ch. 2 is read as a positive assertion of his own authority, I must read this oath in a similar way. Here, however, rather than being a statement that directs the actions of the speaker, it has the effect of directing the actions of the listener. It is not 'I am coming with you', but rather 'you are coming with me'.[159]

The response of Elisha to the woman's declaration (ויקם וילך אחריה, 'so he rose up and followed her', v. 30) is also a direct repetition of his response to Elijah's call (1 Kgs 19.21). This parallel strongly indicates that Elisha is not simply acceding to the request of a distraught woman, but is following the lead of the one in charge.

Gehazi's inability to restore the life of the boy can be read in a number of ways. But even this way of stating the situation biases my reading. The actions of Gehazi correspond perfectly to the command he was given (ושמת משענתי על־פני הנער, 'lay my staff on the face of the child', v. 29 // וישם את־המשענת על־פני הנער, 'and he lay the staff on the face of the child', v. 31). Thus, the failure is that of Elisha.[160] In this instance it

---

158. See Long, 'The Shunammite Woman', p. 17.

159. So Cogan and Tadmor, *Kings*, p. 58. Contra Hobbs, *Kings*, p. 48, who understands this as the woman insisting on accompanying Elisha. While this is possible, I can hardly imagine a story in which the woman stays behind in Elisha's house while the prophet goes to her house to revive her son.

160. Jones suggest that Gehazi's mission is not one of healing (*Kings*, p. 409). However, he is unable to reconcile this view with v. 30, where clearly the woman forces Elisha to accompany her. If Elisha was not intending to follow, I must

is the woman's insistence on Elisha's presence that is prophetic, rather than Elisha's instructions to Gehazi.

The failure of Gehazi to perform the task, even with the staff and assurance of Elisha, also demonstrates the connection between prophetic power and the presence of the prophet himself. Thus, the implication is that a prophetic movement is left without power in the absence of the prophet.[161] In reading this readers learn to associate acts of power with 'great men of old' rather than prophetic communities. Thus, contemporary prophetic communities (i.e. those contemporary with any reader) can be thought of as lacking the ability to demonstrate divine presence, for they certainly lack great men such as Elisha.

The narrative slows again in vv. 32-35. Readers are given a careful step-by-step account of the actions of Elisha and the recovery of the boy. While certainly this is a technique to heighten suspense, the fact that there is suspense to be heightened draws my attention to the provisional nature of Elisha's power. This is clearly the arena of power that belongs exclusively to Elisha, but his previous failure through Gehazi casts doubt on his abilities.

Fuchs notes that this particular miracle is explained in great detail, in contrast to the simple word or seemingly disconnected action that Elisha so often used. She reads this presentation as more medical than miraculous.[162] The contrast with Naaman's healing in 5.10, 11 is particularly striking, as there Naaman appears to expect what this boy receives.

The detail in the action might also affect readers' understanding of

---

presume that he had expected Gehazi to perform the miracle. Gray suggests that Gehazi is sent 'as a pledge of personal engagement and as a means of allaying the mother's impatience' (*Kings*, p. 446), but I wonder how this would have allayed her impatience if it was not meant to be effectual. Conroy understands Gehazi's action as his own attempt at healing (*Samuel*, p. 202), while Slotki notes that according to Jewish tradition Gehazi failed because of his doubt (*Kings*, p. 187). Hobbs vacillates on who is to blame for Gehazi's failure (*Kings*, pp. 48, 52, 54), while Shields simply assumes that Gehazi's failure is Elisha's failure ('Subverting the Man of God', p. 65).

161. Rofé calls Gehazi's character 'a nullity' ('Classification', p. 435). Rofé does not reach the same conclusions I do, for he understands the negative portrayal of Gehazi as a means of highlighting Elisha's holiness and generosity (*The Prophetical Stories*, p. 32 n.10). Readers can conclude for themselves whether they are finding a holy and generous Elisha.

162. Fuchs, 'Literary Characterizations', p. 128.

Elisha's power in another way. Gray understands the pacing in v. 35 as relaxation after exertion.[163] Hobbs understands this as suggesting Elisha's agitation at his initial failure.[164] Deist uses the parallel Elijah story as a contrast, concluding that the story presents Elisha as the weaker of the two prophets.[165] In this way, a passage that highlights the miraculous and powerful works of Elisha can simultaneously undermine the readers' perception of his power.

His success in this regard in no way changes his relationship to the woman. While he is clearly in charge of doing miracles, the moment the miracle is accomplished the text returns power to the woman.[166] Finally, in v. 36 Elisha speaks directly to the woman, for only the second time in the story. While the statement is in the form of a command (שְׂאִי בְנֵךְ, 'take your son'), this accession to her status suggests that he has finally recognized the legitimacy of her claim over him.

Both instances where Elisha speaks to the Shunammite woman (vv. 16, 36) involve Elisha giving the woman a son. The first is the initial prophecy regarding his birth, the second announces to her the boy's return to life. Both instances highlight Elisha as the giver of life, placing him clearly in the position of God (cf. 5.7). This usurpation of the role of God is not likely to endear Elisha to readers.

I need not overlook the prayer of Elisha to YHWH in order to sustain this reading. The brief mention of this action (וַיִּתְפַּלֵּל אֶל־יהוה, 'and he prayed to YHWH', v. 33) can serve as a vestige of what we have been expecting. The prayer is understood as a reminder of the contrast between this healing and that of Elijah in 1 Kgs 17. 17-24. In the Elijah story, not only is the act of praying to YHWH recorded, but so are the words of the two (or four) prayers (vv. 20, 21). The healing of the boy is attributed directly to YHWH (v. 22), and the woman responds to the event by acknowledging the connection between Elijah and YHWH (v. 24). In contrast, in the Elisha story YHWH does not function as an actor, one who acts. While Elisha directs words or thoughts toward YHWH, YHWH is not given credit for either word or deed. It is Elisha who acts, and as we have seen, in a rather non-miraculous way. It is

---

163. Gray, *Kings*, p. 447.
164. Hobbs, *Kings*, pp. 52-53.
165. Deist, 'Two Miracle Stories', p. 82.
166. Contra Rofé, who believes that Elisha is restored to a lofty position at the end of the story. He notes, however, that Elisha's lofty position is also an alienated one (*The Prophetical Stories*, p. 31).

Elisha before whom the woman bows. The credit that should have been YHWH's now goes to Elisha.

The woman responds with the recognition of his power by bowing down to the ground. She then takes her son and removes herself from the sphere of his power (v. 37).[167] In the end, I am left with a picture of a prophet whose claim to power/status arises from his ability to do unnecessary miracles. It is only the supervision of the powerful that constrains him to be responsible for his activities, and to clean up the mess he has created.

Thus the narrative continues to highlight the power of Elisha, here even to the point of his ascension to God-like status. In doing so, it moves beyond the usual relationship of power in which the prophet's power clearly comes from YHWH. The text also presents this power in a context that does not connect with the larger program of the history of Israel, or the larger movement of the will of YHWH. Elisha wanders the countryside in a meaningless journey, giving life where it is not asked for, and providing help only when it is demanded of him. In this way, the narrative questions both the source and the usefulness of Elisha's miraculous activity.

2 Kings 4.38-41: Stew

Chapter 4 ends with two stories in which Elisha interacts further with the sons of the prophets. One of the continuing difficulties for readers is relating the picture these stories paint of Elisha as head of small prophetic communities with the contrasting picture of Elisha as international power broker in regular contact with the king. Whether this contrast leads to confusion or complexity is largely up to the reader.

As usual, the narrator squeezes all relevant (in his eyes) background material into the first few words. He attempts to connect this story to the larger context by having Elisha return (שׁוב) to Gilgal. Gilgal has been mentioned earlier in 2.1, where Elijah and Elisha are coming from Gilgal. This suggests that Gilgal may have been a place of some importance to Elisha, although we are given little evidence to work with.

Here readers are given the necessary social background by being informed that the famine was in the land. Jones suggests that the use of

---

167. Contrast Auld, who reads the story as ending with the woman 'speechless... in her gratitude' (A.G. Auld, *I and II Kings* [Philadelphia: Westminster Press, 1986], p. 164).

the definite article (והרעב, '*the* famine') connects this famine to 8.1-6.[168] Yet Gesenius suggests that there is no reason to look for another instance of the thing just because of the presence of a definite article.[169] Further there is no reason to go searching for famines in order to understand the story. The famine becomes important as I attempt to understand the actions of the characters in the story.

The final piece of relevant material in v. 38 brings in the sons of the prophets, and their relationship to Elisha (ובני הנביאים ישבים לפניו, 'and the sons of the prophets were sitting before him'). Here I can construct a number of scenarios, depending on how I understand ישב ('sitting', cf. 6.1). At this early stage in the story the reader is advised to assume as little as possible, allowing the story itself to fill in (or not) gaps in our knowledge. I remember, however, that there are other stories on which to draw to fill in these gaps. For now I will understand ישב ('sitting') as implying authority but not permanent dwelling, since the rest of the corpus does not allow for a sedentary Elisha.

Elisha then orders his servant to prepare a meal for the sons of the prophets (v. 38).[170] His instructions are brief and in the imperative (ויאמר לנערו שפת הסיר הגדולה ובשל נזיד לבני הנביאים, 'and he said to his servant, "Put the large pot on"', v. 38), which may suggest that the food for the meal is readily at hand, or that the servant is left to his own devices. While in some ways this is part of the introductory material, it sets the plot in motion through the use of direct speech.

Someone then goes out into the field to gather herbs (ארת, v.39). The identity of the person who goes out into the field is unknown. The use of אחד ('one') likely implies that this person is one of the company of the prophets, since there is no indication that Elisha has multiple servants. The reader follows this person out to the field, and watches as he finds a גפן שדה ('wild vine') and gathers some פקעת שדה ('wild gourds') into his garment. This plant has been identified by scholars as a plant that is bitter and has strong laxative properties.[171] While most readers are in no position to argue with the identification of wild gourds in Israel, they might be tempted to be suspicious of a firm identification

---

168. Jones, *Kings*, p. 410.

169. *Gesenius' Hebrew Grammar* (ed. E. Kautzch; rev. A.E. Cowley; Oxford: Clarendon Press, 1910), #126, q-t.

170. Gray's suggestion that the meal is meant 'to have some exciting physical effect' (*Kings*, p. 448) is an unlikely reading given the context of the famine.

171. See Fohrer, *Propheten*, p. 90; Gray, *Kings*, p. 448.

based on so little textual evidence, assuming that this conjecture is available to them.

There is a significant difference between the story in 2 Kings 4 and that same story read through the lens provided by the identification of the gourd. The latter story becomes comical, as I view Elisha heroically using the power of YHWH (presumably) to rescue this group from diarrhoea. For the purposes of this reading, I will bracket this possible identification, and try to take the story seriously as an act of salvation.

Verse 39 reaches its climax at the end, noting their ignorance of the type of plant which he had picked (כי־לא ידעו, 'for he did not know').[172] Readers who ignore scholarly identification of the plant also shares the ignorance of the sons of the prophets. Any reader with any familiarity with eating wild plants will immediately recognize that this is a serious mistake on the part of the man. The man is clearly a fool, and should have known better. Here again the sons of the prophets are portrayed in a negative way, as foolish enough to prepare food with unknown ingredients. Renteria's suggestion that famine leads to the eating of unfamiliar food is possible, but the ease of Elisha's command in v. 38, and the presence of a meal in v. 41, implies that death is not imminent.[173]

Readers continue to follow the movement of the food from garment to stew to pouring out to eating (ויצקו לאנשים לאכול, v. 40). The response of the sons of the prophets is immediate (כאכלם, 'while they were eating'), suggesting that they could tell merely by the taste that something was wrong. The ignorance of the gatherer and the readers is not shared by the eaters.

Elisha is immediately told of the problem. This creates for readers the expectation that Elisha will do something to help. It also reminds readers that Elisha is responsible for this meal to begin with. He initiated its preparation. The story could easily have had a meal prepared anonymously, with Elisha merely present at the event. Readers do not have sufficient information regarding usual procedure of the preparation of food among prophetic groups to expect Elisha to be involved in providing food.

The wording of the cry of the sons of the prophets (מות בסיר איש האלהים, 'man of God, there is death in the pot', v. 40) again connects Elisha with the theme of death. As in the previous story, Elisha is held responsible for life and death. Further, in both stories Elisha is indi-

---

172. Reading the verb as singular, as suggested by BHS.
173. Renteria, 'The Elijah/Elisha Stories', p. 110.

rectly responsible for the presence of death, which he then must miraculously reverse. Thus Elisha's God-like role continues, as does readers' discomfort with this role.

The story ends with Elisha simply ordering the meal to be brought, throwing the meal into the pot and further ordering the redistribution of the food (v. 41). All this is accomplished in ten words, two of them imperatives. One wonders here at Hobbs's suggestion that Elisha is pictured with 'great tenderness'.[174] It would be just as easy to understand Elisha's manner as impatient arrogance.

Not only is YHWH absent from the story, and especially from Elisha's words regarding the healing of the food, but this absence is made more conspicuous when the sons of the prophets appeal to him as 'man of God' (v. 40). Here the parallel made by Robinson is particularly instructive. He notes the similarity between this story and Exod. 15.23-25a, where Moses sweetens the water of Marah.[175] In the Exodus narrative, however, YHWH is mentioned as the clear source not only of the power of the healing, but the instrument, here the wood. In this story, Elisha has no need of YHWH's advice, nor seemingly of YHWH's power. All is accomplished through the personal attention of the prophet. Thus, Elisha replaces YHWH as the source of power, a source that disappears with his absence.

Thus, the story contains the elements that portray positively Elisha as provider of food for the sons of the prophets, and as deliverer from poisonous food. The combination of these two themes in a single story, however, undermine one another, creating a case where two rights make a wrong. It is Elisha who must take responsibility for the poisonous food, since it was prepared under his command.

The movement of the plot is in this way very similar to the previous story. Elisha provided food in time of famine, as he provided a son in time of barrenness. Something goes wrong, which is not directly Elisha's fault. Nevertheless blame is (correctly) placed at his feet. He then is obligated to do another miracle (again depicted in rather non-miraculous terms) in order to make his original offering not turn into disaster.

The power of which Elisha is clearly in possession may contain the foundation for a tradition that venerates the prophets. The tradition, however, when set within the world of Genesis–2 Kings, is unlikely to

---

174. Hobbs, *Kings*, p. 55.
175. Robinson, *Kings*, p. 47.

feel kindly toward a prophet who fails to acknowledge the authority of YHWH as the source of his power, especially in the giving and taking of life. It is also unlikely to be comfortable with a power that is directed toward no larger goal. In this way, prophetic power is simultaneously venerated and undermined, as I become increasingly uncomfortable with this powerful yet godless prophet.

The story also continues the portrayal of the sons of the prophets as a helpless group, unable to supply its own basic needs. The narrative isolates this group from the rest of Israelite society, which allows me to understand them as a sub-culture, a group that operates with its own norms and rules. As quickly as this possibility is raised, it is dismissed as an option for people without continual access to miraculous intervention.

2 Kings 4.42-44: Offerings

Many of the difficulties noted in the previous stories are not found in the final story of ch. 4. In some ways, this final story could serve as another *exemplum*, a place where, like 2.19-22, all the right elements are in the right places. It is no wonder that this is the one Elisha story that has a clear parallel in the Gospels (Mt. 14.13-21; Mk. 6.35-44; Lk. 9.12-17; Jn 6.1-14).[176]

The parallel with this favorite Gospel story cannot help but intrude as Christian readers read the story of Elisha. This is a major hindrance to any inclination readers may have had to read Elisha as a negative example of prophetism.[177] It is perhaps the contrast between this ideal story and the others that highlights for me the strong tone of critique that underlies the rest of the Elisha stories.

The story begins, as do the others, with an opening verse crammed with all the necessary background details to the story. A man from Baal-shalisha comes to a man of God with food. Both the name of the man and the name of the man of God are absent from the introduction, but as readers in the midst of the Elisha stories, it is unsurprising when the man of God is later identified as Elisha. In fact, readers may not have noticed that he was originally unnamed, since the title 'man of

176. See the study of this parallel in Brown ('Jesus and Elisha', *passim*), and the response of Thomas Louis Brodie, 'Jesus as the New?? Elisha: Cracking the Code', *ExpTim* 93 (1981), pp. 39-42.
177. See Long, 'The Shunammite Woman', p. 19.

God' is applied to no other person in the surrounding texts.

As I have been noting in the rest of the stories, there is always some part of the story that makes the reader uncomfortable, makes me question the relative simplicity to which the stories are otherwise given. In most cases, the hitch in the story comes after the initial introduction. Here, however, the hitch occurs in the midst of the introductory verse, almost as if the narrator was attempting to slip the detail past readers.

The problem is clearly the לחם בכורים ('bread from the firstfruits'). The story does nothing to draw this phrase to readers' attention, or to suggest that there is anything unusual in this act. A study of other uses of this phrase suggests, however, that there is good reason for readers to question the general propriety of this act, or at least to note how it differs from the legal requirements.[178]

The instances of the use of בכורים ('firstfruits') can be roughly divided into three categories. The first group, which includes Lev. 2.14; 23.17, 20 and Num. 18.13, directly connect the firstfruits to the priests as those responsible for carrying out the sacrifice. Leviticus 23.20 is the only other instance of the phrase 'bread of the firstfruits' in Genesis–2 Kings. The Numbers passage is especially instructive, since here the firstfruits are expressly given to the priests as their food. The second group, including Exod. 23.16, 19; 34.22, 26, direct the firstfruits to be brought to the 'house of YHWH your God'. It is likely that readers would associate this phrase with the priesthood, but I have distinguished this group because the priesthood is not directly mentioned. The lone exception to the association of firstfruits with priests or the house of YHWH is Num. 28.26. In this passage, neither the verse nor the context make any reference to special persons or places for the celebration of festivals. The command to celebrate is merely given to 'the Israelites' (28.2).

Given this context, readers may be surprised at the action of the man in bringing the firstfruits to someone designated as 'man of God'. Further, readers may be surprised at the lack of general cultic ritual in the story. Is Elisha explicitly rejecting the cultic nature of the event in his command to give the food to the people? Or, given that the first-

---

178. I am not suggesting that the man of Baal-shalisha had access to the written text of the Torah. Readers, however, who has been following the story of the people of Israel, are likely to be working with the idea that the laws given in the earlier books of Genesis–2 Kings are still normative for the people of the land, and especially so for a man of God.

fruits are to be presented to God, is this another indication that Elisha is taking the place of YHWH in the narrative?

The story moves with characteristic speed to the miracle. The wording is especially helpful here. Elisha, with his usual abruptness, commands the food be given to the people (תן לעם ויאכלו, v. 42). When questioned on the sufficiency of the food for so many people, he simply repeats his earlier formulation. He then expands his initial declaration with the addition of the classic explanation, כה אמר יהוה ('thus says YHWH'). This simple addition allows readers, if they so wish, to put aside all earlier difficulties regarding the source of Elisha's speech. Elisha speaks his own word, but here readers are assured that Elisha's word is (always?) backed by YHWH's. Further, v. 44 reports the fulfillment of this prophecy in words that echo both those of Elisha (נתן, 'give') and of YHWH (יתר, 'remaining', אכל, 'eat'),[179] while concluding with the phrase כדבר יהוה ('according to the word of YHWH').

This direct reference to the word of YHWH suggests that whatever discomfort readers may have initially had regarding Elisha's actions should now be put aside as YHWH is clearly present in Elisha's actions. The question remains, however, as to whether this inclusion mitigates readers' earlier discomfort regarding the lack of reference to the word of YHWH, or if in fact it highlights the general absence.

It must also be noted that YHWH's words are not presented in direct speech. Readers have only Elisha's word that YHWH ever said these things. If there is room in the readers' world for miraculous actions without the aid of the power of YHWH, then it is possible to read this as another demonstration of Elisha's power while attempting to suggest to his audience (i.e. both the servant and ourselves) that all his actions are backed by the word of YHWH.

This is still a story that is easily read as one that correctly clarifies the connection between YHWH and Elisha. One could argue that this is the most obvious way to read the story. There remain, however, the three factors that allow me to continue in my suspicion. First is the inclusion of 'firstfruits', which places the passage in clear contradiction to the commands of YHWH. Second is the lack of direct speech from YHWH. Given the earlier parallel between Elisha and Elijah stories, I note that the Elijah stories contain six direct quotations from YHWH, as well as two instances of direct speech by the angel of YHWH. Thus, it is entirely

---

179. Note, however, the use of יתר ('remaining') in 4.7, where overabundance is attributed to the word of Elisha.

appropriate for readers to expect to see words directly from YHWH.

Third, there continues the movement from producing to sharing which I noted in 1 Kings 19.[180] While Elisha here is shown as one who provides for those who are (presumably) hungry, it is not his own produce. If the people are reliant upon Elisha for their provisions, they are in need of outside production, even if Elisha can multiply it to sufficiency. Further, if the people remain reliant upon the presence of the man of God, he is unable to provide for them outside the miraculous. Thus the community of those surrounding the prophet lacks the means to sustain itself economically, and thus is not a viable alternative to the larger Israelite social structure.

2 Kings 5: Naaman

Thus far Elisha has been encountered in a number of different settings. We have seen him working among the sons of the prophets (2.1-18; 4.1-7, 38-41), among the ordinary people of Israel (2.19-25; 4.8-37, 42-44) and with the king and army of Israel on a military campaign (3.4-27). He has been geographically associated with Abel-meholah, Gilgal, Bethel, Jericho, the Jordan, Mt Carmel, Samaria, Shunem and Baal-shalishah.

In this story, Elisha for the first time is shown encountering people from outside Israel/Judah. Further, he is described as being at home (5.9), presumably in Samaria if the word of the little Israelite girl is to be believed (5.3). In isolation, this story portrays a sedentary prophet who dispenses healing to all who come to his door. In many ways, I am tempted to read this story in isolation, since the Elisha pictured here is so different from the one I have encountered thus far.

One of the factors that keeps me from reading the story in this way is its importance for what follows. This is the first encounter between Elisha and Aram, an encounter that will dominate much of the rest of his life. Further, I have been expecting Aram to play a part in the story right from the beginning, since Hazael of Aram is mentioned along with Elisha and Jehu as the three final missions in the life of Elijah (1 Kgs 19.15-16).

The first verse of ch. 5 begins by subtly reminding me of this connection. While it begins with Naaman, and goes into great detail in describing his social standing (שׂר־צבא מלך־ארם היה איש גדול לפני אדניו ונשׂא

---

180. See above, pp. 50-51.

נפים, 'commander of the army of the king of Aram, he was a great man and in high favor with his master', 5.1),[181] readers are quickly reminded that YHWH has an interest in victory for Aram (כי־בו נתן־יהוה תשועה לארם, 'for by him YHWH had given victory to Aram', 5.1). Like the other initial verses of the stories studied thus far, much of the relevant background detail is given right away. Included is the conflict that allows the plot to move forward. In this case, the conflict is initially internal to the character, a conflict between sickness (מצרע, 'leper') and social status (גבור חיל, 'mighty warrior').

Modern readers, however, should not be blind to the social nature of the conflict. Until the final word of the first verse, they have been given an entirely positive picture of Naaman. The picture is so convincing that von Rad adds to the military and social indicators the conviction of Naaman's 'excellent character'.[182] But מצרע ('leper') as used in Genesis–2 Kings, is in Israel cause for social segregation (Lev. 13.45-46; Num. 5.2). While it may be that leprosy as we know it today was unknown in Israel of that period,[183] Gray's suggestion that this is not a form of leprosy that debarred someone from society is out of place,[184] since Genesis–2 Kings makes a very clear distinction between diseases that do and do not cause social segregation, and those that do are labeled מצרע ('lepers', see Lev. 13). Thus, readers are likely to assume that Aramean views on leprosy differ from those in Israel.

The story continues with Aram going out with raiding parties (גדודים, v. 2). While this action is not directly connected to Naaman, there is no semantic reason for readers not to connect this action with the actions of Naaman as commander of the Aramean forces.[185] While the group which went out is characterized as גדודים ('raiding parties'), which suggests that this is not a formal battle *per se*,[186] it is still Aram that goes out, and Naaman is responsible for the Aramean forces. Hobbs chooses

---

181. Note the parallel between Naaman as גדל ('great' [man]) and the Shunammite as גדלה ('great' [woman]) (4.8), which suggests a parallel between the two characters.

182. Gerhard von Rad, 'Naaman: A Critical Retelling', in *idem*, *God at Work in Israel* (Nashville: Abingdon Press, 1980), p. 48.

183. Würthwein, *Könige*, p. 299.

184. Gray, *Kings*, p. 453.

185. Contra Gray, *Kings*, p. 453.

186. Note the use of גדוד ('raider') in 1 Sam. 30, where some Amalekite raiders destroy Ziklag. The group is of considerable size, given that 400 escape from the otherwise complete destruction (v. 17).

to skirt this issue by stating that the girl 'found her way' into Naaman's household,[187] but this is not what the narrative says. Von Rad adds a theological flavor to this narrative by seeing the girl as an instrument God offers to save Naaman.[188] The fact that the little girl ended up in Naaman's household further links the actions of the raiders to the official army of Aram.

As Cohn has noted, this story stands out from the other Elisha stories due to its length and complexity.[189] It is not one simple plot line, but a complex of vignettes. The narrator adopts various terms for and attitudes towards the characters, and the characters themselves move beyond the boundaries of mere types.[190] For the purposes of this study, focus will remain on the picture of Elisha as prophet.

While the story retains coherence throughout, it can easily be divided into parts according to the movement of the plot. The story begins with a general introduction (vv. 1-7), followed by the activities of Elisha in resolving the tensions that the introduction creates (vv. 8-14).[191] This initial conflict having been resolved, the story could easily end there. But the narrator has prepared for a continuing story by telling us of the gifts that Naaman brought along (5.5), while not saying anything about their distribution. This affords the opportunity for Naaman to return to Elisha to utter his confession of faith, and inquire as to the possibility of worshiping YHWH in a foreign land (9-19a). The story could easily conclude after 19a. There is no unresolved tension, there are no loose ends to tie up. Thus, the final vignette (19b-27) must create its own tension, and find its own resolution. It is connected to the larger story by continuity in chronology and characters.

The interest in Elisha as prophet is quite central to the story itself. It is as הנביא אשר בשמרון ('prophet who is in Samaria', v. 2) that Elisha[192] is introduced into the story (v. 3). Further, it is as נביא בישראל

---

187. Hobbs, *Kings*, p. 59.
188. Von Rad, 'Naaman', p. 48.
189. Cohn, 'Form and Perspective', *VT* 31 (1983), p. 171.
190. Contra A. Rofé, 'Classes in the Prophetical Stories', in G.W. Anderson (ed.), *Studies on Prophecy* (Leiden: E. J Brill, 1974), pp. 3-64 (147).
191. V. 8 is set apart grammatically by the ויהי (but [it happened that]) which begins the verse. While v. 7 also begins with a ויהי this latter one acts as signal for chronological transition.
192. While the identity of the prophet is not clear until v. 8, any but the first-time reader will assume that this is one of the Elisha stories until otherwise informed. One can note also the phrase שר־צבא מלך ('commander of the army of

('prophet in Israel', v. 8) that Elisha intrudes into the king's dilemma. It is also הנביא ('prophet', v. 13) that the servants of Naaman, and thus presumably Naaman himself, believe they are consulting.

The first indication of the role assigned to a prophet is found in the mouth of the captive Israelite girl.[193] Her belief in the power of the prophet extends at least to his ability to cure Naaman of his leprosy (v. 3). The readers' willingness to believe the word of this girl is heightened by the immediate action taken by Naaman (v. 4). If a foreign army commander is willing to believe this statement, how much more easily should readers accept it!

The initial confidence readers have gained (or been reinforced in) in the healing ability of a prophet is immediately contrasted with the acknowledged inability of the king to perform this act (v. 7). While it is certainly possible to read the king's response as a mockery of royal authority,[194] readers should not make too much of the comedic aspects of the portrayal of the king. It is highly unlikely that readers would expect the king to have the ability to heal leprosy. Healing has not been part of the role of the king in the past. Rather, readers are more likely to be surprised by the king's reaction precisely because even a servant girl knows that it is prophets who heal. Thus, it is the ignorance of this particular king that is highlighted, rather than the general impotence of kings. The message to readers is to recognize the specific duties assigned to each category of people: kings reign, prophets heal. Further, since kings do not heal, it is also likely that prophets do not reign. This small extension of the logic of the passage reinforces rather than undermines the royal authority structure.[195]

The narrator makes this point not by dogmatically inserting it into the reportorial voice but by letting Elisha himself make it. It is Elisha who reminds the king that it is prophets who heal (v. 8). In this way, Elisha acts in service to the king, rather than in any way undermining the king's authority. In fact, by first creating and then resolving this mini-tension, and by placing these words in the mouth of Elisha, the narrator allows readers to laugh at the king and cheer for Elisha while still

---

the king') in 5.1, which designates the same social group that Elisha claims influence over in 4.13.

193. It is ironic that here Elisha is praised by a נערה קטנה ('small girl'), whereas earlier he has caused the death of forty-two נערים קטנים ('small boys', 2.23).

194. So Cohn, 'Form and Perspective', p. 175.

195. Contra Cohn, 'Form and Perspective', p. 176.

4. *Elisha*

maintaining the subordinate role of the prophet.

Elisha is allowed to retain total authority within his own sphere of influence. It is Naaman who must come to him and stand (ויעמד) at the entrance to Elisha's house. In response, Elisha merely sends a messenger with the necessary formula for healing (v. 10). This affront to the position of Naaman is keenly felt, and the reader listens to his words of complaint (v. 11). But the affront is displayed toward an Aramean army commander, and thus poses no threat to the social structure of Israel.

One can see this also in the wording of Elisha's message to the king of Israel (v. 8). The message is worded in the imperfect (יבא), which here is read as a jussive ('let him come'), rather than using an imperative such as שלח ('send'). In this way the message is a suggestion for the use of royal authority, rather than a usurpation of that authority.[196]

The authority of the prophet within his own sphere of influence is total. His authority is linked also to his position as 'man of God' (vv. 8, 14, 15, 20). This connection between Elisha and the presumed source of Elisha's power is not as strong as it might be, however. The name of YHWH is mentioned by the narrator in v. 1, in connection with Naaman's military victories, and by Naaman himself in v. 11 in connection with his expectation, but does not otherwise appear in connection to the healing.[197]

One notices this also when comparing the rhetoric to that in the Elijah stories. Elijah's actions are often clearly directed toward the knowledge that there is a God in Israel (1 Kgs 17.1; 18.24, 36, 37, 39; 2 Kgs 1.3, 5, 16). But in this story Elisha directs his intentions toward his own status, rather than that of YHWH (v. 8b). Even the reporter's record of the final outcome is different. The fulfillment of Elijah's word is regularly traced to כדבר יהוה אשר דבר ביד אליהו ('according to the word of YHWH that he spoke by Elijah', 17.16b, see also 2.17), or similar phrases that directly connect Elijah's word with YHWH's word, and resultant actions with the work of YHWH. But in this story Naaman is healed, כדבר איש האלהים ('according to the man of God', v. 14).

There is clearly nothing in this story to indicate that any other source

---

196. Fretheim recognizes the importance of the issue of 'the nature of proper prophetic leadership' (Terrence E. Fretheim, *The Deuteronomic History* [Nashville: Abingdon Press, 1983], p. 145). The question which remains is 'proper from whose perspective?'

197. Würthwein has noted this lack of connection, and suggests that all references to 'YHWH' and 'man of God' are secondary (*Könige*, p. 297).

of power than YHWH is possible for the healing. Further, the lack of any reference to Baal in 2 Kings 2–9 does not allow for any other source of extra-human power.[198] There is, however, still clearly a lack of direct connection between Elisha's action and the word of YHWH. There remains also the continuing problem of the nature of this connection, should readers presume it to exist. Again, readers do not know whether Elisha acts at YHWH's direction, or vice versa.

In all of this, Elisha, too, remains in the background. The story is carried by the words and actions of others. Even the words of Elisha are only recorded indirectly, as I read the message to the king (v. 8), and hear the voice of the messenger speaking to Naaman (v. 10). Readers can, with Fretheim, read this as an attempt to focus on the *way* the prophet works, rather than on the prophet himself.[199] But given the rather oblique way the narrator portrays the prophet's methods, I suspect that something else is happening here. For this reason, I turn to the third part of the story to understand why this story is being told in this particular way.[200]

Naaman's response to the proclamation of Elisha's servant further highlights the questionable connection between Elisha and YHWH. It is Naaman who points out the lack of reference to YHWH in Elisha's oracle, as he had expected (וקרא בשם־יהוה אלהיו, 'and call on the name of YHWH his God', v. 11). If even a foreigner can see this omission, how much more should the Israelite reader have noticed. Readers may even be slightly embarrassed at having a foreigner point this out to them, and thus feel the omission more keenly.

The omission is not merely a lack of the name of God. Rather, Naaman has noted that the role that he expects of a prophet, namely that of an intermediary, has not been taken up by Elisha. It is the servant who has acted as intermediary, in bringing out the message. This leaves Elisha in the role of God.

This change in status can be seen clearly when compared to Exod. 7.1. In that story, YHWH clearly indicates that the prophet is to act in

---

198. Binns attributes Elisha's silence regarding Baal to pragmatism, suggesting that Elisha would have been unsuccessful in combating Baal worship (*From Moses to Elisha*, p. 232). Binns's picture of ubiquitous Baal worship is in sharp contrast to the text's picture of Israel devoid of Baal worshipers.

199. Fretheim, *Deuteronomic History*, p. 145.

200. Fretheim also notes the importance of vv. 15-27 for the readers' understanding of the text (*Deuteronomic History*, p. 144).

the role of an intermediary. Aaron becomes Moses' prophet when he speaks for Moses. Thus Aaron is to Moses as Moses is to YHWH. There is nothing disquieting about this particular scenario, since it is commanded directly by YHWH for a particular reason. What makes the Elisha story suffer by comparison is the lack of YHWH's voice and lack of reason for the intermediary. If YHWH does not command the use of Gehazi as prophet, and if there is no clear voice from YHWH that is conveyed through Elisha, through Gehazi and thence to Naaman, I have good reason to be suspicious of the word that presents itself as prophecy. This is especially true if the suspicion is raised by the voice of Naaman (v.11).

The story takes on a much more confessional tone in vv. 15-19a. The story also shifts from a series of monologues to a dialogic form.[201] This affords Naaman the opportunity to speak his confession, and to make his request directly to YHWH's representative, giving it more force in my mind, for surely the man of God would see through any attempt at false declaration.

Gunkel has noted the uniqueness of the scope of Naaman's confession.[202] Elisha responds in kind, making a direct link between his action and the action of YHWH (אשר־עמדתי לפניו, 'in whose presence I stand', v. 16). Elisha also responds to Naaman's offer of a gift, and places his refusal within an oath to YHWH (חי־יהוה, 'as YHWH lives', v. 16). In this way, readers are informed that the proper financial conduct of the prophet does not include the acceptance of reward. While this does not surprise readers familiar with the activities of the biblical prophets, they may notice the contrast to the office of the priest, whose services cost 10 per cent.[203] This contrast assures the financial survival of the priestly caste, while disallowing any such mechanism for the prophet.[204]

Elisha's oath (חי־יהוה, 'as YHWH lives', v. 16) allows readers to

---

201. Cohn, 'Form and Perspective', p. 178.

202. Gunkel, *Geschichten*, p. 39. Cf. Rick Dale Moore, *God Saves: Lessons from the Elisha Stories* (JSOTSup, 95; Sheffield: JSOT Press, 1990), p. 78.

203. The exception to this rule is in 1 Sam. 9.7-8. There Saul states that some sort of gift is necessary in order to receive an oracle from a man of God. The text appears a bit embarrassed at this, however, in its insertion of the comment regarding the seer (הראה, v. 9). Verse 9 connects the gift, then, not to the present order of נביא ('prophet') but to the past order of ראה ('seer').

204. A Christian reader may recall how Jesus remains within this tradition, and lives largely without financial resources of any kind.

safely assume that YHWH has been active through Elisha throughout the story. It may also, however, reinforce the readers' concern regarding the absence of YHWH in the earlier material. Is Elisha really acting as servant of YHWH, or is this merely a formality on Elisha's part? The choice is the readers', and is likely to be made unconsciously as they move quickly through the story.

Naaman's second request continues, and the narrative presents us with an archetypal confession of a believing foreigner.[205] In this way, the narrative brings readers into its world without resorting to lecture or diatribe. Rather, readers rejoice with Naaman as he recognizes the truth of the faith which the narrative engenders. The words are placed in the mouth of the newly-healed army commander: ידעתי כי אין אלהים בכל־הארץ כי אם־בישראל ('I know that there is no god in all the earth except in Israel', v. 15).

This unique confession reinforces my understanding of the power available to the man of God, a power that comes from YHWH. But the confession has certain beliefs and practices that 'naturally' are associated with it. Thus, Naaman links the belief in YHWH with two other images. The first is the soil of Israel (v. 17a), and the second is the cultic acts of burnt offering and sacrifice (v. 17b).

Von Rad has suggested that Naaman asks for the soil to act as 'an insulating layer' against heathenism.[206] This is a possible explanation for the motivation of a character, but does not illuminate the effect of the narrative on the reader. Others such as Gunkel have answered this question by talking about the connection between Israel and its soil.[207] But none of these responses notes the rather sharp distinction between this type of confession and the concerns of the prophet Elisha that we have seen until now.

It is at this point that readers can attempt to read between the lines, to observe more closely the worlds that are not being fully constructed in my reading. Looking either backwards or forwards in the Elisha stories, readers are given no indication that Elisha has any interest in the soil of Israel or its sacrificial cult. In fact, as I have shown above in 4.42-44,

---

205. Moore calls this a 'theological victory', but does not indicate who the victor is (Moore, *God Saves*, p. 80).

206. Von Rad, 'Naaman', p. 52.

207. Gunkel, *Elisha*, p. 40. Rofé uses this to date the text to late eighth or early seventh century, noting the idealization of land and altar abroad (Rofé, 'Classes in the Prophetical Stories', p. 148).

Elisha even acts in direct contravention of cultic law. And I can hardly imagine Elisha carrying mule loads of earth on his trip to Damascus (8.7).

These, however, are observations of the silences in the text. Thus, readers are given nothing concrete that would invite a contrast between Naaman's ideal (from the narrative's point of view) confession and an alternative cultus that might arise from Elisha's followers. On the surface of the text, the connection between the work of Elisha and the 'normal' cultic practices of Israel remains intact. Readers are led to accept this cultic world not only through law and judgment (Deut. 12), but through emotive scenes such as the healing and confession of a foreign army commander. There remain, however, indications within the text that hegemonies are maintained at the expense of alternative ways of constructing societies. Thus, if I read for indications of a prophetic alternative, I should not be surprised that the text does not offer it to me in a straightforward manner.

Naaman's speech continues in v. 18 as instruction from narrative to reader. I can certainly imagine the possibility that such a text may have been used as a apologetic for the actions of Israel in Babylonian captivity or later in the diaspora.[208] But this reading ignores the fundamental principle that the narrator wishes to reiterate, which is the connection between knowledge (ידעתי, 'I know', v. 15), burnt offering and sacrifice (עלה וזבח, v. 17) and worshiping in a house of god (here בית־רמון, house of Rimmon, v. 18).

In this way, readers are assured that even a foreigner recognizes that cultic activity takes place inside a house of God, which for the reader of Genesis–2 Kings is naturally the temple in Jerusalem. Even in the stories of northern prophets, who give no indication of any loyalty to the Jerusalem cultus, the idea of the centrality of the temple for the true worship of YHWH is reinforced in the mind of the readers.[209]

This principle is overlooked by commentators precisely because it appears to be so 'natural' within the world of the text. If Elisha had made any indication that Naaman needed to go to Jerusalem to truly worship, readers would likely note the incongruity between this and the rest of Elisha's words and actions. And if Naaman had volunteered to visit Jerusalem to worship YHWH, readers would likely feel the

---

208. So Rofé, 'Classes in the Prophetical Stories', p. 148.
209. While the stories of Elisha are 'about' northern Israel, the perspective remains Judahite.

incongruity between this action and the usual north-south tension that the text is building. So Naaman offers a little speech about his own dilemma as a foreigner, a natural enough dilemma for one so close to the official cultus of another nation, and in doing so is used by the narrative to again remind readers that any intelligent individual worships in a house of god.

Elisha's reply to Naaman (לך לשלום, 'go in peace', v. 19) is finally rather non-committal, although it suggests that Naaman's request for pardon (יסלח, 'may I be pardoned', v. 18) has been granted. It is certainly characteristically short. It in no way intrudes on the lesson we have just learned. The prophet has nothing to add to the new-found faith of the foreigner. Having connected knowledge, sacrifice and temple, the individual has no need of further word from the prophet. These alone will suffice until further disease threatens. Elisha is not allowed the status of cultic advisor, but is relegated to the role of healer in service of the king. The matter has passed beyond the boundaries of his role, and he does not intrude, not even to confirm the pardon of the foreigner. Pardon for sins is not part of the prophetic role.[210]

The vignette that follows Naaman's departure allows me to see the various worlds of the text as they interact with one another.[211] We have seen Elisha in the context of the sons of the prophets, in his relationship to Gehazi, and in relationship to kings and army commanders. In this story the three worlds of Elisha are brought together, thus lessening the feeling of fragmentation. Somehow the narrative must show us how these various worlds interact with one another.

Thus, Gehazi enters the story (ויאמר גיחזי נער אלישע, 'and Gehazi, servant of Elisha, said', v. 20), allowing readers to believe that he was the messenger of vv. 8, 10. His place is clearly defined, as servant of a man of God. The text is always careful not to make any reference to a possible continued succession. Gehazi is not the next prophet in line in a series of leaders.

Gehazi is further disallowed from prophetic office by being portrayed in the most negative light. An oath is placed in his mouth (חי־יהוה, 'as YHWH lives') which shows him in direct contradiction to the 'proper' attitude of Elisha (חי־יהוה אם־אקח, 'as YHWH lives, I will not take',

---

210. Again, the Christian reader will note how the Gospels affirm the limits of this role, by noting that Jesus' power of healing confirms his prophetic office, but his granting of forgiveness is met with anger (Lk. 5.17-26).

211. See Gunkel, *Elisa*, p. 43.

v. 16).²¹² Gehazi is shown to recognize the duplicity of his own actions by placing his request in the mouth of Elisha (v. 22). Thus Gehazi is clearly not the sort of person one would want in the role of prophet.

The fact that Gehazi places his request in the mouth of Elisha further derogates the role of the prophet. If Elisha is presented in the text as God, the giver and taker of life, then Gehazi acts as Elisha's prophet. Verse 22, then, represents the dark side of the prophetic role, namely that the prophet puts his own words in the mouth of God, and the listener has no way to tell whether the prophet is telling the truth. This possibility is raised in a largely harmless context, one in which the reader is clearly informed of the falsity of this particular message (v. 19). Still the possibility remains disturbing, and induces a certain disquiet into the readers' confidence regarding the reliability of the prophetic word.

Gehazi further removes his request from his true intentions by asking both on behalf of Elisha and on behalf of the sons of the prophets. In this way the text offers readers an intersection of the worlds of Elisha. And they intersect in a very clear set of economic practices. Naaman, here representing the elite, has kindly offered gifts from his excess to the prophet, who declines. The sons of the prophets are placed in their usual position of beggars, in constant need of economic handouts. Gehazi acts as intermediary, however falsely, between these two worlds.

Readers are left with little choice about which is the more likely route to economic security. Naaman goes to the prophet for healing, brings gifts in excess of the wildest imaginings of most readers and utters marvelous confessions of faith. The sons of the prophets come for simple economic handouts, offer nothing and are subsequently removed from the story. In fact, the sons of the prophets are not even granted full reality within this story. The narrator acknowledges their existence, but only introduces them in the imagination of Gehazi. Readers are not asked to accept that these two sons of the prophets actually exist, but they are asked to accept this as their likely place in the story should they exist.

It is tempting to read the basic plot itself as a common morality play.²¹³ Bad Gehazi chases after good Naaman and lies to get his money, then lies to Elisha about doing it, and is rightly punished for

212. See Nelson, *Kings*, p. 180.
213. So Jones, *Kings*, p. 419; Cohn, 'Form and Perspective', p. 183.

these actions. The difficulty with this reading is the problem of ascertaining the motivation of Gehazi and the nature of his wrong deed. Gehazi himself explains his actions to us by accusing Elisha of sparing (חשׂך) Naaman by not taking something that he offered (v. 20). Gehazi further provides motivation by calling Naaman 'this Aramean' (v. 20).

The narrator provides another accusation of Gehazi, when he recounts Gehazi's lying speech to Naaman regarding the purpose of the gifts (v. 22), and the further lie Gehazi tells Elisha regarding his actions (v. 25). This tempts me to think the motivation is greed, but it is a rather subdued greed, given the small size of the gift in relation to Naaman's resource (v. 5). Finally, Elisha's judgment provides readers with his own perspective on these events, a perspective that is quite difficult to understand.

Commentators have offered various explanations for v. 26. Moore considers the list to be the spoils of war.[214] Hobbs and Cohn parallel this verse to 1 Sam. 8.14-17, a similar list that recounts the evils of kingship.[215] Jones translates v. 26b as 'time to accept money *for* clothes...'[216] None of these adequately answer the question of what precisely it is that Elisha is accusing Gehazi of doing. What is this 'time' (עת) that Elisha refers to? This ambiguity allows the punishment to appear rather arbitrary.

All this would have been rather more straightforward had we been given Elisha's motivation for not accepting the gifts in the first place. Readers are generally uncomfortable with unmotivated action by a main character in a story, and are likely to try to fill it in themselves (as most commentators do). Further, the mere presence of significant unmotivated action for the hero of the story calls into question his status as hero. Good guys act for pure motives. Characters who act without obvious motivation, at least in modern literature, are usually written off as lunatics or psychopaths.

Again, Elijah provides for us the obvious parallel. And it has been shown above that Elijah's motivations are always clearly spelled out (word of YHWH, knowledge, fear and so on) These are the motivations of the pure biblical hero. Elisha is not allowed this status. His actions are continually clothed in ambiguity. His power is seldom questioned,

---

214. Moore, *God Saves*, p. 84.
215. Hobbs, *Kings*, p. 68; Cohn, 'Form and Perspective', p. 182.
216. Jones, *Kings*, p. 421.

4. *Elisha*

but lacking clear direction and motivation he becomes more an unbridled force than a folk hero.

Verse 26 does provide us with one additional piece of information regarding Elisha's power. His question to Gehazi (לֹא־לִבִּי הָלַךְ, 'did not my spirit go with you') is surely rhetorical, but also puzzling. Its meaning is explained immediately, namely that Elisha is able to observe events without being physically present (הָפַךְ־אִישׁ מֵעַל מֶרְכַּבְתּוֹ, 'someone alighted from his chariot', v. 26; וַיִּפֹּל מֵעַל הַמֶּרְכָּבָה, 'he jumped down from his chariot', v. 21). This power will again be commented on in 6.12. Readers may or may not be amazed by this particular power, since they have seen few limits thus far on what Elisha is capable of. Again there is no specific reference to YHWH as the source of this power, and in fact Elisha's words come very close to attributing this power to his own puissance.

This disturbing possibility is enhanced by the phrase מְצֹרָע כַּשָּׁלֶג ('white as snow') in v. 27. This phrase parallels Exod. 4.6 and Num. 12.10,[217] where it is used to emphasize the extreme power of YHWH. In the Exodus passage, Moses' hand is turned white as snow as a sign to motivate belief in the power of YHWH (4.8). In Numbers, Miriam is turned white as snow because she doubted the word of Moses. In both cases, the action is clearly attributed to YHWH. In 2 Kgs 5.25-27, YHWH remains unmentioned and readers might infer that the power resides in Elisha himself.

Finally, to whom is Elisha useful? To YHWH? Not specifically, for Elisha's actions are not connected to the will of YHWH. To Israel? No, for this story is soon followed by renewed fighting between Aram and Israel (6.8-23; 6.24–7.20). To the king? Yes, insofar as Elisha is able to diffuse a perceived threat from Aram. The narrator maintains tight control over the activity, the motivation and the utility of prophetic power.

Through all of this, there is no overt condemnation of either prophets or prophetic activity. The narrator sticks to reporting the events as they happened, and the narrative never wavers from its portrayal of prophetic power. Yet disquieting notes appear with continuing frequency. Elisha, with his miraculous power, assumes the role of God, while Gehazi his prophet puts words in the mouth of this ersatz God. Prophetic power may be undoubtable, but it has little usefulness for the

---

217. So Jones, *Kings*, p. 421.

larger history of Israel, or even for its immediate needs. Naaman's healing does not result in a cessation of Aramean incursions into Israel (6.8), neither does it further the task assigned initially to Elijah in 1 Kings 19.

The prophet thus has no place within the larger history of the people of Israel. He is reduced to the role of a magician, a wonder worker in a slightly unreal world. The exception to this uncomfortable portrayal comes as Elisha acts in service to the distraught king. Elisha is useful insofar as he aids the king in a time of distress, dispelling the threat which Naaman poses to the peace of Israel.

2 Kings 6.1-7: The Floating Axe

Between the mighty acts of international consequence that engage the prophet Elisha in the surrounding stories, this story presents a much less grand picture of prophetic activity. Here readers are back in the world of the sons of the prophets, a world where the miraculous pertains more readily to daily survival than to military conquest or defeat. They are also in a narrative that is much more stark, where 'restraint governs the setting and the telling'.[218]

Readers are also asked again to significantly alter their perceptions of Elisha's abode. While previously Elisha has been connected with Samaria (2.25; 5.3; cf. 6.32), and in the following story he is in Dothan (6.13), here he appears living with (ישבים שם לפניך understood as 'we live there under your charge' [so NRSV], v. 1) or acting as itinerant instructor for (ישבים שם לפניך understood as 'we meet with you' [so Cogan and Tadmor[219]]) the sons of the prophets. The crux of the issue is whether one understands ישבים as 'sitting' or 'dwelling'. Thus, readers are allowed to maintain a picture of Elisha the wandering prophet, with various possible homes available to him should he chance to be there.

It is important to note, however, that the stories of the sons of the prophets do not concern themselves with the larger world. They do not recognize the centrality of Samaria, or the importance of the cities. Thus, they do not easily read as simply part of the wanderings of Elisha. Their world is self-contained, sufficient unto itself. The prophet is always there in every story, and they cease to exist without him. This

218. Long, *Kings*, p. 80.
219. So Cogan and Tadmor, *Kings*, p. 69.

does not allow for a leader who is only occasionally present.

Thus, readers are forced to make a decision regarding the way the various worlds of the stories are to be entered. They can choose to read the story sequentially as a representation of unified world, or they can enter into the world of the individual stories, and mentally place them in groups according to similarity of world-view. If they take the former approach, then they would understand that Elisha has left his home in Samaria to call upon the sons of the prophets. In the latter approach, they see Elisha as permanently dwelling with the sons of the prophets. This, of course, forces readers to choose between various 'Elishas', for Elisha cannot permanently dwell in two places.[220]

Neither choice is very satisfying. Readers forced to choose between worlds must consequently lose faith in the reliability of the narrator, who otherwise has worked very hard to establish his credibility. The reader who chooses a unified world is left with a disjointed character, who appears now here and now there in various guises, with the only consistent aspect being his miraculous power. Forced to choose between an unreliable narrator and a disjointed character, I suspect that most readers of Genesis–2 Kings would choose the latter. But this uncomfortable choice would likely result in further erosion of the readers' comfort regarding the status of the prophet, for the readers' discomfort is not with the personal characteristics of Elisha, but precisely with his role in society. Where, precisely, does this *prophet* (his role) fit into the story of Israel, a story that wants to become *our* story.

There is a further aspect of the story that has caused modern readers some discomfort. This is the miracle itself. Nelson has noted that modern readers have difficulty sympathizing with the loss of a simple tool.[221] Further, Jones understands Elisha's action in v. 6 as simply cutting off the stick and fishing out the axe head.[222] While I agree with Hobbs that the grammar of the narrative argues against the rationaliza-

---

220. While readers might alternately choose to understand the stories representing the various stages of Elisha's life, the implicit chronology does not easily allow this reading. Further, this world, either world, is not one that easily allows for major role changes that would accompany this movement.

221. Nelson, *Kings*, p. 184. Presumably by 'modern reader', Nelson means relatively wealthy readers. One wonders also whether more wealthy ancient readers had a similar perspective, which would cause them to denigrate the sons of the prophets, rather than celebrate the power of the prophet.

222. Jones, *Kings*, p. 422; cf. Gray, *Kings*, p. 460.

tion of the miracle,[223] the impulse to rationalize also arises from within the narrative. The impulse arises because of the general picture of the ineptness of the sons of the prophets.

This attitude toward the sons of the prophets arises slowly from the story. Besides the initial confusion regarding Elisha's dwelling, which causes readers to begin the story in an uncomfortable position, readers are shown a group of people who plan to go to the Jordan, cut down one log each and build a new accommodation. Whether or not readers are willing to believe that the Jordan is a good place to find house-building material,[224] any reader familiar with building houses likely recognizes that one log per occupant is clearly insufficient to build a wooden structure. While one might presume a stone building with wooden supports, the plan still suggests a rather unusual division of labor.

The attitude is compounded by the apparent unwillingness of the sons of the prophets to proceed without Elisha being present. While the narrative clearly requires his presence for the miracle, there are other ways to indicate this rather than the blunt request of v. 3. Thus, readers arrives at the miracle with a good deal of discomfort, whether acknowledged or not. It is no wonder that the discomfort is transferred by the modern scientific mind to the miracle itself. Readers may be willing to lay aside their discomfort for the sake of the narrator, who has demonstrated his reliability, and thus believe the outline of the plot. But they then often resort to naturalistic explanations for the supposed miracle. The story does not allow for easy participation in its world, and readers exercise the right of non-participation precisely at the point where the power of the prophet is demonstrated.

This story adds further to our picture of the sons of the prophets. Gray notes this indirectly when he says that 'if this were simply a case of practical sagacity on the part of the prophet, its elevation to a miracle may be apologetic for the practical ineptitude of the man who lost the axe and had not the resource to try to recover it'.[225] I suspect that not even the miracle can save us from reaching these conclusions regarding the person who lost the axe, especially if we prefer a naturalistic explanation for the 'miracle'.

Würthwein states this conclusion much more clearly: 'Die Verbundenheit zwischen Meister und Jünger ist so stark, dass diese nichts

---

223. Hobbs, *Kings*, p. 76.
224. Hobbs argues that it is not (*Kings*, p. 76).
225. Gray, *Kings*, p. 460.

ohne jenen unternehmen und in jeglicher Not zu ihm kommen, aus der er mit seiner Wunderkraft hilft' (The bond between master and disciple is so strong that the latter undertakes nothing without the former, and comes to him in every trouble, to help him with his miraculous powers).[226] This is precisely the conclusion of the credulous reader. And it is not complimentary toward the sons of the prophets, especially if they are given no indication of the continuation of the office of the master. While Würthwein notes that this is similar to the student-teacher relationship in later Judaism, here Elisha acts not as teacher but solely as miracle worker. Thus, readers are informed that the continuity of the sons of the prophets is dependent upon the presence of the miracle-working master. In the absence of this particular type of 'man of God' (v. 6), the group has no means to sustain itself.

The stories move regularly back and forth between the various worlds with which Elisha interacts. In the stories of the sons of the prophets, readers are invited into a possible world led by prophets, an alternative to normal Israelite society. This world, however, is presented as obviously non-sustainable, as it only exists due to the constant miraculous intervention of the prophet. The sons of the prophets are unwilling to build a place without his presence, and are unable to build without borrowed tools and miracles that would be unnecessary for an intelligent woodcutter.

Elisha as man of God is a constant and unwavering source of power, but he is not presented as someone who presents for readers a critique of the 'normal' power structure in Israel (king/palace/temple). The narrator never intrudes with any sort of explicit critique of prophetic power, but subtly influences me to prefer a prophet who is under the control of more practical leaders.

2 Kings 6.8-23: The Triumph of Prophetic Power

This particular story represents a high point in the story of Elisha. It is a story that presents Elisha at his most powerful, dealing both with the king of Israel and the army of Aram. It is a story in which the connection between Elisha and YHWH is made without question. Were I to choose a story to highlight the power of Elisha from all the options, this would be a very good choice. We have here the construction of an

226. Würthwein, *Könige*, p. 303.

almost ideal plot, with good use of repetition and thematic development to enhance the readability of the narrative.[227]

The story begins with an historical overview of the events that led up to the central incident of the story. Elisha[228] is portrayed as a highly useful source of intelligence for the king of Israel. Gray's suggestion that Elisha, as a mobile person, 'would naturally be well informed on current affairs and topography',[229] makes little sense in the context of the narrative world. Neither does Gottwald's belief in a prophetic underground that would provide Elisha with information.[230] The story makes no mention of any details regarding Elisha's method, which clearly leads me to assume the use of Elisha's (or YHWH's?) special power.

The narrative follows with an account of a discussion in the palace of the king of Aram (vv. 11-13). This is an unusual foray, even for the omniscient biblical narrator. For modern readers, this may be a difficult leap, since we prefer our historians to relate discussion to which they might actually have been privy. It is possible for readers to assume that the conversation is a hypothetical reconstruction, except that the narrative produces one speech with a particular amount of force.[231] This is the speech of the servant of the king of Aram in v. 12.

לוא אדני המלך כי־אלישע הנביא אשר בישראל יגיד
למלך ישראל את־הדברים אשר תדבר בחדר משכבך

(no, my lord king, for Elisha the prophet who is in Israel tells the king of Israel the words that you speak in your bedroom)

As in 5.15, it is an Aramean who offers one of the central declarations of the entire Elisha corpus. It is this servant who first names Elisha, in contrast both to the narrator in v. 9 and the namelessness of both the king of Israel and Aram. It is the servant who focuses on

227. See Robert LaBarbara, 'The Man of War and the Man of God: Social Satire in 2 Kings 6:8–7:20', *CBQ* 46 (1984), pp. 637-51 (639-45).

228. Although not named until v. 12, there is no doubt in the present context who this 'man of God' is. The use of title here focuses readers' attention more closely on the words of the Aramean servant in v. 12.

229. Gray, *Kings*, p. 464.

230. Norman K. Gottwald, *All the Kingdoms of the Earth: Israelite Prophecy and International Relations in the Ancient Near East* (New York: Harper & Row, 1964), p. 75.

231. On the concept of force in narrative, see Bal, *Death and Dissymmetry*, pp. 130-35.

Elisha as הנביא ('prophet').²³² It is this speech that informs readers that the role of the prophet is to serve the king of Israel. And it is this speech that highlights the power available to Elisha even beyond that granted by the narrator (בחדר משכבך, 'in your bedroom'). In many ways, this would be considered a confession of faith, were it not for the lack of any reference to YHWH or even God.

One must be careful here not to impose too much of the modern secular/sacred distinction on to an ancient narrative. The narrative leaves little room for any power beyond that of YHWH. But as I have shown, occasionally the Elisha narratives stray into a rather grey area, where the attribution of power is not as clear as it is in the Elijah stories. In this case, however, the mention of YHWH in the mouth of a servant of the king of Aram would be out of place, and thus can be read as an Aramean understanding of the workings of YHWH (recognition of power without attribution of source).²³³

The force of this statement is found not only in the quantity of information it contains, nor only in its 'confessional' quality, but also in its placement in the mouth of an Aramean. Christian readers are reminded of the examples in the Gospels of faith statements by Gentiles, which for the Jewish reader would function to produce shame at having a lesser faith. Here the effect is felt automatically, for the story allows no Aramean readers.²³⁴

One should also note the contrast here between the prophet as all-knowing servant of the king, and the picture in 6.1-7 of the man of God doing silly miracles for incompetent followers. Readers are likely to choose the portrait of the prophetic role found in the mouth of the Aramean, and thus relegate prophets to the status of royal servant.

The chariots, horses and army of the king of Aram arrive at Dothan apparently unmolested and uncontested. Further, the king of Israel is given no warning of this incursion, and neither, presumably, is Elisha. The lack of such detail does little to heighten suspense. I can easily

---

232. Würthwein, *Könige*, p. 305.

233. Here again Gray's suggestion of leaks through Israelite prisoners or concubines is clearly outside the world of the narrative (*Kings*, p. 464).

234. The effect of the story is the *production* of 'Israelite' readers. Despite the fact that I am not Israelite, I find myself consistently reading from within the Israelite perspective, as I identify with the Israelite people and their fate. Thus, the text does not *assume* Israelite readership so much as it *produces* it. See Sternberg, *Poetics*, pp. 48-50.

imagine an oral storyteller elaborating further on the size of army, the stealth of the march or the danger to the city. The narrative does not pause for these details. The suspense is barely initiated (v. 14) before it is alleviated (v. 16).

It is given a brief moment of prominence in v. 15, as readers look through the eyes of the attendant of the man of God at the army of Aram, and hear his fear. Until now, however, Elisha's servants have been notoriously unreliable in their perception of events.[235] Thus, readers are likely not to feel his fear too keenly, and instead comfortably await the miraculous rescue that is sure to follow.

As commentators have noted, the text clearly indicates a contrast between fear (ירא) and seeing (ראה), a contrast that readers experience to some degree. Readers, however, are always given 'true' sight, or at least clear indications of false or incomplete sight (through the use of the prophet's attendant). In this case, true sight involves seeing the chariots and horses of fire that surround *Elisha* (v. 17).[236]

One of the more striking aspects of the presentation of this narrative is the presence of three prayers to YHWH (vv. 17, 18, 20). These are the only three instances of recorded direct speech from Elisha to YHWH in the entire corpus.[237] The first is certainly an example of the prophetic ideal. Elisha asks (פקח־נא, 'open please', v. 17) and YHWH responds. In this way, readers clearly understand that the power belongs to YHWH, and the prophet is efficacious only insofar as he is able to have his requests granted. The same formula is repeated in v. 18 (ויתפלל ... הך־נא, 'he prayed ... strike please according to the word of Elisha'), but in this instance the narrator undermines the initial position by recording the fulfillment with the awkward formula כדבר אלישע ('according to the word of Elisha', see also 2.22). In the stories of Elijah, readers have become used to the formula כדבר יהוה ('according to the word of YHWH'), which is used repeatedly in reference to the miraculous. It is not since Moses (Exod. 8.9, 27) that this formula has been used in this

---

235. See the discussion above on 4.14, 4.31 and 5.19b-27, and especially the parallel use of משרת ('servant') in 4.43.

236. LaBarbara notes that חיל ('army') is lacking from this description, and suggests a chiasm indicating Elisha as the place where the חיל ('army') of YHWH is concentrated ('Man', p. 641, cf. Long, *Kings*, p. 36). The chiasm he diagrams is weak, however, and readers may wonder if it not precisely the lack of army which leads to Elisha's actions which follow.

237. Elisha also prays to YHWH in 4.33, but his words are not recorded.

manner.²³⁸ In the third prayer, Elisha's words to YHWH are recorded as ויאמר ('and he said') rather than ויתפלל ('and he prayed'), but still clearly fit under the category of prayer. This time Elisha commands rather than implores (פקח, 'open', is an imperative), and the command is followed by action from YHWH.

This is surely one of the strongest indications to readers that Elisha is to be revered as a great prophet and man of God. It is certainly a subtle indication, but in this context the prayers are jarring enough to cause the reader to wonder at them. In the second prayer, the wording is jarring enough that English translations move away from the formula they have been using for parallel expressions of YHWH's power (NRSV: 'according to the word of the Lord' [1 Kgs 17.16]; 'as Elisha had asked' [2 Kgs 6.18]). There is a clear movement here from prophet as mere channel of power to prophet who can direct the power.

In the narrative thus far, we have often seen how the nature of Elisha's power has been ambiguous. In this passage, all ambiguity is removed as power flows clearly from YHWH to Elisha, but with Elisha gaining the power to significantly influence the actions of YHWH, if not direct them.²³⁹ In this way, the narrative allows me to comfortably remove all doubts I have been harboring regarding Elisha and his prophetic mission. I am returned to the world of YHWH's actions and human attempts to follow YHWH's direction.

The story continues with ever increasing wonders. A great deal of credulity is required on the part of the reader in order to imagine this story happening. Not only are the Arameans made blind (v. 18),²⁴⁰ but then they encounter the man they are to capture, and follow him through hilly country to Samaria. One wonders also at the credulity of the Arameans in following so silently, so obediently. But this is of no concern to the narrator, who overlooks this detail with a simple report

238. One should also note the use of the phrase כדבר-X ('according to the word of X') in other places such as Exod. 12.35; 32.28, Lev. 10.7 and 2 Sam. 13.35; 24.19. These, however, are in regard to instructions given rather than miraculous events.

239. Note that in Exod. 8, Moses is acting under the explicit direction of YHWH (see 8.1-4), but here Elisha is acting apparently on his own initiative.

240. LaBarbara, citing Jirku, suggests that this blindness (סנורים) is not the inability to see, but more precisely the non-correspondence of sight with reality ('Man of War', p. 643). While this makes sense in this context, it does not alter the size of the miracle, nor does it lessen my wonder at the thought of the Aramean army following Elisha many miles through the hills to Samaria.

(ויהי כבאם שמרון, 'and when they came to Samaria', v. 20).

Brueggemann notes the silence of the Arameans throughout vv. 19-22, suggesting that the narrative portrays them as 'passive recipients of the actions'.[241] This is largely true, except for the phrase in v. 20, והנה בתוך שמרון ('they saw they were in Samaria'). This detail is already known to the reader in the beginning of the verse, and thus the presence of והנה indicates that the statement is from the perspective of the Samarians. Readers are briefly allowed to feel their surprise and likely horror at being in the middle of Samaria. This is certainly the last place they want to be.

But why is this? What is happening to me as I encounter this rare emotional note in the middle of an otherwise unemotional narrative? Once again I am being reinforced in my perception that there is something totally natural about the centrality of Samaria for Elisha, and indeed for the entire world of the narrative. I am not allowed to pause to wonder why Elisha leads them to Samaria, rather than back home or out into the desert. Rather, I am shown the shock of the Arameans at being in Samaria, and thus are carried into the world where Samaria is naturally the place where these soldiers should have been taken.

This impression is strengthened by the appearance of the king of Israel in v. 21. Here again readers encounter the theme of seeing. The king sees, but the word order of the Hebrew records first his speaking and then his seeing (ויאמר...כראתו). It is important here to remember that Genesis–2 Kings has little interest in saying anything positive about the Omride dynasty. Thus, here there is another typical king whose name is not worth recording, who speaks before seeing. But it is still the king who speaks, and whose perceptions are recorded. It is not the elders, nor is it the people, nor does Elisha give commands to the army without going through the king's agency.

In his reading of this story, Brueggemann sets up a contrast between royal power and the way of the prophet. But this is not the contrast of my narrative. Royal persons may be the object of mockery, but there is no suggestion that the prophetic way is capable of setting up as a real alternative to royal power. Elisha acts in ways unavailable to the king, but still brings prisoners to Samaria, still responds to the questions of the king and still acts through his agency.

This is not to suggest that the narrative is other than an ideal

241. W. Brueggemann, 'The Embarrassing Footnote', *TTod* 44 (1987), pp. 5-14 (10).

4. *Elisha*

presentation of prophetic power. The king speaks before seeing, calls Elisha by the honorific אבי ('my father', v. 21), and acts on his command (שים, 'set', imperative, v. 22). While v. 23 records the actions of the king (while the subject of the verbs is not given, one can assume that the king is carrying out the commands of Elisha), the final triumph belongs to Elisha.

If this particular story represents the triumph of prophetic power, it is helpful to highlight the various aspects of this idealization, in order to recognize the nature of the world being constructed. In this story, the prophet is the locus of an exceedingly great quantity of power. The power is of YHWH, but the prophet's requests are all granted, even to the point where the prophet commands the power (note כדבר אלישע, 'according to the word of Elisha', in v. 18, and the lack of נא ('please') in Elisha's speech to YHWH in v. 20).

While the prophet is the locus of this power, the focus of the power is Samaria. Elisha acts to inform the king regarding the movement of enemy troops (v. 9, and especially v. 12). It is to Samaria that the Aramean soldiers are taken, and it is the king who speaks in Samaria. I note this focus because of the alternative recorded in the stories in which the sons of the prophets appear. Their world is not centred in Samaria, but it is clearly not the 'real' world of soldiers and non-miraculous bread.[242]

Despite the focus on Samaria, the text still affords a great deal of power to Elisha, especially in respect to foreign relations and royal prerogatives. If this picture of Elisha was sustained throughout the corpus, it is likely that my reading would fail. The prophet is without peer in terms of power, and in terms of his access to YHWH. There is a real possibility in this narrative of prophetic power eventually overshadowing royal power and creating an alternative, Yahwistic society. I can imagine a line of prophets whose access to divine power finally renders the royal line unnecessary.[243]

I do not know if there is something inherently disquieting about such a scenario, or if it is the narrative that creates this disquiet.[244]

---

242. The king no more bakes the bread than does Elisha in 4.43, but the king's acquisition of enough bread to feed an army is 'natural', whereas Elisha's is 'miraculous' (again, these terms are not in the text, but they are certainly found in the commentaries, which suggests that they are part of the narrative world).

243. Modern legends such as Disney's *Aladdin* explore just such a scenario.

244. Again, *Aladdin* is the perfect example.

Nonetheless, the story does not long allow readers to ponder this possibility. The victory of Elisha is total. Not only is he not captured (this was the initial conflict in the narrative), but his solution creates a period of military peace between Israel and Aram. The Arameans are overmastered, and slink quietly into their homes. Not only does the army return home, even the raiding parties (גדודי ארם, v. 23) cease to harass Israel.[245] Yet the entire edifice comes crashing down in 6.24.

The connection between v. 23 and v. 24 is quite explicit. The reader is not allowed to suppose that 6.24-7.20 represents an earlier incident. Verse 24 begins with the explicit chronological marker ויהי אחרי־כן ('and after this'). Even the versification connects the stories, as 6.24 begins the only story in the Elisha corpus that spans chapter divisions.[246] Modern readers, accustomed as they are to definite chapter divisions in modern literature, will find it difficult to ignore this directive.[247]

The reversal is total, and in fact moves beyond simple reversal. Verse 6.24 moves beyond v. 23 in narrative detail. The simple גדוד ('raiding party', in v. 23) are replaced by כל־מחנהו ('the entire army', v. 24). The unnamed king is replaced by Ben-Hadad, and the simple excursion to capture Elisha is succeeded by a siege of Samaria. The defeat is clearly Elisha's.

Modern commentators scramble to undo the damage done to the prophet's reputation. Gray states that the phrase ויהי אחרי־כן ('and after this') 'need not necessarily connect with the preceding passage, but with some other matter which has been omitted by the compilers'.[248] Cogan and Tadmor argue that this phrase 'carries no chronological significance for the modern reader'.[249] While this may be true for the

---

245. The narrative makes no distinction between the various military endeavors of Aram (חיל מחנה גדוד) in regards to their connection to the Aramean authority structure. It does not suggest that some are under royal authority while others are not (cf. 5.2).

246. Hobbs chooses to deal with chapters individually, and thus deals with 7.1-20 as a separate unit (*Kings*, p. 82). There is little reason to afford the versification such control over reading, but it certainly highlights the fact that most of the stories in 2 Kgs follow chapter divisions.

247. Würthwein says that 6.24aα is added to install composition into its context, but makes no mention of the impact the connection has on the narrative (*Könige*, p. 310).

248. Gray, *Kings*, p. 470.

249. Cogan and Tadmor, *Kings*, p. 78.

reader who reads independent narratives as constructed by modern scholarship, it certainly does not hold for readers of Kings. Further, even if I worked with the (re)constructed original units, I would certainly concede that the compiler produced a text that creates a definite connection between individual stories. This is especially true given the similarity of theme, character and action between the two stories.

The phrase ויהי אחרי־כן ('and after this') is also found in 1 Sam. 24.6; 2 Sam. 2.1; 8.1; 10.1; 31.1 and 21.18. In the first example, David has cut off the corner of Saul's cloak while he was sleeping. Afterward (ויהי אחרי־כן), David responds with remorse, and then Saul leaves the cave (v. 8). This suggests that there cannot have been a significant period of time between David's action and his remorse.

The other instances of this phrase do not necessarily signify such a short period of time. They do, however, always indicate that the narrative is following the same chronology as the story, that the reader is not being presented with stories that are chronologically displaced. Thus, this instance of the phrase indicates that something that is not supposed to happen, namely Aram attacking Israel (2 Kgs 6.23), does indeed happen (6.24).

Thus, in three short words the credibility of Elisha collapses.[250] The failure rests clearly with the prophet, just as the credit did. The exact nature of the damage is difficult to assess, for it would depend upon the reaction of the individual reader to this unexpected turn of events. It is possible for readers to ignore the connection, and thus to salvage the reputation of the prophet. They could only do this, however, at the cost of intellectual honesty. It is entirely possible that the readers' need to think positively about a prophet would outweigh other considerations. While I am attempting to record the narrative's desire to contain and even mock prophetic power, I am not able to reach any firm conclusions regarding its success in this venture.

As I note the question of the shadow that 6.24 casts on the positive picture of Elisha's miraculous intervention, it should also be recognized that Elisha in this story is portrayed as useful in saving himself and the king of Israel from Aramean attack. Given the expectation created by 1 Kgs 19.17, I wonder why Elisha does not bring the Arameans into Samaria and then turn them loose to destroy the house of Ahab. It is

---

250. Readers might wonder about the credibility of the narrator, except for the discrepancy between גדוד (v. 23) and מחנה (v. 24), which allows them to read v. 23 as ironic.

disturbing to see Elisha act as advisor to Ahab's son. The role of prophet as royal oracle is only created at the expense of the role of prophet as YHWH's sword.

2 Kings 6.24–7.20: The Siege of Samaria

This story is the longest and most complex in the Elisha corpus. It contains six interconnected subplots, which will be read together in order to fashion a coherent picture of narrative movement and narrative motivation. Each subplot contributes to the overall picture, and each is even allowed to briefly dominate the story. Yet the story is held together by the interweaving of the subplots, which do not make sense outside the whole.

The story begins, as I have already noted, with the siege of Samaria by Ben-Hadad, king of Aram. Commentators are divided as to the 'real' chronological location of the events presented here, noting that the king of Israel is consistently unnamed, and the disjunction of v. 23 and v. 24.[251] For readers of Kings, the king of Israel remains Jehoram/Joram (3.1; 8.16, 25). The conflict produced by the siege itself ('how will Samaria survive the siege?') is resolved in 7.6-7, in a narrative/chronological aside. Thus, this is not the central conflict of the story, only the one that engenders the rest of the events.

The secondary nature of this conflict can also be seen in 6.25, as the focus of the story shifts to the famine. The famine is clearly presented as a result of the siege, and nothing is said of the food supply in the rest of Israel. In fact, nothing is said at all about the rest of Israel. This is in keeping with the general tone of Genesis–2 Kings, where capital cities 'are' the nation.[252] Given this context, readers should be aware that it is unlikely that they are truly seeing a narrative produced by peasants to satirize the political system.[253] While this particular king is presented in a negative light, the lack of alternative system suggests that the hegemony of the monarchic system is not challenged.

As quickly as the conflict changes from siege to famine, it further changes when the petition of the woman is introduced (v. 26). Readers might believe that both siege and famine were pretexts for this incident,

---

251. Gray, *Kings*, p. 470; Cogan and Tadmor, *Kings*, p. 478.
252. Note, e.g., 2 Kgs 19, where YHWH is concerned to defend Jerusalem, but seemingly unconcerned about the plight of the rest of the cities of Judah.
253. Contra LaBarbara, 'Man of War', p. 651; Nelson, *Kings*, p. 191.

were it not for the fact that the conflict introduced by the woman is never resolved. This lack of resolution is a major clue regarding the role of this subplot in the movement of the narrative, and will be dealt with below.

As many commentators have noted, this story presents a clear parallel with the incident in 1 Kgs 3.16-28. Stuart Lasine has presented a clear and thorough reading of these contrasting stories, detailing the many points of inversion in plot, theme and resolution.[254] While Lasine treats this story apart from its narrative context, his conclusions impact on the reading of the whole. For the purposes of my reading, it must be remembered that this incident is narrated from within the Elisha corpus, and his non-presence in the conflict must be questioned.

The woman's initial petition (הושיעה אדני המלך, 'help, my lord king', v. 26) is one which would engage the sympathy of readers. The woman is not a prostitute, as in the Solomon story, and there is initially nothing to indicate that readers cannot identify with her plight. The fact that the woman's petition is directed to the king can also be perceived as natural. The king remains the highest form of human authority. Further, the king is also granted a degree of access to YHWH in much of Genesis–2 Kings, especially in the ideal cases of David and Solomon.

The king's initial response is a rather surprising confession of both faith and helplessness. The statement contrasts the source of power available to the king (threshing floor and winepress = economic power) to the unlimited power of YHWH.[255] This confessional reply opens the possibility of the king as a sympathetic figure. This would be a rather unusual role for the king in the Elisha corpus, but the clearly emotional nature of the king's words may initiate an emotional response in readers, one which may well be sympathetic. I must not rely too heavily on general impressions of character in reading an individual story, for good narrative is capable of allowing sympathetic insights into the portrayal of an otherwise antagonistic character. This sympathetic response would be heightened by the reading of the woman's complaint. If I read this as a plot unto itself, the king is clearly the 'good guy'.

---

254. Stuart Lasine, 'Jehoram and the Cannibal Mothers (2 Kings 6.24-33): Solomon's Judgment in an Inverted World', *JSOT* 50 (1991), pp. 27-53.

255. LaBarbara suggests that threshing floor and winepress are indications of the king's reliance upon Baal ('Man of War', p. 646). This is clearly unlikely in the midst of the Elisha corpus, which allows no reference to the existence of other deities.

Lasine is certainly right in perceiving a comic element in this story.[256] While modern readers may be too revolted by the story to allow any sympathetic characters, it is possible that other readers more acquainted with death and survival would be amused by the woman's unawareness of the horrible nature of her actions, and the complete lack of 'just' outcome for this story.

Readers may also note that her actions correspond to the curses in Deut. 28.52-57. In this case, the actions of the woman are a judgment upon the people of Israel, who presumably did not 'serve the Lord your God joyfully and with gladness of heart for the abundance of everything' (Deut. 28.47, NRSV). This parallel turns comedy into tragic condemnation, and shifts the blame from prophet to people. Readers are again reminded that this is Israel, the ultimate destruction of which is a result of their sin (2 Kgs 17.7).

Readers who were surprised and delighted by the outcome of the Solomon story are likely wondering how this particular king will produce such a just solution. Solomon's solution cannot be applied to this story, for a division of the child is precisely the outcome desired by the petitioner. Further, even the pretext of the solution does not apply, since a 'true' mother has already killed and eaten her own child (and it was a son!). Thus, readers are likely not surprised that the king of Israel is unable to produce a resolution. This is not a failure on the part of the king. The king has done what he could (from the threshing floor and winepress), and has correctly identified the only possible source for a solution.

Further, readers are allowed to look through the eyes of the people of Samaria (וירא העם, 'and the people saw', v. 30) at the sackcloth that the king wears under his clothes. This is an unusual change in perspective, since the narrator could have easily have noted the sackcloth without showing it through the eyes of the people. In Kings, sackcloth is a sign of contrition and humiliation. It is used together with terms like כנע ('be humble', 1 Kgs 21.27-29), נאצה, תוכחה, צרה ('disgrace', 'rebuke', 'distress', 2 Kgs 19.3), and more generally to show humility (1 Kgs 20.31). It is always done for someone else, whether for God (1 Kgs 21; 2 Kgs 19) or for an enemy (1 Kgs 20).[257] Thus, a public showing of this garment is a sign of great distress, and a sign of petition. The people are

---

256. Lasine, 'Jehoram', p. 33.
257. Long notes that kings in sackcloth are associated with God-sent trouble (Long, *2 Kings*, p. 92).

shown the depth of the distress of the king, and consequently esteem him for his private suffering before YHWH on behalf of the city (for to whom else could the king be petitioning?).[258] This is what is happening inside the world of the narrative. For readers, the king is viewed briefly through the eyes of his adoring subjects. Since readers are more likely to identify with the citizens of Jerusalem than either king or prophet, their sympathetic reading of the king is enhanced by their identification with the adoring populace.

The king's reaction in v. 31 (כה־יעשה־לי אלהים וכה יוסף אם־יעמד ראש אלישע בן־שפט עליו היום, 'so may God do to me, and more, if the head of Elisha, son of Shephat, stays on today') has generated a number of responses from commentators. Jones notes the lack of reason given for the reaction, which to him suggests that this section was a later addition.[259] Gray also argues that it is an unreasonable response, and says that the king blames Elisha to divert attention from himself.[260] Hobbs, on the other hand, indicates that Elisha is held responsible due to his actions in the preceding story.[261] All three positions are helpful in noting the effect of the story on readers.

Jones's argument stems from an important point, the lack of narratorial motivation for the king's outburst. While Jones's solution is not available to a narratological reading, the importance of the lacuna should not be overlooked. Readers clearly must supply the missing motivation for the king's response. This is what Gray does, in suggesting diversion. Yet Gray's idea of diversion is precisely the opposite of what the reader is likely to feel. After all, readers are expecting this to be a story about the actions of Elisha. They are not expecting the king to really solve anything. The king has already reminded readers of the real power in the story (6.27; also the sackcloth, v. 30), and they know that it is the prophet who mediates the power of YHWH in Israel.

---

258. Nelson uses the reference to city walls (vv. 26,30) as an indication that 'this story offers the perspective of history's common folk who suffer below the walls upon which kings walk' (*Kings*, p. 191). Yet one should note that walking on city walls clearly allows the people access to the king. It also allows the greatest number of people to see the sackcloth. This is clearly not a portrayal of a king who is unaffected by the suffering of his people. The view from below shows the king in a very good light.
259. Jones, *Kings*, p. 434.
260. Gray, *Kings*, p. 471.
261. Hobbs, *Kings*, p. 80.

Hobbs is correct in showing the connection between this story and its context. Readers know that not only is Elisha the likely source of salvation (Moore reminds us of the continued importance of Elisha's name[262]), but he is culpable in regards to the origin of the action. Perhaps if he had not allowed the Aramean army to go free earlier, Samaria would not be in this difficulty.

This places readers in a difficult situation. I have been developing an uncharacteristically sympathetic response to the king of Israel. Further, I have noted the discrepancy between 6.23 and 6.24. The situation in Samaria is truly horrendous, for the picture in v. 29 clearly depicts the breakdown of society.[263] Yet are readers ready to blame a prophet for not acting sooner? The response of commentators to this situation suggests that they are not. Even Hobbs quickly rescues the prophet from such negative possibilities. Only Lasine is willing to admit the possibility that the story may challenge the usual pro-prophetic stance of Genesis–2 Kings.[264]

I suspect that the inclination of readers to always understand the action or inaction of the prophet in the most positive light comes more from the general view of prophecy in the rest of the Bible (Hebrew or Christian) than from a careful reading of this particular story, or more generally the Elisha corpus. The narrative certainly opens itself to a positive reading of prophetic activity, a reading that can be sustained through the remainder of the story, although not without difficulty.

The king of Israel's pronouncement is followed by his action, as he dispatches a messenger (v. 32).[265] The scene then shifts spatially to Elisha, sitting with the elders in his house. This shift of scene is not without narrative consequence. While one might surmise from 5.8-9 that Elisha had a residence in Samaria, the preceding story placed him in Dothan. The presence of the elders is also curious, both because they are found with Elisha and because they enter the story at all.

The elders are such a curiosity to readers that commentators feel the need to account for their presence. The assumption usually is that they

262. Moore, *God Saves*, pp. 36, passim.
263. Lasine, 'Jehoram', p. 31.
264. Lasine, 'Jehoram', p. 47.
265. Shifting, with the *BHS* notes, וישלח איש מלפניו ('and he sent a man from his presence') to the beginning of v. 32. The shift is the only way to make sense of the sending of the messenger, since the obvious subject of וישלח ('and he sent') is the king.

represent a conservative element in Israel,[266] possibly representing an alternative to the current monarchy.[267] Cogan and Tadmor state that the elders 'no doubt wait for an oracle of deliverance'.[268] This suggestion may or may not account for the presence of the elders in the story, but it certainly represents the perspective of the reader. The city is besieged, famine has caused social chaos, the king is humbling himself before YHWH and Elisha is present. I am allowed to wonder why Elisha has done nothing until now.

The idea of waiting for an oracle is certainly helpful in relieving Elisha of responsibility. Yet readers have been given little indication that Elisha needs to wait for an oracle. While 4.27 might suggest that Elisha relies on YHWH for his special knowledge, a reliance that has its limits, the rest of the stories indicate a prophet who can all but command the actions of YHWH. It is readers who are waiting.

Elisha is quick to use his special power, but he does so initially to save himself (v. 32).[269] The picture of a group of elders hastily barring the door against the intrusion of the king and his messenger hardly stands as a great demonstration of YHWH's power. It is the king who summarizes for readers the situation as they are to perceive it (v. 33). The trouble is from YHWH. This perspective on the actions of YHWH foreshadows the final condemnation of Israel made by the narrator (2 Kgs 17.18). Yet here there is no explicit mention of Israel's sin, nor of actions on the part of king or people that have made this situation unavoidable. Since readers are not likely inclined to believe that the actions of YHWH are unmotivated, I must presume that the king is speaking not so much about cause as solution.[270]

The second statement of the king can be understood as a challenge to Elisha. The statement is straightforward in translation, but ambiguous as a presentation of the state of mind of the king. 'מה־אוחיל ליהוה עוד'

---

266. LaBarbara, 'Man of War', p. 647; Gray, *Kings*, p. 471.

267. Ahlström states that Elisha 'may have been encouraging them and others to favor a change in government' ('Jehu', p. 57).

268. Cogan and Tadmor, *Kings*, p. 80.

269. Culley notes that all of Elisha's actions in this story have an aspect of self-vindication (*Themes*, p. 90).

270. Of course, readers might also note that all of YHWH's actions in the Elisha corpus are without explicit motivation, except in response to the request/demand of Elisha.

has been paraphrased 'no use going to God for help',[271] or understood as concern that hurting Elisha might make matters worse.[272] Hobbs understands it as a suggestion that the king has understood that the siege has served God's purposes.[273]

The statement also acts as a foil for Elisha's reply, and thus as a window of doubt that is quickly closed by Elisha's response. In this way the narrative allows for the healthy expression of doubt and uncertainty on behalf of readers, so long as it is not given any time to develop. Yet the answer is not without ambiguity of its own. Should the king wait for YHWH because of YHWH's concern for his people, or should the king wait only because Elisha is there? Long states that the king 'threatens Yahweh's prophet ... but nothing comes of it'.[274] Yet it is precisely the king's threat that initiates the oracle. Elisha's words, and by inference YHWH's words, are a response to the questions of the messenger/king.[275] The king remains correct in his assessment of the situation, at least in the world of the narrative.

Insofar as 7.1 represents Elisha's response to the situation, I need to ask precisely which situation he is responding to. The words he utters are clearly a response to the famine, and a direct contrast to the earlier words of the narrator (6.25). It is almost as if Elisha has been listening to the narrator, and wishes to respond to his challenge. In the context of the plot, Elisha is still presumably in some danger from the king, having only the elders barring a door against the potential of military might (note the presence of the military office in 7.2). This threat is itself a response to the petition of the cannibal mother. Given the larger narrative context, the words of the oracle are surprising. Elisha predicts the price of commodities at the gate of Samaria. In this way, he indirectly answers the challenge of both king and mother by restoring more normal staple goods at more normal prices.[276]

---

271. Jones, *Kings*, pp. 434-35. Similarly understood by Cogan and Tadmor, *Kings*, p. 81; Long, *Kings*, p. 93.

272. Gray, *Kings*, p. 472.

273. Hobbs, *2 Kings*, 81.

274. Long, *Kings*, p. 93.

275. Many translators prefer to substitute מלך ('king') for מלאך ('messenger') in 6.33. This is unnecessary, give the spatial relation between them related by Elisha (v. 32), and the conflation of messenger's and sender's voice in Hebrew narrative.

276. Commentators are divided as to whether these prices represent unusually low rates or more usual rates. This detail is lost in the mists of time, yet readers

Reader may have numerous ways of responding to this type of information. The narrative focuses readers' attention on the question of how the return of normal food prices will be accomplished by placing doubt in the mouth of a bystander. The official[277] offers one scenario for the fulfillment of this oracle, and dismisses even that as inadequate.[278] Elisha then responds to his doubt by offering a further, albeit cryptic, oracle concerning the fate of the officer.

Again, the narrative has allowed for the possibility of doubt concerning the possible fulfillment of Elisha's word in the mind of readers by placing this idea in the mouth of a character. In this case, the character is one with whom readers are unlikely to identify, since a military officer is out of his league when dealing with a prophet, and besides, the military is a non-presence in the entire siege story.[279] The narrative also minimizes further doubt by decreeing the fate of those who doubt the word of the prophet, namely seeing but not partaking.

This dialogue maintains the various roles which we have seen throughout the Elisha corpus. The king is ineffective but necessary. The prophet is powerful, almost without limit, yet the prophet acts in service to the king. This particular story has added certain details to the picture. Readers have been given an opportunity to view the king as a sympathetic character. On two occasions, the narrative has allowed for doubt to enter my mind, and has quickly quashed these with oracles, oracles which, as will be seen, quickly come to pass.

The character YHWH has reappeared, three times in the speech of the king (6.27, 33), and twice in the speech of Elisha (7.1). YHWH is not given any lines to speak, and thus always remains under the control of the other characters. The king has spoken about YHWH, and recognized YHWH's complicity in the events of the story. The king has also invoked YHWH, albeit indirectly (אלהים, 'God', v. 31), as a guarantor

have little difficulty understanding that these represent a drastic shift from the prices in 6.25.

277. Gray notes the parallel between this individual's role and that of Naaman in 5.18 (*Kings*, p. 470).

278. LaBarbara takes the reference to ארבות ('windows') as an indirect reference to Baalism ('Man of War', pp. 647-48). While the narrative has no control over the associations that readers might make between its world and the world of the readers, it is clear that Baal is not considered a force to be reckoned with in the Elisha corpus.

279. Except for ch. 3, readers might almost get the impression that Israel had no army at this time.

of his own word. It is Elisha who speaks for YHWH, and readers soon realize that he speaks correctly, as the oracle soon comes to pass. Yet they do not hear YHWH speaking directly.[280]

The lack of direct speech from YHWH clearly changes YHWH's role as a character in the story. YHWH ceases to be an actor, one who causes action to happen. The ones who cause action to happen are the king and Elisha. The figure YHWH is given both blame (6.27, 33) and credit (7.1) for the action that is to occur, but this comes not from YHWH but from the actors. It is Elisha's action (his speaking) which causes the king to stop his attack upon Elisha. Even the narrator fails to give YHWH explicit credit for action, as he attributes the קול ('voice') to אדני ('my lord') rather than YHWH (7.6). In this way, the role of God is transferred from YHWH to Elisha. Elisha speaks, and it happens. YHWH becomes a figure, a sign that indicates that something is about to happen, but is not the cause of the action.

The scene shifts dramatically to the plight of a group of four[281] lepers sitting outside the gate of the city. After the Naaman story, there is a certain irony in finding lepers sitting outside the city gate while Elisha is sitting comfortably inside with the elders (as Jesus notes in Lk. 4.27). This might serve as another reminder that in both stories Elisha acts in response to the distress of the king, rather than the suffering of others.

The tale of the lepers, while initially tragic, quickly becomes comic and even humorous. The plight of the lepers dominates the beginning of the scene (vv. 3-4), their greed dominates the middle (v. 8), and their report dominates the end (vv. 9-10). In between the first two sections, the story of YHWH's deliverance lies almost buried. The flight of the Aramean army is merely a piece of background information that allows the story of the lepers to move from tragedy to comedy.

The order in which is given information is important here. The story I construct as I read tells me that the Arameans had already fled before the lepers had their discussion. Yet it is through the eyes of the lepers that I see the empty Aramean camp (note the והנה, 'and behold' [often left untranslated] in v. 5). Thus the report in vv. 6, 7 is asynchronous,

---

280. It is also important to note that YHWH is not invoked by Elisha in 7.2. This will be important later in the recitation of the oracular fulfilment. Carlson has understood this to mean that events of the story are less important than prophetic speech ('Elisee', p. 401).

281. As LaBarbara has pointed out, the number four (ארבעה, 7.3) is certainly a pun on ארבות ('windows') in 7.2 ('Man of War', p. 648).

4. *Elisha*

relaying information of what has previously occurred. The narrative continues in 'real time' in v. 8. The focus remains on the lepers.

There is, however, considerable detail regarding the flight of the Aramean army. This is also picked up again in v. 15, where the path of the flight is observed by the two soldiers. The flight is attributed to אדני ('the Lord'), who causes them to hear the sound (קול) of horses, chariots and a great army (7.6). This is the only use of אדני in the Elisha corpus as a reference to YHWH. While clearly the rest of Genesis–2 Kings directs readers to understand this as a reference to YHWH, the figure of Elisha has been taking over the role of God in much of the rest of the Elisha corpus, and thus the identification is not automatic. The reader might note the parallel in 1 Kgs 22.6, where the 400 prophets of the king of Israel prophesy victory for the king as coming from אדני, but Micaiah prophesies from יהוה (22.19). Thus, the narrative is able to distinguish between Lord and YHWH in other passages as well.

The story continues in the comic mode by opposing the מצרעים ('lepers', v. 3) to the מלכי מצרים.[282] The power of YHWH is clearly displayed for readers (kings of Egypt, v. 6), but it remains buried in the comedy of lepers and kings. This further lessens the readers' focus on the power of Elisha. In this story, the power of Elisha is purely oracular, and he disappears from the story until the reminder in v. 17.

The lepers then decide to report to the city what they have found, out of fear of punishment (מצאנו עון, 'we will be found guilty', v. 9). This motivation keeps them from being sympathetic characters, since readers are likely sympathetic to the plight of the people of Samaria. Since the actions of the lepers can be contrasted with the actions of the king, a non-sympathetic reading of the lepers allows readers to continue with a largely sympathetic reading of the king.

Readers know what has happened in the camp of the Arameans, but they also know that the king does not know. There is no reason for the king to simply accept the story of the disappearance of the Arameans, since Elisha has said nothing about how YHWH will bring about the change in commodity prices. Thus, the king's caution in v. 12 is a likely scenario, and makes good military sense.[283] Clearly military strategy is not the point of the story, but it is still valued by readers. Military

---

282. Narrative credibility is established by the Hittites, comedy by the Egyptians.

283. Hobbs notes the parallel between this story and Josh. 8 and Judg. 9 (*Kings*, p. 91). For the opposite view, see La Barbara, 'Man of War', p. 650.

strategy has been an important element in Genesis–2 Kings, and the king shows his own acumen by painting a picture of cunning strategy on the part of the enemy.

Elisha is absent from the discussion between the king and his servants. This is not surprising, since military strategy is not his area of expertise.[284] What is somewhat more surprising is the absence of any reference to YHWH. YHWH has been consistently invoked in this story as the means of deliverance (6.27, 33), and is given credit for the event which brings about deliverance (7.6-7), yet neither the king nor his servants consider consulting YHWH. This is also true of the story of the lepers, where the lepers never consider YHWH as the source of their fortune.

Yet the text contains no condemnation of this 'secular' method of problem solving. Readers may note the contrast here with 2 Kgs 1.2-3, where the king of Israel is condemned for consulting a foreign god. My passage allows for no foreign deities of any temptation to Israel, and thus the king is left to his own wisdom. And his own actions are clearly contrasted with the actions of YHWH, who is always linked to the prophet Elisha.[285] Yet it is the king who comes off rather well in this narrative, and consequently both Elisha and YHWH are shown in a less positive light.[286] Even when YHWH is shown as the deliverer of Israel, he is shown as inactive until cannibalism breaks out, until the king forces Elisha to act. YHWH as deliverer is also hidden both by chronological displacement and by narrative placement in the middle of a comic interlude.

Thus, LaBarbara is correct in pointing out that 'always standing behind Elisha is the God he serves'.[287] Readers, however, would be justified in feeling rather uncomfortable with the YHWH/Elisha pairing which the text continues to present. Since readers are unlikely to maintain a negative attitude toward YHWH, it is likely that discomfort will be transferred to the figure of Elisha.

Interestingly, the narrative concludes with the option for readers of distancing YHWH's action from that of Elisha. Verse 7.16 concludes this section of the story with a recitation of oracular fulfillment, ending

---

284. Note the lack of strategy in 3.16-19. Elisha's words are predictive, but have little information regarding the means by which events occur.
285. See LaBarbara, 'Man of War', p. 651.
286. Contra LaBarbara, 'Man of War', p. 651.
287. LaBarbara, 'Man of War', p. 651.

with the phrase כדבר יהוה ('according to the word of YHWH').²⁸⁸ Yet the story cannot end here, for there is another oracle to be fulfilled (7.2). This is accomplished in the rather lengthy description of 7.17-20, which includes a recitation of the entire encounter.

The repetitious nature of vv. 17-20 is a departure from the usual laconic style of the narrative. It contains the indirect report of direct speech (ויהי כדבר איש האלהים אל־המלך לאמר, 'for when the man of God had said to the king', v. 18), which is also an unusual feature. Further, the word is credited to Elisha (כאשר דבר איש האלהים, 'as the man of God had said', v. 17), which in contrast to v. 16 suggests that the fulfillment also is. Even the placement of the fulfillment formula is unusual, since the story ends with ויהי־לו כן ('it happened thus to him', v. 20), with no mention of agency except the people (העם).²⁸⁹

Thus, readers are given two contrasting stories of the fulfillment of oracles. One involves YHWH, whose actions result in the end of siege and famine, and who accomplishes his own work (ואדני השמיע, 'for the Lord had caused', 7.6). The other involves Elisha, who works to kill a doubting officer through the agency of the people. The power of Elisha to bring his word to fulfillment is never in doubt, but the effect of the action is hardly complimentary toward prophets, bringing death in the midst of rejoicing.

Thus, the final conflict of the story is resolved. There is a certain necessity to the order of resolution, although the narrative could have resorted to another chronological displacement to conclude with the fulfillment in v. 16. One must remember the importance of recency in creating a final impression. Verses 17-20 are a rather comic tale, with many obviously entertaining features, a light-hearted treatment of oracular fulfillment. This is the readers' final impression of Elisha in his actions during the siege of Samaria. The king is concerned with the suffering of his people, YHWH works to cause the Arameans to flee, but Elisha is concerned with his personal vendetta against a particular

288. This is the only time in the Elisha corpus that the narrator independently affirms that the word of Elisha that he claims is from YHWH is actually from YHWH. This is the exception which proves the rule.

289. Gray considers this change of style to be a shift from 'history' to 'prophecy-fulfilment' (*Kings*, p. 473-74). Yet this does not account for the fulfillment formula in v. 16, nor the stylistic discrepancy between this fulfillment story and the others of the Elisha corpus.

officer. The narrative ends with death (וַיָּמָת, v. 20), whereas the story continues with the celebration of the people of Samaria.

2 Kings 8.1-6: The Shunammite Woman Returns

Many of the narratives I have been explaining up to this point have followed a similar pattern in presentation. They begin with a short introduction that gives the necessary background to the story, and then quickly move to the details of the plot. This introduction also presents one or more of the main actors in the story.

In this instance, the narrator begins with Elisha, who had spoken to הָאִשָּׁה אֲשֶׁר־הֶחֱיָה אֶת־בְּנָהּ ('the woman whose son he had restored to life', v. 1). Here readers are reminded of the earlier story of Elisha and the Shunammite, and the order of the words (ו + subject + verb) suggests that Elisha's speech may have taken place at that time. Elisha subsequently disappears as an actor in the story, reappearing only as the subject of conversation (leading one commentator to presume his death).[290] Elisha's initial words stand as the reason for the conflict that ensues (the woman's loss of land), yet he is not directly involved in the resolution.

The reappearance of the Shunammite woman is interesting. Rofé suggests that this is not the same person as in 4.8-37,[291] yet the story clearly hinges on the retelling of the earlier incident (v. 5), and includes Gehazi, who played an important role in the earlier story. Her position within society has also caused concern, since the narrative continues to depict her as the head of her household (בֵּיתֵךְ, 'your household', v. 1; בֵּיתָהּ, 'her household', v. 2). Montgomery takes this as an indication that she is now a widow.[292] Jones places her husband's death during her time in Philistia, since in the text (v. 3) it is only the woman who returns from Philistia.[293] Cogan and Tadmor take the phrase אֶל־בֵּיתָהּ וְאֶל־שָׂדָהּ ('for her house and for her land') as indicating that she had land possibly from a former marriage.[294] I can find no indication in the narrative that it shares the commentators' squeamishness concerning land-owning women. It is certainly an anomaly in the text, but then

---

290. So Jones, *Kings*, p. 438.
291. Rofé, *Stories*, p. 33.
292. Montgomery, *Books of Kings*, p. 391.
293. Jones, *Kings*, p. 440.
294. Cogan and Tadmor, *Kings*, p. 88.

4. *Elisha*

ordinary citizens are an anomaly in general in a text focused on kings and prophets.

The action around which the plot focuses is initiated by the word of Elisha, who claims divine guidance. Würthwein has helpfully reduced the plot to its basic components by considering as secondary v. 1, 'whose son he had brought back to life', v. 2 'and did according to the word of the man of God', and all of vv. 4, 5 and 7b 'and all the revenue ... '[295] This leaves us with a story about warning concerning famine, moving, returning and restoring. It leaves out all the sections that add complexity to the story, and which might cause readers to pause and wonder (e.g. why has this woman reappeared? Why is Gehazi the leper sitting next to the king? Why is all the revenue from the land returned?).

The famine is necessary to the plot. The woman needs some reason to go to Philistia. Verse 8.1 bears a strong resemblance to 1 Kgs 17.1, where Elijah proclaims a famine upon Israel. In neither case is any reason for the famine given in the initial verse, although readers may suspect that 1 Kgs 16.31-33 has provided the impetus for YHWH's action through Elijah. Readers are subsequently informed that this presupposition was correct, when in 1 Kgs 18.18 Elijah connects his actions with the Baalism of Ahab.

This parallel has a disquieting effect upon the story. It is the Shunammite woman, not the king, who is warned regarding the famine. We have just finished a story that allowed a sympathetic reading of the king's character, and are unaware of any serious violations of YHWH's will on his part except for the formulaic recording of his continuance of the sins of Jeroboam (back in 3.3). While famine was likely a common occurrence in Israel in those days, the prophetic warning would suggest divine initiative is involved.

This is especially true in a famine of seven years (v. 1). As Gray has pointed out, the number seven is a sacred number, used in legal texts such as Exod. 21.2 and Deut. 15.1-18. As a famine, seven years is also lengthy, causing great suffering to the many people dependant upon subsistence farming. Famine also tends to be a factor in the transfer of land ownership from farmer to landholding elite, since debt accumulates when the farmer is unable to pay for the food that his (or in this case her) land fails to provide. Thus, land ownership is transferred to

---

295. Würthwein, *Könige*, p. 317.

the creditor in lieu of payment. Insofar as commentators view this as a story 'from below', the economic displacement of an extended famine needs to be accounted for as the action of YHWH.

This is especially true if readers remember the story of Joseph in Genesis 41. In 41.28-36, Joseph uses the knowledge of the coming famine to outline a plan of action for the Pharaoh. While this famine is not linked specifically to any sin, foreknowledge leads to preparedness, which would possibly lessen the impact on farming communities. There is no indication in this text that Elisha so uses his knowledge.

So the woman acts כדבר איש האלהים ('according to the word of the man of God', v. 2). This story makes a very clear distinction between prophetic word and word of YHWH. The word of YHWH (presumably) comes to Elisha, and what he does with it is his responsibility. In this case, he uses his special knowledge to aid a friend. The word that Elisha speaks to the woman is not part of the word of YHWH. The scene could be seen as very humanizing in the portrayal of an otherwise distant character, were it not for the complete silence of the text regarding the reason for the famine and the other actions of Elisha in this seven-year period.

Readers are also likely to be uncomfortable with the woman's destination. Since the time of David, Philistia has long ceased to be a factor in Genesis–2 Kings. Yet readers are likely to have strongly negative associations with the Philistines, given their prominence in the story of David. The place is of the woman's choosing, and does not detract from our picture of Elisha. It does, however, hinder us from identifying too strongly with the woman.[296]

The identification of Philistia as the place of the woman's sojourn may also remind readers of Isaac in Genesis 26. In that story, however, it was YHWH who instructed Isaac to remain in Philistia (v. 2), while here YHWH's role is again taken over by Elisha. The parallel is also another reminder of the sins of Israel, in that YHWH promised Isaac possession of Philistia as a reward for obedience (Gen. 26.3, 5).

The woman returns to צעק ('plead', v. 3) to the king of Israel concerning her house and her fields. Bar Efrat parallels this term with

---

296. There is a parallel between the woman's actions and those of David in 1 Sam. 21.10-15 and 1 Sam. 27–31. One wonders, however, if readers do not feel discomfort with David's actions, given the ongoing battles between Philistia and Israel.

2 Sam. 19.28 and suggests that it is a complaint against injustice.[297] This is similar to the argument of Cogan and Tadmor, who presume that the woman has legal right to the land, and that it has been taken away by 'unlawful appropriation'.[298] The exact legal status of her land is difficult to ascertain.[299] While in general the law assumes that land is someone's possession in perpetuity (see Lev. 25.23-25), it is difficult to know how the law would deal with land abandoned for seven years. Again the Elijah corpus provides a parallel with the story of Naboth's vineyard (1 Kings 21), but there the question is sale and murder, not abandonment and legal claim.

It is also important to note that it is to the king that the woman appeals. The legal statutes suggest that her land may need to be redeemed (Lev. 25.23). The rights of the king over land ownership is certainly one of the issues in the Naboth story, and the king is there accorded little power over the matter. Readers could certainly be excused for initially reacting against such a move. Given the lack of clarity regarding the legal status of the land, and the history of kings and land ownership (see also 1 Sam. 8.14), the sympathies of readers do not easily extend toward the woman's claim.

Yet there remains the problem of Elisha. It is he who suggested her move, which provides a certain divine initiative to her action. Surely YHWH would not abandon one whom he has called to sojourn (remember Elijah and the ravens). Yet Elisha clearly has no authority regarding the distribution of land. The idea of the prophet forcing the return of the woman's land is foreign to the text. Even Elijah, proclaiming the direct word of YHWH, does not order the return of Naboth's land to his kin (1 Kgs 21.17-24). Thus, the king remains the logical one to whom someone would appeal in regard to a land dispute. Power continues to

---

297. Shimon Bar-Efrat, *Narrative Art in the Bible* (JSOTSup, 70; Sheffield: Almond Press, 1989), p. 271.

298. Cogan and Tadmor, *Kings*, p. 88, citing Skinner.

299. In general, the narrative assumes that the characters are constrained by the Law. Polzin, however, notes the contrast between *authoritarian dogmatism* and *critical traditionalism* in the books of Deuteronomy and Joshua, the latter of which 'recognizes the constant need for revision and varying interpretations of the traditions' (Robert Polzin, *Moses and the Deuteronomist* [New York: Seabury, 1980], p. 84). Thus I must be careful not to expect too rigid an application of legal statute in narrative text.

be carefully divided in the narrative, especially in regards to the limits of prophetic power and authority.

The following verse demonstrates this point very effectively. The disquiet of readers regarding the king's authority and good will in relation to land ownership is stilled by the totally positive depiction of the king of Israel. The king is shown speaking to Gehazi, requesting to hear stories of the great deeds (הגדלות, v. 4) of Elisha. In showing the king in such a positive light, the narrative suggests a favorable reading of the woman's request.

Yet there remain a number of questions regarding this surprising depiction. Why is a descendant of Ahab portrayed as a fan of Elisha's? What has become of Gehazi's leprosy (5.27)? Where is Elisha? These questions detract strongly from the credibility of the story. The image of a leprous Gehazi sitting beside the son of Ahab cheerfully recounting stories of Elisha at the request of the king does not easily correspond with the images I have been constructing thus far.

The credibility gap affects my entire attitude toward the Elisha stories, and by extension affects my attitude toward Elisha. If one story is incredible, how can I know the others are true? Perhaps the entire corpus is purely imaginary, as are the great deeds I have been reading about.

Again here the narrative attempts to program the readers' attitude toward the prophet. This attitude is placed in the mouth of the king, just as other directives have earlier been placed in the mouth of characters (5.11, 15; 6.12). Here the king directs my attention to the prophet as doer of great things (כל־הגדלות אשר־עשה אלישע, 'all the great deeds which Elisha did', v. 4). Elisha continues to emerge as puissant wonderworker, but one who has no other role in his society. Stories of Elisha are told for general amusement.[300]

The focus on Elisha as wonder worker continues in v. 5 with the triple repetition of the phrase אשר־החיה ('whom he had restored to life'). This is the place of Elisha in the story. He has nothing to say

---

300. Cogan and Tadmor see this as a clue to the original transmission of the Elisha tradition (*Kings*, p. 88). They fail to note, however, the contrast between stories of interest to be performed to regale audiences, and stories that are used as traditions to create societies. In the Elisha corpus, readers are drawn away from the notion of the prophet as ultimate authority on the will of YHWH, and toward a more cynical attitude toward prophets, as transient wonder-workers who wish to take the place of YHWH.

regarding the return of real estate. He has nothing to say regarding the actions of this particular king. Even his word regarding the leprosy of Gehazi seems to have been forgotten, since one can hardly imagine the king sitting beside a leper.[301] Yet he is not absent. His presence is reinforced by the mention of his name at the end of v. 5. This is still a picture of a world with Elisha in it. Elisha is merely confined to his proper place, as object of entertaining stories.

The woman is asked to repeat her story, and she does so. Her story is obviously about the raising of her son, rather than her sojourn in Philistia. The king is not likely to be entertained by the story of her being warned of the famine, since he appears not to have been warned. The reader might suspect that the son of Ahab would not have been pleased to hear of another famine announcement from a prophet, having likely lived through the three-year famine announced by Elijah.

Having heard the report of the woman, the king dispatches (literally 'gives to her' ויתן־לה) a eunuch (סריס) to enforce the return of all that is hers,[302] including the produce (תבואת) of the land during the time of her absence (v. 6). The details of the return of the woman's property are placed in the mouth of the king himself. Thus a story that began by quoting an earlier speech of Elisha (v. 1) ends with a speech of the king (v. 6). It is the king who finally overcomes the difficulty created by Elisha's actions. This is completely opposite to the pattern we might expect.

Readers familiar with the stories of Genesis–2 Kings are, on the whole, rather likely to expect the king and the prophet to be on opposite sides of whatever discussion is going on. I think of Samuel and Saul, Nathan and David, or more recently Elijah and Ahab or even Elisha himself and this same Jehoram (3.14; 6.31). Yet here they are clearly depicted on the same side, on the side of the woman. Elisha acts initially to save her from the famine, and the king acts later to rescue her from poverty and landlessness. The king even exceeds Elisha's kindness by restoring the produce of the land.

---

301. Any suggestion that this was a form of leprosy that did not cause exclusion is outside the world of the narrative. The narrative clearly shows the place of the leper to be outside the gate (see 7.3).

302. The inclusion of a eunuch in a story concerning a woman, her son and her inheritance is both humorous and interesting. It forms a definite contrast between the action of the king (restoration of produce) and the action of Elisha (production of children).

It is in this excess that my sympathy is lost. This is clearly not a case of 'economic justice'.³⁰³ The narrative has not clearly established the authority of the king over landholdings, and has in fact suggested a lack of authority in this regard (1 Kgs 21). Further, there is clearly no justice in returning to her produce from land that she has not farmed, and whose yield has likely sustained someone through a seven-year famine. It must be remembered that this is an אשה גדולה ('great woman', 4.8), and not a subsistence farmer. Both the actions of the king and of Elisha are directed toward helping someone who already had considerable resources. Her appearance before the king suggests access to authority that is unlikely to be available to most Israelites.

Thus, Nelson would be correct that the narrative directs readers toward a response similar to the king's—be convinced and act³⁰⁴—were it not for the excess that concludes the story. There are simply too many narrative anomalies in the story for readers to be sympathetic toward the final outcome. Readers are able to overlook many inconsistencies in a story that ends with the hero winning against the odds. The narrative is too fraught with problematic actions and too short of heroes to create a sympathetic reading. As Hobbs observes, 'that the story "legitimates" Elisha in any sense is unlikely'.³⁰⁵

The final negative judgment on prophecy is highlighted when this story is compared to the story of Naboth's vineyard in 1 Kings 21. In the Elisha story, the king acts to restore inheritance to a woman whose son has been brought back to life. In the Elijah story, the king (or rather Jezebel) acts to take the inheritance of a man by means of murder. The Elijah story concludes with prophetic condemnation that comes as the result of the direct word of YHWH (1 Kgs 21.17-19), followed by royal confession (v. 27) and partial divine forgiveness (vv. 28-29). This is clearly the 'ideal' story. The Elisha story only includes YHWH indirectly in retrospect ('Elisha had said, "... YHWH has called for a famine"', 2 Kgs 8.1), the king is the one who wields power (through a eunuch), and restoration is enacted by taking produce away from the producer. The stories operate as mirror images of each other.

Thus the picture of Elijah, servant of YHWH in the cause of justice, is undermined by the opposite picture of Elisha, still powerful, still claiming the word of YHWH, but ultimately acting in service of the wealthy,

---

303. So Nelson, *Kings*, p. 192.
304. Nelson, *Kings*, p. 192.
305. Hobbs, *Kings*, p. 97.

for the amusement of the king, and in no particular cause whatsoever. Readers may be impressed by Elisha's power, and are reminded to heed the warnings of these men, but are certainly less impressed by the purity of their motivation and the usefulness of their actions.

2 Kings 8.7-15: Transition

In the previous story I noted many details that reminded me of the Elijah corpus, including the famine, the restoration of a dead person to life and the actions of a king regarding a piece of land. In the present story, we will see further reminders of the work of Elijah, and will be reminded in more concrete ways of the word of YHWH that came to Elijah. In this way, this story, together with the one that precedes and the one that follows, forms a transition between the Elisha corpus and the return of Elijah as the major player in the history of Israel. Elijah will continue to be dead, and Elisha's death is not recorded until ch. 13, but, as we will see, the dominant force in Israel will once again be Elijah.[306]

The return of Elijah to centre stage is foreshadowed in the opening words of the narrative. Elisha is in Damascus. While the narrative makes no direct connection with earlier events, the connection is made through the lack of motivation for Elisha's action.[307] Readers, wishing to supply motivation for the actions of a key character in the story, are likely to turn to 1 Kgs 19.15-18, since here the actions of Elisha are at least indirectly connected to the city of Damascus. In the earlier story, it is Elijah who has been ordered to anoint Hazael as king of Aram. Elijah is now dead, so it would not be surprising to readers for Elisha to be carrying out Elijah's mission.

Thus, the narrative suggests to me a return not only to the Elijah story for an explanation for current actions, but also a return to the world of Elijah. Elijah's mission was always political, in the sense that it involved confrontation with kings. Elisha, by contrast, has been largely

---

306. Cogan and Tadmor consider this story and 1 Kgs 19.15-18 to be independent stories that are not harmonized (*Kings*, p. 92; cf. Würthwein, *Könige*, p. 321). Jones believes that the reasons for Elisha's presence 'may now be lost because the narrative has been extracted from its original context' (*Kings*, p. 442). Whatever the history of these passages, the readers are likely to make this connections, and deal with the harmonization problem as it arises.

307. Gray, *Kings*, p. 477.

apolitical, or at least non-confrontational.[308] Suddenly Elisha's actions are taking on a very Elijah-like character.

Ben-Hadad, king of Aram, is informed of Elisha's presence. This creates the impression of Elisha as a very important figure on the world stage. Elisha no longer needs servant girls (5.2) to make his fame known. Ben-Hadad then sends Hazael to inquire of Elisha regarding his illness. The mention of Hazael by name is unusual, since messengers are generally anonymous. Furthermore, Hazael's request can clearly be contrasted with the inquiry of Ahaziah in 1.2.[309] Thus, I have in the opening lines of the narrative three indications that I am returning to the world of Elijah. 'Damascus' and 'Hazael' remind me of 1 Kings 19 and the explicit instructions of YHWH concerning the future YHWH wishes to bring about; the inquiry of Ben-Hadad reminds us of Ahaziah, and I again find myself in a world where the kings of Israel are portrayed in opposition to the will of YHWH. These elements, namely of YHWH's will and evil kings, have been largely absent from the Elisha corpus, but form central themes of the Elijah corpus.

The contrast between 8.8 and 1.2 also allows the narrative to place in the mouth of an important figure another statement concerning the 'correct' role for the prophet. Prophets are there for the purpose of ודרשת את־יהוה ('inquiring of YHWH', v. 8). This expression places the initiative in the hands of the one inquiring, in this case the king. It places the prophet in a subservient role, as intermediary, a useful functionary in the king's court. Readers may be returning to Elijah's world, but that world has been influenced by the Elisha narratives, which severely limits the role of the prophet in Israelite society.[310]

The inquiry of Ben-Hadad, as I have noted, is directed through Hazael. Readers might expect the narrative to use a more standard phrase such as וישלח המלאך לאמר ('and he sent a messenger saying, see', e.g., 1.2; 5.8, 10; 6.9, 10). The mention of Hazael in vv. 8 and 9 warns readers that Hazael will be important in the story. Another feature that calls attention to Hazael is the difference between the words of the king (v. 8) and the actions of Hazael in carrying out this word (v. 9).

---

308. Insofar as no action is truly apolitical, Elisha has shown no inclination to this point to be involved in the reform of the monarchy, nor does he pose any challenge to the current monarchic hegemony.

309. Cogan and Tadmor, *Kings*, p. 90.

310. Again, 'Israelite society' understood as a product of the text, rather than the basis for the text.

4. *Elisha*

The texts are very similar except for the mention of וכל־טוב דמשׂק משׂא ארבעים גמל ('all the good things of Damascus, forty camel loads'). This is clearly in excess of the expectation of readers, even given the munificence of Naaman in 5.5. In this case, the excess is highlighted as the action of Hazael, rather than Ben-Hadad.

Hazael is highlighted by the narrative, and he is also not above some politicking of his own. In his speech to Elisha, he points to his own role by using the phrase מלך־ארם שׁלחני ('the king of Aram has sent me', v. 9). This is a departure from the standard messenger formula, which often uses the speech of the sender as sufficient to indicate that the message was relayed (e.g. 5.8, 10). The use of the unusual messenger formula, and the repetition of the message, thus allows readers to perceive a rather self-important messenger.

The story is also not above mocking the name of the king of Aram. The kingly name Ben-Hadad is a title, meaning 'the son of (the god) Hadad'.[311] In v. 9, Ben-Hadad becomes Ben-Elisha, at least in the speech of Hazael (בנך, 'your son'). The irony here is subtle, which reinforces the readers' impression that there is really only one god. In this case, the god appears to be Elisha.

The reply of Elisha is muddled by an interesting qere-ketib difference (v. 10). The qere reads לו, and would translate 'say *to him*, "You will indeed recover..."' The ketib is לא and would translate 'say, "You will *not* recover..."' Either reading produces a text which makes sense, but the qere is the one that introduces the conflict in the story, and makes sense of v. 11. Given the manuscript evidence, it is likely that the ketib is 'a late scribal alteration of MT which sought to avoid implicating Elisha in a falsehood'.[312]

Besides the complete reversal of opinion between the two halves of Elisha's speech, there is also a change in attribution. The addition of והראני יהוה ('YHWH has shown me', v. 10) may suggest to readers that the first part of Elisha's speech is not part of YHWH's intent. While the scribes may have had difficulty with a lie coming from Elisha, the narrative itself has difficulty with a lie coming from YHWH. Yet the outcome of the story is clearly part of the intent of YHWH as expressed in 1 Kgs 19.15, an outcome that is in part generated by the lie.

Verse 11 is difficult to understand because of the difficulty in understanding the subjects of the various verbs. While it is natural to assume

311. Cogan and Tadmor, *Kings*, p. 78.
312. Cogan and Tadmor, *Kings*, p. 90.

that the subject continues from the previous verse, the mention of 'man of God' at the end of the verse might suggest that the subject of the previous verb(s) may be Hazael. The difficulty is with the sociological implications of עד־בש ('until ashamed'). Elisha may have been ashamed because he has told Hazael to lie to his master without explanation.[313] Elisha may have been embarrassed because he realizes that Hazael has already been plotting the murder of his master.[314] It might have been Hazael who was ashamed, possibly because of guilt or because of Elisha's stare.[315] Alternately one might avoid the whole problem by translating עד־בש as 'for a long time'.[316] Certainty may only come when more is known about the role of shame in ancient cultures. Given this uncertainty, I would translate without adding subjects to the sentence, and allow the modern reader to deal with the ambiguity of the Hebrew.[317]

Even with this ambiguity, readers are given ample clues in the rest of the narrative to construct motivation for the characters. Elisha weeps because of the knowledge he has concerning the future actions of Hazael (v. 12). Hazael's tendency toward self-aggrandizement has already been noted (v. 9), which allows me to read the self-description הכלב ('the dog', v. 13) as false modesty.

Ruprecht has also noted that v. 11 is a wordless pause between the speeches in v. 10 and v. 12.[318] This silence builds tension, leading up to the emotional climax in v. 12.[319]

Elisha weeps over the picture he paints regarding the future of Israel at the hands of Hazael. It is a picture whose fulfillment is clearly recorded in 10.32 and 11.17-18. Yet despite the clear intention of YHWH as recorded in 1 Kgs 19.15-18, readers can hardly be expected to think positively about these events. The death of kings and evil queens is one matter, but the murder of children and pregnant women moves well beyond the bounds of simple punishment.[320] Given that

---

313. So Montgomery, *Books of Kings*, p. 394; Hobbs, *Kings*, p. 102.
314. Ruprecht, 'Entstehung', pp. 76-77.
315. Jones, *Kings*, p. 444; Nelson, *Kings*, p. 193; Gray, *Kings*, p. 477.
316. Cogan and Tadmor, *Kings*, p. 90; Long, *2 Kings*, p. 104.
317. NRSV: He fixed his gaze and stared at him, until he was ashamed.
318. Ruprecht, 'Entstehung', p. 76.
319. Ruprecht, 'Entstehung', p. 77.
320. Jones remarks that the list of evils 'falls outside the interest of the narrative

readers are unlikely to think ill of YHWH for this description, blame is likely to be placed on Elisha for reminding them of the horror of war, and for implicating YHWH in this horror.[321] This is made more likely given the lack of moral comment of Elisha to Hazael in an attempt to ward off this evil.[322]

The narrative continues in its subtle play on the question of prophetic word as word of YHWH. In v. 12, Elisha's foreknowledge is characterized as ידעתי ('I know') as opposed to the attribution הראני יהוה ('YHWH has shown me') in v. 10. Readers are unlikely to attribute this knowledge to anything besides the word of YHWH, but the semantics certainly allows readers a certain comfortable distance between YHWH's word and the slaughter of children. This is not a conclusion that readers are likely to ever express concretely, but the text does allow them to subtly connect these horrible actions with Elisha rather than YHWH. This is further demonstrated by the return to הראני יהוה ('YHWH has shown me') in v. 13.

In all of this, I am left wondering at the reason for Hazael's prominence in the narrative, given that he is merely a servant to the king of Aram. It is finally Hazael who asks my question, כי מה עבדך (v. 13), which triggers Elisha's reply, and fills in the missing information. This delay creates a good deal of tension in the narrative, and also allows the final oracle to be linked closely with the following actions of Hazael.

Hazael then repeats the message that Elisha has told him to give to the king of Aram.[323] Readers keeping track of possible lies will note that there have been no lies told in this story. Elisha tells Hazael what to say to the king of Aram. This is a command, not a lie. Hazael tells the king of Aram exactly what Elisha said to him, and thus does not lie. His words are an exact repetition of the message he was given.

There is a clear parallel here with the story of Micaiah in 1 Kings 22.

---

as a whole' (*Kings*, p. 444). This assumes that readers can know the interests of the narrative apart from the actual words of the narrative.

321. The horror is emphasized by the description הדבר הגדול הזה ('this great thing'), placed in the mouth of Hazael (v. 13).

322. Cogan and Tadmor note that the story 'lacks a moralizing judgment, which the reader of Kings has come to expect' (*Kings*, p. 92). We have seen that the Elisha stories usually lack moralizing judgment, but readers might still expect Elisha to defend the interests of the children of Israel (although we remember 2.24).

323. The king of Aram ceases to be important once his death has been announced, and thus also becomes nameless.

The parallel is thematic, and relates to the truth of the prophets' words. In the Micaiah story, the focus is clearly upon the true word of YHWH (ויאמר מיכיהו חי־יהוה כי את־אשר יאמר יהוה אלי אתו אדבר), 'Micaiah said, "As YHWH lives, what YHWH says to me I will speak"', v. 14). It is Micaiah who chooses not to speak the true words of YHWH (v. 15), although they are clearly known to him (vv. 17, 19-23).

In the Elisha story, the question is more the truthfulness of Hazael. Elisha clearly commands Hazael to lie, even though both Elisha and Hazael are aware of the truth. It is Elisha's word that Hazael can choose to relate accurately or not, but obedience for Hazael is the telling of something that he knows is false.

The parallel Micaiah story allows another inference regarding the role of Elisha. In 1 Kgs 22.20-23, YHWH places a lying spirit in the mouth of the prophets. The lie originates from the mouth of YHWH, rather than from the messenger. In the Elisha story, the lie originates from Elisha, which thus places him in the role of God not only as the origin of the message through the messenger Hazael, but as the origin of the lie itself.

Immediately following the repetition of the message, the actions of Hazael toward his master are recorded, and the king of Aram dies. The readers' lack of knowledge regarding ancient bed coverings and medicinal treatments allows some commentators to make no connection between Hazael's action and the king's death.[324] Yet the narrative juxtaposition of these events, as well as the careful description of Hazael's actions leave little room for serious doubt that Hazael murdered the king.[325]

The murder of Ben-Hadad is caused by the word of Elisha. While readers might wonder, given Hazael's self-aggrandizing tendencies, whether this would have happened soon in any case, the prophetic word is not merely predictive but causative or at least catalytic. Readers may wonder, therefore, about the causative connection between Elisha's word and the death of Israelite children and pregnant women. Did he also cause this to come about?

Thus is recorded the fulfillment of the first of YHWH's instructions to

---

324. Most notably Gray, *Kings*, p. 479. Both Cogan and Tadmor and Hobbs are noncommittal (Cogan and Tadmor, *Kings*, p. 91; Hobbs, *Kings*, p. 102).

325. Nelson suggests that the death report sounds like partial knowledge of an event in a far-off palace (*Kings*, p. 194). Given the direct speech recorded and the detail regarding Hazael's actions, this is precisely what it does not sound like.

Elijah (1 Kgs 19.15-18). Given that the final one has already been fulfilled (Elisha is anointed as prophet in Elijah's place), readers only await the anointing of Jehu as king of Israel. This expectation brings readers further into the world of Elijah. Not only are the words of YHWH to Elijah being fulfilled, but Elisha is slowly disappearing from the scene, as he does not directly carry out the final directive, but appoints another to do so (9.1). I am back on more comfortable ground, with direct word from YHWH being fulfilled by the actions of a prophet, although not by odd prophet Elisha. As I will soon see, the transition will be complete in ch. 9, but the legacy of Elisha will not die so easily in the narrative.

2 Kings 8.16-29: Transition Continues

With the second fulfillment of the instruction to Elijah, the text moves to fill in detail regarding changing monarchs and international conflicts on other borders. Modern readers are likely to feel more comfortable in this setting, with the difficult miracle stories behind them. Nelson exemplifies this comfort by stating that 'one could easily imagine that this is contemporary news'.[326]

The transition to a more comfortable narrative further increases the distance between readers and the world of Elisha. The world of Elisha seems less 'real' when compared to the concrete details of succession, and of failure or success in the eyes of the narrator. Readers are given very explicit instructions regarding what to think of each monarch, how they acted and what their relationship was to YHWH. Thus the narrator gives me much more firm ground for evaluation of the characters and the action. Elisha suffers by comparison. As has been seen, the world of this prophet, and by extension all prophets, is full of ambiguity, of unresolved tension and of unclear motivation. This further discredits prophetism as a viable alternative to the dominant hegemony.

This section also continues the transition to the world of Elijah, a prophet who is much more firmly engaged with the world of the kings. Just as 3.1-3 has provided the initial transition into the world of Elisha, now another accession formula smooths our way out of this world. Suddenly some of the characters that readers may remember from the Elijah story reappear, like Ahab (vv. 16, 18, 25, 27, 28, 29), and Omri

---

326. Nelson, *Kings*, p. 197.

(v. 26), as well as the place-name of Jezreel (v. 29). Hazael begins to inflict damage upon Israel (v. 28), as expected.

Readers, however, are not allowed a smooth transition into Elijah's world. Perhaps the murky world of Elisha is influencing the regnal succession stories by mere proximity. The formula in 8.16 is marred both by the change in name of the king of Israel (3.1—Jehoram; 8.16—Joram), and the suggestion that Jehoshaphat was king in Judah while Jehoram became king of Judah. While both of these are conflicts with plausible explanations, it is important to note that readers are not brought smoothly into the world of the kings.

Just as in ch. 3, regnal succession is followed by a confused battle report (8.20-22). The battle is compacted into one short verse (v. 21), with no prophetic intervention to blame for the disorder. Nonetheless, it creates a surprising parallel with ch. 3, as they represent likely the two most confused battle reports in Genesis–2 Kings. Again, plausible explanations are possible, but readers are forced to work very hard to create the orderly story which the narrative does not supply.

The narrator hastily supplies the regnal details for Ahaziah, king of Judah (8.25-27), and creates the conditions necessary for the following story of Jehu. Again there is a battle report that is brief to the point of non-existence, and appears to exist merely as an explanation for 9.16. This brevity creates the impression that these monarchs are only important insofar as they advance the narrative to the point where Jehu can come on to the scene. Readers are clearly being led to make a distinction between important and unimportant events, as well as important and unimportant characters.

2 Kings 9–13: Elijah Returns

Elisha is named in 9.1, then disappears from the story until 13.14. His disappearance coincides with the return of Elijah as an actor in the story. Since Elijah is clearly dead, the actions of Elisha in 9.1-3 are narratively necessary. Elijah cannot initiate action. Chapter 9 is a fascinating narrative, and an interesting story. Yet for my purposes, I will study it only as it has an impact upon our understanding of Elisha.

Elisha is introduced as הנביא ('the prophet') in 9.1. While I have noted no consistent distinction between הנביא and איש האלהים ('man of God') in the narrative, the specific use of הנביא ('prophet') in this context allows an easier transition into the world of Elijah. While

Elijah, too, is called איש האלהים ('the man of God') in 1 Kings 17 and 2 Kings 1, in these instances the title is conferred by a character, and not by the narrator, and thus might be understood as a case of mistaken characterization. Further, in 1 Kings 19 it is as prophet that Elijah designates himself (vv. 10, 14), and it is by this title that Elisha is to carry out his mission from YHWH (v. 16). Thus in 2 Kgs 9.1 Elisha returns as prophet to finally complete his mission, and returns readers to the world of Elijah and the kings.

Verse 9.1 is not only the last mention of Elisha for a while, but the last time the sons of the prophets are mentioned in Genesis–2 Kings. It is somewhat surprising that they are mentioned in connection with the anointing of a new king. They have been generally apolitical until this point, being given an isolated existence on the margins of Israelite society. Their appearance here highlights their subsequent disappearance. Their accession to the world of monarchic politics removes them as an alternative to its hegemony.[327] Thus their story parallels Elisha's, and they seemingly cannot survive without his presence. Insofar as they represented in the narrative an alternative to the world of the kings and the cities, they disappear when the wonder worker disappears. They continue to be wholly dependant upon him for existence.

In 9.11, Jehu's companions use the term המשגע ('the madman') to describe the prophetic messenger. For Gray, this 'indicates the comparatively low esteem in which the meaner members of the prophetic guilds were held'.[328] Yet this description needs to be read also in light of the response of the officers to the anointing. If they truly held this individual to be crazy, they would not have been likely to proclaim Jehu as king on his word alone.[329] This contrast of impressions is quite similar to the impression we have been forming of prophets as we follow Elisha. The power of Elisha to predict the future or float iron is never doubted, but he is not presented as someone to be emulated, or as

---

327. Note that the narrator never really allowed them to appear as a true alternative. While always before us was dangled the possibility of a different way, the promise was quickly dashed through their presentation as inept, slightly crazy hobos.

328. Gray, *Kings*, p. 488.

329. I realize that other societies handle what we call mental illness in a radically different way than we do. Nonetheless, the proclamation of Jehu as king on the word of one individual suggests that 'low esteem' only captures part of the picture.

someone to be followed. Thus this story again confirms my impression of הָאִישׁ וְאֶת־שִׂיחוֹ ('the men who babble', v. 11).

Verse 9.1 also sets in motion the final chapter of the history of the Ahab dynasty.[330] Verse 9.2 is the first mention of Jehu since 1 Kgs 19.17. Thus, the transition to the world of Elijah continues with the fulfillment of YHWH's final instruction to Elijah. As will soon be seen, the transition is soon complete, with the return of all the long-forgotten characters who enlivened the life of Elijah.

The member of the sons of the prophets does as he is told. He goes to Jehu, takes him into a private chamber, and repeats, with minor modification, the words he is told to say. He then continues with a major addition to the words of Elisha (vv. 7b-10). Commentators are divided as to whether these words are[331] or are not[332] later additions. For my purposes, what is important to note is not that these words are additional. Often in Genesis–2 Kings the words of the messenger are longer than the original message we have recorded.[333] Rather, the difficulty for readers is that the words spoken to Jehu by the messenger are words from Elijah's world rather than Elisha's. Elisha has been totally unconcerned with the actions of the Ahab dynasty. He has totally ignored the 'blood of my servants the prophets, and the blood of all the servants of YHWH' (v. 7). These were the concerns of Elijah.

The discrepancy between this proclamation and its original, and more broadly between the worlds of Elijah and Elisha, have suggested to van Seters that, with the exception of chs. 3 and 9, the Elisha collection 'has not been integrated in any way into the Deuteronomist's history, nor does it show any signs of his editing'.[334] While this judgment is clearly outside the interests of this study, it does provide evidence for the separation that the text makes between these two otherwise rather similar characters. Van Seters has reached the conclusion which the narrative wishes him to reach. The world of Elisha does not fit with the world of Elijah or the rest of the world of Genesis–2 Kings. It cannot

---

330. While strictly speaking the dynasty is Omri's, Ahab continues to bear the brunt of displeasure from the narrator.

331. So Jones, *Kings*, p. 456; Gottwald, *Kingdoms*, p. 78 n. 83; Binns, *Moses*, p. 233.

332. So Hobbs, *Kings*, p. 111; Ahlström, 'Jehu', p. 47.

333. See Alter, *Art of Biblical Narrative*, pp. 97-104. Note also the incisive study of this chapter by Miscall, 'Elijah', pp. 73-83.

334. Van Seters, *In Search of History*, p. 305.

4. *Elisha*

sustain itself when faced with real political decisions, with the 'real world'.

That we have firmly re-entered the world of Elijah is confirmed by the continuing entry of characters from the Elijah narratives. Jezebel appears in v. 7. This is probably the most surprising absence in the Elisha corpus. Readers are suddenly reminded that Jezebel has been alive all through the life of Elisha. Yet he has had nothing to say regarding her presence. Readers are left to wonder about her influence as queen mother on the reign of Jehoram in Israel and as queen mother-in-law on Jehoram and Ahaziah of Judah. How can she have been alive this whole time, given the silence of Elisha and the disappearance of Baal? For the narrative still accords her a place of considerable prominence in its rogues' gallery.

Naboth is mentioned in 9.25. The house of Ahab is still held responsible for his blood, and the death of Joram is linked by prophecy (כדבר יהוה, 'according to the word of YHWH', v. 26) to the death of Naboth. Finally Elijah himself reappears in 9.36, and then again in 10.10, 17. These verses also demonstrate the more usual formula for the fulfillment of prophecy, all attributing the דבר ('word') to YHWH, with Elijah as the messenger.

Finally, the mention of Baal in 10.18 completes the transition. Like Jezebel, Baal has been conspicuous by his absence. While the total number of Baal worshipers turns out to be quite small (Gottwald notes that they all fit into one room in 10.21[335]), it must also be remembered that the fight against Baalism was central to the initial program of Elisha's call (1 Kgs 19.18). The absence of references to Baal in the Elisha narratives is truly remarkable, although absences are more difficult to track for the reader. It is only the return of the missing element that causes the reader to re-examine the earlier narratives in this new light.

The transition into Elijah's world is complete, and Elisha disappears from the story of Jehu. Thus, I am left to reach conclusions regarding the world of Elisha. The narrative separation allows for a general contrast with Elijah, not only as a characters but as a representative of an alternate world. Yet the choice is not completely straightforward.

---

335. Gottwald, *Kingdoms*, p. 79. For Gottwald this suggests that Ahab checked the spread of Baalism in Israel. I still wonder at the inaction of Elisha in this regard.

Elisha will continue to influence our understanding of both the role and the limitations of prophecy.[336]

The narrative continues with the details regarding the actions of Jehu as he becomes king and secures his throne. Gottwald has noted the silence of the prophets in the rest of Jehu's deeds, which he considers difficult to understand.[337] Yet readers really have no quarter from which to expect prophetic intervention. Elijah is dead, and while his word lives on, it lives only until it is fulfilled. The sons of the prophets have not shown any interest in the affairs of kings. Elisha is there if Jehu needs him, but has been rather passive unless specifically called upon, or unless the king is in definite trouble. Now he has fulfilled the mission of Elijah, and thus there remains to readers little reason to expect continued involvement.

Thus he disappears. He is not even necessary for Jehu to receive the word of YHWH (10.30). If any place were left to the prophet, it would surely be this. Now that the kings can access the word of YHWH directly, the role is forfeit. Note that the disappearance of the prophetic word does not coincide with the death of Elisha. He is not yet dead, and thus the reader can only assume that he has no important role to fill. If YHWH has use for the prophet, surely his deeds would be included in the story.

There remain some loose ends in the Elisha story, and also in the Elijah story. While the references to Elijah cease at 10.17, the final destiny of Hazael has not come about. Thus Elijah/Elisha cannot disappear from memory until all things have come to pass. Readers are reminded of this with the continuing references to Hazael in 10.32; 12.17-18; 13.3, 22-25. These recall the prophecy of destruction which both YHWH (1 Kgs 19.17) and Elisha (2 Kgs 8.12) spoke. They are also a reminder of the brutality of Hazael that Elisha predicted.

Thus the narrative seeks to mitigate the severity of Hazael's conquest. This allows readers to overcome the tension between the

---

336. Gottwald concludes that the prophets were inept and unhelpful with regard to long-range domestic and foreign policy (*Kingdoms*, p. 85). I believe this is precisely the conclusion the narrative wishes him to reach. While Gottwald has presented a different analysis of the Elisha stories in his more recent Introduction (*The Hebrew Bible: A Socio-Literary Introduction* [Philadelphia: Fortress Press, 1985], p.344-445, 351-52), I cite his earlier work for I believe it to be a valid possible conclusion for a reader.

337. *Kingdoms*, p. 81.

4. *Elisha*

success of Jehu in eliminating Baalism, and the continued oppression of Hazael. If Jehu has eradicated Baalism within Israel, why is Hazael allowed to continue his war upon Israel?

Verses 13.2-3 address this question to some degree, reinterpreting the oppression of Hazael in light of the refusal of Jehoahaz, son of Jehu, to depart from the sins of Jeroboam. Yet here the salvation of Israel comes not through Elisha or any prophet, but through a מוֹשִׁיעַ ("'savior', v. 5), who is more reminiscent of the judges than of Elisha.

The narrative continues, doing its best to confuse readers with Jehoash/Joash on the throne of Israel/Judah (13.10-13), just as earlier it has placed Jehoram/Joram on these same thrones (8.16-24). It is almost as if some sort of monarchic confusion must act as a transition to the world of Elisha. In this case, the confusion is confounded by the record of the death of Joash of Israel (13.13), who is then reintroduced alive into the story of Elisha (13.14).

Jones notes that the chronology of the narrative makes Elisha about 85 or 90 years old.[338] While a detail like this is only likely to be noted by the most chronology-fixated reader, it is certainly true that Elisha's reappearance is quite surprising. So, too, is the friendly and even dependant relationship between Elisha and Joash which is implied in 13.14. Given the response of Elisha, the words of Joash (אבי אבי רכב ישראל ופרשיו, 'my father, my father, the chariots of Israel and its horsemen', v. 14) can be understood as a request. Once before in the stories of Elisha this phrase has been used for divine intervention in the human world (2.12), and a similar phrase was used in 6.17 to indicate divine aid in time of trouble. Thus, here I can read 'Help me with the chariots of Israel (and of fire)'.

The fact that the words of the king are only interpretable in light of the response highlights the ambiguity of the statement. The gap between statement and understanding gives opportunity for readers to feel the incongruence between Joash's presumed description of Elisha (for this is how the statement originally appears to function) and Elisha's actual role in Israel in the previous narrative. Hazael has continued to oppress Israel, as does his son Ben-Hadad (13.3), and a savior has arisen in the role that presumably should have been that of Elisha.[339] Elisha has been

---

338. Jones, *Kings*, p. 501.
339. After all, as Moore continues to point out, Elisha's name means 'God saves' *(God Saves*, passim).

conspicuous not as רכב ישראל ופרשיו ('chariots of Israel and its horsemen', v. 14) but by his absence.

Elisha provides an oracle that is unusually dependant upon action, rather than word. While in many respects one might draw parallels between the king's obedience and that of Naaman, there is the added element of Elisha placing his hands upon the king's hands (v. 16). Power here is firmly placed in the hands of Elisha, and not just in a metaphorical sense. While credit is still given to YHWH (v. 17), it can even be understood as Elisha providing YHWH with a victory. While readers are unlikely to adopt this reading, the narrative continues to muddy the relationship between Elisha and YHWH.

The initial oracle of Elisha (v. 17) is quickly weakened by the further actions of Elisha and the king, which also produce an oracle (v. 19).[340] In this case the king again does as he is instructed (הך ... ויך, 'strike ... and he struck', v. 18), but this time his obedience results in anger rather than an oracle of deliverance. The narrative here gives the characters the same amount of information that readers have. Readers do not have special knowledge unavailable to the king. This allows readers to walk with the characters in their actions. As I read through the narrative, I am likely to think well of the king, who is doing precisely as he is told. He does not vacillate or ask for explanation, or make complaint. The king in this text can be contrasted to Naaman or the officer of the king in 7.2. Insofar as obedience is the correct response to prophetic command, the king is fulfilling his obligation perfectly.

Thus, readers are likely to be surprised at the anger of Elisha, and his reprimand of the king for not striking five or six times (v. 19). The king has received no indication that more would be better. I can easily imagine the king standing there in bewilderment, wondering how he was to know. Even in proclaiming victory, the narrative does not easily allow a fully sympathetic reading of Elisha. It would have been simple to suggest hesitancy or questioning on the part of the king, and allowed readers to fully blame the king for the incomplete victory of Israel over Aram. While it is still possible to blame the king, there remains the shadow of obedience without reward that lingers over the actions of the king.

Thus, with this final enigmatic action, Elisha dies and is buried. The

---

340. Note that neither oracle is presented as a response by Elisha to a word from YHWH, but reads as an initiative of Elisha. This again calls into question whether Elisha is acting as messenger or as God.

4. Elisha 169

place of his burial is not named. This is unusual, since the vast majority of burials in Genesis–2 Kings record the place of the burial (Gen. 23.19; 25.19; Num. 20.1; Deut. 10.6; and so on). An exception to the norm is Isaac (Gen. 35.29), but there one might presume that he was buried in his last known location, Mamre (35.27). Given that 2 Kgs 13.14-19 provides no location (except west of Aphek, v. 17), and the narrative provides many possible sites for the king to visit Elisha (Dothan, Samaria, Carmel, with the sons of the prophets), the lack of place for Elisha's burial remains a mystery.

The final act of power credited to Elisha is posthumous (13.20b-21). The miracle is straightforward, and obvious in its demonstration of power. One can certainly imagine that the grave of Elisha would become a major pilgrimage site should its location be known. But even here, the story is still set up to place the miracle in the context of the continued harassment of Israel by its enemies. If Elisha's bones really wanted something to do, why did they not stop the raids? Readers are never allowed a story without some flaw in performance.

The story of Elisha has a few more loose ends to clean up, before the memory of the prophet can safely be tucked away. Hazael's oppression of Israel ends with his death (13.22-24), and Joash defeats Hazael's son three times (v. 25), to fulfil the final oracle of Elisha. All the loose ends of Elisha's life are now tied up.

There remains for me only the question of the 'seven thousand' mentioned in 1 Kgs 19.18. Readers may choose to supply 'seven thousand' as the number of Israelites sent into exile in 17.6, but the number is not given, and I would suspect a much larger number if 'none was left' (17.18). This problem, however, is a problem in Elijah's world, and not in Elisha's. The ambiguity in the Elisha stories is not the limit of his power.

2 Kings 14–25: Prophetism after Elisha

There remain a number of references to prophets in the rest of 2 Kings that need to be mentioned in order to sustain my argument that Elisha comprises the end to prophetism. These references can be divided into two groups, those which name the prophet involved, and those which do not. This distinction can be made because the unnamed prophets do not function as *actors* in the story, that is, they do not 'cause or undergo *functional* events'.³⁴¹ Their role could just as easily be played by a talking horse or writing on a wall as by a human character.

1. *Named Prophets*

The prophet Jonah, son of Ammitai, is mentioned briefly in 2 Kgs 14.25. The role that Jonah plays is precisely the role which is allowed for the prophet in the Elisha stories, namely as oracle for the king. Even here, however, there remain some of the disquieting features of the Elisha stories. The king whose victories Jonah has prophesied is characterized as one who did 'evil in the eyes of the Lord' (v. 24), much as Elisha is shown as providing aid to the line of Ahab.³⁴² Further, the prophecy is only mentioned after the event prophesied has already occurred, which might cause readers to wonder whether the prophecy itself is *post factum*.

Huldah is the next prophet mentioned in the story. King Josiah's servants go to her as a direct result of the king's command to 'inquire of the Lord for me' (2 Kgs 22.13). It is curious that these men go to Huldah, as the king appears later to have a number of prophets in his company (23.2). Nonetheless, her reply is directed to 'the man who sent you to me' (22.15, see also v. 18). Thus, again she fulfills the role that the Elisha narrative has allowed for the prophet.

The final prophet named in Genesis–2 Kings is Isaiah (2 Kgs 19-20). Again, Isaiah is portrayed as one who acts as an oracle for Hezekiah. His actions are either in response to an inquiry or request from Hezekiah (19.2-7; 20.8-11), or as YHWH's response to a prayer directly from Hezekiah (19.14-34; 20.2-6), or as the response of YHWH to Hezekiah's actions (20.1, 15-18). In all these instances, he does not stray from the role of oracle, either in an attempt to play a larger role in Israel outside the royal court, or in an attempt to play a larger role inside the court.

2. *Unnamed Prophets*

There are five references in 2 Kings 14–25 to prophets who are not named. The fact that they are not named allows readers to make a distinction between prophets as actors in the story and prophets as abstraction. As a narrative with a continued belief in a deity who is active in

---

341. Bal, *Narratology*, p. 25, emphasis hers.

342. The narrator immediately records the reason for YHWH's intervention on behalf of Israel at this point (vv. 26-27), a mitigation which Elisha was never allowed.

Israel, there must be some means for that deity to convey messages to the people. One of the ways the narrative allows for this to happen is through oracles, who are labeled 'prophets'. The narrative is much less comfortable, however, with instances of the actual individuals who come to take on this designation as a title. We have already seen this as it is worked out in the Elisha stories.

As unnamed abstraction, there is still room in the world of the narrative for the prophetic oracle. The abstraction, in fact, is allowed certain roles that actual prophets are not portrayed as filling. Thus, in 2 Kgs 17.13, prophets are said to have warned the people concerning their evil ways. Considering that the reason for the final destruction of Israel is given as the refusal of the people to heed the warning of the prophets, it is all the more notable when the prophets fail to fulfill this mandate in any way. This is one way in which the narrative casts doubt upon prophetism in the Elisha stories, by showing a prophet who warns neither kings nor people concerning their evil ways.

The fact that 2 Kgs 17.13 does state clearly that prophets did warn the people concerning their evil ways might suggest that prophetism does not end with Elisha. Given, however, that the narrative does not record any actual instance of a prophet post-Elisha actually doing this, readers are left either to hypothesize that these prophets lived before Elisha (e.g. Elijah in 1 Kgs 18.36-39), or to wonder where these prophets were, given their absence from the text after the Elisha stories. In either case, I am left to ponder their absence from the (hi)story of Israel precisely at the time when they appear to be most needed.

The next mention of unnamed prophets is found in 2 Kgs 17.23, where the destruction of Israel is said to have been 'foretold through all (YHWH's) servants the prophets'. This is likely a reference to 1 Kgs 14.15-16, the words of the prophet Ahijah concerning the final end of Israel. Thus, this is a reference to prophetism that precedes Elisha.

The nation of Judah is also the subject of the words of unnamed prophets in 2 Kgs 21.10-15. Here the prophets bring judgment upon Judah in response to the 'abominations' of Manasseh. While these prophets clearly spoke after the time of Elisha, the role in which they are presented is precisely the role allowed for prophetism in the Elisha narrative, that of royal oracle. The audience for these prophecies is not named, neither is the situation of their presentation, nor of their reception. While the narrative allows the conclusion that the audience is the people, the primary target of the prophetic word is the actions of

Manasseh, which suggests that Manasseh is more likely to be the primary audience for these words. Further, the complete lack of narrative setting for these words might cause readers to wonder whether these words were meant to be efficacious in any way, or whether the condemnation is one that could not be withdrawn. If the latter, then the words act merely as *post factum* explanation for the destruction of Israel, rather than as warning or censure.

The use of the plural (נביאים, 'prophets') is also interesting. While the plural is also used in 17.13, 23, there it could easily refer to a number of individuals scattered over a long period of time. Here, the plural in association with a specific prophetic word (לאמר, 'saying') suggests a gathered group of prophets.

As we have seen, groups of prophets such as the בני־הנביאים ('sons of the prophets') are not upheld by the narrative as positive characters. Other references to prophets in the plural have similar connotations. Groups of prophets are associated with Saul in 1 Samuel 10 and 19, in passages that can easily be read as derisive. The other social location for prophets is in the royal court (1 Sam. 28.6, 15; 1 Kgs 18, 19, 22; 2 Kgs 3.13).[343] These groups of prophets are also subject to negative judgment in the narrative, being portrayed as unreliable (1 Kgs 3.13) or untrustworthy (1 Kgs 22), again despite the fact that their designation as נביא ('prophet') is never called into question. Thus, however small the role allowed for the individual prophet in Israel, they are still to be preferred over prophets who act in group. Socially, this further decreases the ability of prophetism to have a significant impact upon social structures and organization.[344]

Another group of prophets accompany Josiah as he reads the words of the book of the covenant in 2 Kgs 23.2. As already noted, this reference is interesting in that, when Josiah's officials go to inquire of YHWH for Josiah, they go to Huldah rather than to these prophets (22.11-14). While it may be that Huldah is to be thought of as part of

---

343. While the prophets of YHWH mentioned in 1 Kgs 18, 19 are not placed directly in the royal court, the parallel between these prophets and the numerous prophets of Baal and Asherah who 'eat at Jezebel's table' (18.19) does suggest a connection with the royal court.

344. I can imagine a scene where a lone prophet is pitted against the hosts of priest and court functionaries. Any attempt by the lone prophet to gather a support community around him- or herself further arouses the misgivings of any audience who have read Genesis–2 Kings.

this category of 'the prophets' in 23.2, the narrative distances her from this group by specifically focusing on her in 22.14, even in a society with multiple נביאים ('prophets').

In either case, the prophets in 23.2 act not as those who bring the word of YHWH, but those who listen, with the others, to the word of YHWH as found in the book of the covenant. In this way, prophetism is placed beneath the written word as a means of accessing God's will. Prophets are also mentioned after priests and just before העם ('the people') in the list of those going to the temple, a list that can easily be read hierarchically. Thus, not only are prophets placed beneath the authority of the written word, they are placed after the guardians of the word in the hierarchy of Judah.

Another prophet is briefly mentioned in 2 Kgs 23.18. This is a reference to the prophet from 1 Kgs 13, a prophet who lived before Elisha. The 1 Kings story is instructive in that it provides a clear distinction between נביא ('prophet') and איש־האלהים ('man of God'). In this story, it is the man of God who brings the word of God to the king, while the prophet is relegated to the role of tempter. While the Elisha stories failed to provide this clear a distinction between the two roles, the late reference to a story that does make this distinction again denigrates the role of the prophet, placing in the readers' minds a negative association with the term נביא ('prophet'). The narrative continues to do this while maintaining the prophet's connection to the deity. The negative associations remain subtle; their effect is cumulative.

The actual words of the text in 2 Kgs 23.15-18 are also instructive. Reference is made to the fulfillment of the words of the man of God (23.16 // 1 Kgs 13.2, 3), yet no mention is made of the actions of the prophet. The story instructs us that prophets are (dead) people whose bones are not to be disturbed, rather than living people whose actions are crucial for the survival of the nation.

The final reference to prophets in 2 Kings is in 24.2. This is a record of the fulfillment of the word of YHWH regarding the destruction of Judah כדבר יהוה אשר דבר ביד עבדיו הנבאים ('according to the word of YHWH that he spoke by his servants the prophets'). There are a number of specific prophecies that are referred to here, namely Isaiah's prophecy in 20.17, Huldah's in 22.16-20, or the general words in 23.27. This final word is not placed in the mouth of a prophet, but readers are likely to assume that the messenger role would have been played by a prophet.

This note regarding fulfillment is itself ambiguous in it significance. On the one hand, it demonstrates that the word of YHWH as spoken through the prophets needs to be taken seriously, since it will come to pass. On the other hand, readers may be reminded of one of the main difficulties with predictive prophecy, namely that readers can be sure it is the true word of God only after it has been fulfilled (see Deut. 18.22). This is not a particularly useful criterion for distinguishing the true word of God from the false word of God (I am reminded of the story of Micaiah in 1 Kgs 22, and its parallel in 2 Kgs 3), since the entire nature of prediction dictates that this type of prophecy is only useful when prediction is entirely trustworthy.

The limitations to the role of the prophet that were shown in the Elisha stories are thus continued in the remainder of 2 Kings. Further, the doubt that was cast upon the usefulness of prophetism also continues. From here it is only a small and entirely logical move for me to prefer a world without the institution of prophetism. In a world without kings, the prophet has no role at all. Given that the word of God has now been codified within the narrative itself, there remains little need for a word outside that which can be accessed by the priest. Prophetism can now[345] be understood as a useful phase in the history of Israel, but one devoid of ongoing purpose or power.

---

345. 'Now' in the sense of the 'present' of any reader, since all readers live in a postexilic time.

Chapter 5

CONCLUSION

The stories concerning the prophet Elisha raise and then dismiss various options for my understanding of the role of the prophet. These options are also those found in the larger world of Genesis–2 Kings. Elisha, as a prophet of YHWH and successor to Elijah, is enlisted in the task of fighting Baalism and bringing the people back to a true worship of YHWH (I Kgs 19.16). Included in this task is the termination of the line of Ahab, which would presumably also mean the death of Jezebel.

Most of the stories of Elisha pay no heed to these expectations. Both Baal and Baalism are absent from the main body of the stories. It is almost as if Elijah had truly won the battle on Mt Carmel, and the death of the prophets of Baal had succeeded in eradicating Baalism from Israel. Yet Baal hovers in the background as an unexplained absence. The flight of Elijah from Jezebel after his supposed victory on Mt Carmel (1 Kgs 19.3) allows for the possibility of a return of Baalism in Israel. Further, YHWH focuses our attention on Baal as the true enemy of Elisha (1 Kgs 19.18).

Jezebel, too, is a present absence. Aside from the oblique reference to her in 2 Kgs 3.13, she has no apparent influence upon the mission of Elisha. It is only her reappearance in 2 Kings 9 that alerts readers that she is not dead. It is as if Elisha is unaware of the prophecy of Elijah concerning Jezebel's death.

In a less obvious way, YHWH is also absent from the world of Elisha. The most obvious factor is the absence of direct speech from YHWH. This creates an interesting paradox for my understanding of the prophet: how is the prophet a messenger for YHWH in the absence of the divine word? Elisha still claims the divine word (2.21, 24; 3.16; 4.43; 7.1; 8.1, 10, 13; 9.3), but the narrator is not consistent in assuring me that this is so (compare 2.22 and 4.44).

The loss of the voice of YHWH parallels the absence of a general sense of prophetic mission. The text continually presents Elisha as either prophet or man of God. These titles suggest specific roles which are to be performed. If Elisha is not at work opposing Baal, what exactly is he there for? He does not lead Israel as Moses and Samuel did. He does not challenge the people to return to YHWH as Elijah did. He does not act as conscience to the king of Israel as Nathan did. He brings no ethical imperative to either king or people.

Instead Elisha wanders the countryside doing miracles. These miracles are alternately set within the world of the kings (2 Kgs 3; 5.1-18; 6.8–7.20; 8.7-15) or the people of Israel (2; 4; 6.1-7), or a combination of the two worlds (5.19-27; 8.1-7). The stories concerning the people of Israel are often specifically set in the context of the sons of the prophets (2.1-18; 4.1-7; 4.38-41; 6.1-7), or more generally within the context of the citizens of Israel (2.19-25; 4.8-37, 42-44).

In each of these situations, the actions of Elisha highlight various options regarding the proper role of the prophet, which readers are subtly directed to accept or reject. In the context of the sons of the prophets, Elisha aids an impoverished group by providing food (4.38), and aiding them in times of distress (4.2, 40; 6.6). He is depicted as their leader (2.15; 4.38; 6.3), as one in authority over them. This world is one without king or army, without concern for foreign invasion or foreign deities. It would be idyllic, were it not for the continuing picture of a helpless, hopeless group unable to provide for its own needs. The inability of the sons of the prophets to feed itself (4.38-41), care for its widows (4.1), or solve basic problems (6.5) without the aid of a wonder worker makes it difficult for readers to perceive this group as an alternative to the social structure of the larger society. The alternative presented here is only an option for a group with easy access to the miraculous. This sub-culture is otherwise unsustainable.

The role of Elisha as miracle worker is demeaned by the association between his miracles and the helpless sons of the prophets. If the sons of the prophets are subtly presented as a non-sustainable group, then surely it cannot be the role of the prophet to provide for such people. At the very least, his work among these people is not as important as his presence in the world of the king. The miracles among the sons of the prophets provide comic relief for the larger narrative, but do not form an integral part of the ongoing story of Israel.

In the stories of Elisha and the citizens of Israel (2.19-25; 4.8-37, 42-44), the focus is also on Elisha the miracle worker. This is a world

5. Conclusion

between the world of the sons of the prophets and the world of the king. The king is not present as an actor in these stories, but he is a character in the larger world (4.13). The narrative, then, gives us a picture of Elisha in the context of the ordinary people of Israel.

The stories focus on Elisha having power over fertility (2.19, 21; 4.16), hunger (4.43) and even death (2.21, 4.32-35). Yahweh is mentioned in each of these stories as the power behind the miracle (2.21, 24; 4.33, 43), but all except the last story also cause some concern for readers as to the nature of the connection between the miracle and the word of YHWH (note the כדבר אלישע, 'according to the word of Elisha,' in 2.22, the picture of 42 mauled children in 2.24, and the lack of reference to YHWH in 4.11-16).

The connection between Elisha's miracles and the word of YHWH is also questioned by the lack of specific ethical or teleological framework for the miracles. The miracles may be welcomed (2.19) or gratuitous (4.16), but they do not function to bring Israel back to YHWH or to root out evil in the land. The miraculous power of Elisha serves no larger purpose for the people of Israel or for YHWH.[1]

In the stories of Elisha and the kings, Elisha's power clearly surpasses that of the kings. This is seen in his ability to provide water in the desert (3.16-20), healing from leprosy (5.7-8), counsel regarding the position of enemy soldier (6.8-9, 12), and victory in the face of defeat (7.1). Each of these things is something the king could not do. This allows the prophet to be viewed as someone able to provide for Israel better than can the king. The answer to Israel's plight in their request for a king (1 Sam. 8.20) is a prophet, not a king.

Yet as soon as the narrative allows this possibility, it closes it off by making the king a necessary part of the story. It is kings who instigate military endeavors (2 Kgs 3.6), and who provide the military strategy (3.8; 7.12). It is the king who is appealed to in time of distress (5.6; 6.26). While the prophet provides advice, it is the king who acts (6.23). Finally, the removal of an evil king in Israel is naturally accomplished by someone who is to be king (9.1-3).

---

1. Of course, the fact that human needs are met outside the framework of divine intervention need not be read in a negative way. Perhaps readers would prefer a world where feeding and healing can take place outside the control of religious functionaries. The fact that readers are returned to the 'ordinary' world of Elijah and the kings, however, suggests that this narrative does not lead in this direction.

Elisha also uses his miraculous power to aid the kings. Yet even here the function of the miraculous is questioned in a number of ways. First, why is it that Elisha is shown to aid these kings at all? Why is the son of Ahab and Jezebel repeatedly rescued by YHWH's prophet? Given the relationship between Elijah and Ahab, and the end of the line of Ahab pronounced by YHWH (1 Kgs 19.16) and Elijah (1 Kgs 21.22), readers might wonder why Elisha does not allow Jehoram to be killed.

Second, the connection between Elisha and YHWH is questioned in these stories. This is most notable in the story of Naaman, where Elisha clearly points to himself as the power in Israel (2 Kgs 5.8, cf. 1 Kgs 18.37), and then employs a messenger, thus taking the place of God in the narrative (2 Kgs 5.10, 11; note also 4.13).

The connection between Elisha and YHWH is also called into question as the narrative is unclear as to the relationship between Elisha and the word of YHWH. Does Elisha receive the word of YHWH when he wishes it (3.15)? Is his word predictive or causative (7.1; 8.10)? Who instigates the miracles which accompany this word (5.8)? While readers may accede to the prophet the ability to command the power of YHWH in the service of YHWH, how comfortable are they with the prophet who commands YHWH in service to himself?

Third, the role of the prophet as miracle worker in service of the king is questioned by the failure of the miraculous (3.27; 6.23-24). At two major points in the narrative, the word of the prophet is almost but not quite fulfilled. The failure is not such that it would place in question the status of Elisha as true prophet of YHWH. It is just enough so as to cause me to hold back on my enthusiasm for the miraculous intervention of the prophet. If this is what readers are looking for in a prophet, they are warned that it does not always succeed.

I am left with one positive framework within which the prophetic role can be carried out. As an oracle to the king of Israel, Elisha consistently acts to save the king and the people of Israel in times of distress. His actions within this context are in response to the request of the king, or in response to the command of YHWH (8.10; 9.1). Thus, Elisha serves as a functionary for the royal court, although not within the royal court. His role is an important one, but it never supersedes the royal office. No matter how ineffective the king is portrayed to be, the prophet remains as his servant, coming to his aid when called upon.

The sole exception to this rule is when Elisha must act to replace the king at the command of YHWH (9.1). Even here, however, the focus

5. *Conclusion*

remains on the royal court. Elisha replaces the king by anointing another as king, rather than by taking the reins of power himself. The larger task assigned by YHWH (1 Kgs 19.17-18) is then transferred to the new king, who is able to accomplish the will of YHWH without the intervention of the prophet (2 Kgs 9.25-26; 10.11, 17, 18-27).

All this is accomplished without direct judgment or explicit direction from the narrator. The point is made without readers necessarily becoming conscious of it. This makes readers much less able to judge whether or not this portrayal of the prophet is to their liking. It does not allow me to choose between viable alternatives. The prophet serves in the court of the king, or he no longer serves as 'prophet'.

BIBLIOGRAPHY

Ackroyd, Peter R., *Exile and Restoration* (Philadelphia: Westminster Press, 1968).
Aharoni, Y., 'Mount Carmel as Border', in K. Galling (ed.), *Archaeologie und Altes Testament* (Tübingen: J.C.B. Mohr [Paul Siebeck], 1970), pp. 1-7.
Ahlström, G.W., 'King Jehu: A Prophet's Mistake', in A.L. Merrill (ed.), *Scripture in History and Theology* (Pittsburgh: Pickwick Press, 1977), pp. 47-69.
Ahuis, Ferdinand, 'Das Märchen im Alten Testament', *ZTK* 86 (1898), pp. 455-76.
Albright, W.F., 'The Chronology of the Divided Monarchy of Israel', *BASOR* 100 (1945), pp. 16-22.
Alter, Robert, *The Art of Biblical Narrative* (New York: Basic Books, 1981).
—'How Convention Helps Us Read', *Prooftexts* 3 (1983), pp. 115-30.
—*Motives for Fiction* (Cambridge, MA: Harvard University Press, 1984).
—*The Pleasures of Reading in an Ideological Age* (New York: Simon & Schuster, 1989).
—'Sodom as Nexus: The Web of Design in Biblical Narrative', in Regina Schwartz (ed.), *The Book and the Text* (Cambridge, MA: Basil Blackwell, 1990), pp. 146-60.
—*The World of Biblical Literature* (New York: Basic Books, 1992).
Alter, Robert, and Frank Kermode (eds.), *The Literary Guide to the Bible* (Cambridge, MA: Harvard University Press, 1987).
Amihai, Miri, George W. Coats and Anne M. Solomon (eds.), *Narrative Research on the Hebrew Bible* (Semeia, 46; Atlanta: Society of Biblical Literature, 1989).
Andersen, K.T., 'Die Chronologie der Könige von Israel und Juda', *ST* 23 (1969), pp. 69-114.
Arnold, Patrick M., *Wildmen, Warriors, and Kings* (New York: Crossroad, 1992).
Astour, M.C., '841 B.C.: The First Assyrian Invasion of Israel', *JAOS* 91 (1971), pp. 383-89.
Auerbach, Erich, *Mimesis* (New York: Doubleday, 1957).
Auld, A.G., *I and II Kings* (Philadelphia: Westminster Press, 1986).
—'Prophets and Prophecy in Jeremiah and Kings', *ZAW* 96 (1984), pp. 66-82.
Austin, J.L., *How to Do Things with Words* (Cambridge, MA: Harvard University Press, 1975).
Bal, Mieke, *Death and Dissymmetry* (Chicago: University of Chicago Press, 1988).
—*Lethal Love* (Bloomington: Indiana University Press, 1987).
—review of *The Literary Guide to the Bible* (Cambridge, MA: Harvard University Press, 1987), edited by Robert Alter and Frank Kermode, in *JAAR* 57 (1989), pp. 373-83.
—*Murder and Difference* (Bloomington: Indiana University Press, 1988).
—*Narratology: Introduction to the Theory of Narrative* (trans. Christine van Boheemen; Toronto: University of Toronto Press, 1985).
—*On Storytelling* (Sonoma, CA: Polebridge Press, 1991).
Bar-Efrat, Shimon, *Narrative Art in the Bible* (JSOTSup, 70; Bible and Literature, 17; Sheffield: Almond Press, 1989).

Barnes, W.E., *The Second Book of Kings* (Cambridge: Cambridge University Press, 1928).
Barr, James, 'The Meaning of "Mythology" in Relation to the Old Testament', *VT* 9 (1959), pp. 1-10.
Barrick, W. Boyd, 'Elisha and the Magic Bow: A Note on 2 Kings xiii 15-17', *VT* 35 (1985), pp. 355-63.
Bartlett, J.R., 'The "United" Campaign against Moab in 2 Kings 3:4-27', in J.F.A. Sawyer and D.J.A. Clines (eds.), *Midian, Moab and Edom: The History and Archaeology of Late Bronze and Iron Age Jordan and North-West Arabia* (JSOTSup, 24; Sheffield: JSOT Press, 1983), pp. 135-46.
Battenfield, James R., 'YHWH's Refutation of the Baal Myth through the Actions of Elijah and Elisha', in A. Gileadi (ed.), *Israel's Apostasy and Restoration* (Grand Rapids: Baker Book House, 1988), pp. 19-37.
Baumgartner, W., *Eucharisterion* (Göttingen: Vandenhoeck & Ruprecht, 1923).
Beck, Jonathan, review of *The Pleasures of Reading in an Ideological Age* (New York: Simon & Schuster, 1989), by Robert Alter, in *Diacritics* 21 (1991), pp. 76-90.
Beek, Martinus A., 'The Meaning of the Expression 'the chariots and the horsemen of Israel' (2 Kings ii 12)', in M. Beek (ed.), *The Witness of Tradition* (Leiden: E.J. Brill, 1972), pp. 1-10.
Begg, Christopher T., 'The Chronicler's Non-Mention of Elisha', *BN* 45 (1988), pp. 7-11.
Belsey, Catherine, *Critical Practice* (London: Routledge, 1980).
Bergen, Wesley J., 'The Prophetic Alternative: Elisha and the Israelite Monarchy', in R.B. Coote (ed.), *Elijah and Elisha in Socioliterary Perspective* (Semeia Studies; Atlanta: Scholars Press, 1992), pp. 127-38.
—'Why Are Kings: A Study of Elisha' (STM thesis, St Andrews College, Saskatoon, SK, 1989).
Berlin, Adele, *The Dynamics of Biblical Parallelism* (Bloomington: Indiana University Press, 1985).
—*The Poetics and Interpretation of Biblical Narrative* (Sheffield: Almond Press, 1983).
—'Point of View in Biblical Narrative', in Stephen Geller (ed.), *A Sense of Text* (Winona Lake, IN: Eisenbrauns, 1983), pp. 71-113.
Bernhardt, K.H., 'The Political Situation in the East of Jordan during the Time of King Mesha', in A. Hadidi (ed.), *Studies in the History and Archaeology of Jordan* (London: Routledge & Kegan Paul, 1985), pp. 163-67.
Berquist, Jon L., review of *2 Kings* (FOTL, 10; Grand Rapids: Eerdmans, 1991), by Burke O. Long, *JBL* 112 (1993), pp. 329-30.
Beyerlin, Walter, 'Geschichte und heilsgeschichtliche Traditionsbildung im Alten Testament', *VT* 13 (1963), pp. 1-25.
Bin-Nun, S.R., 'Formulas from Royal Records of Israel and Judah', *VT* 18 (1968), pp. 414-32.
Binns, L.E., *From Moses to Elisha* (Oxford: Clarendon Press, 1929).
Blenkinsopp, J.A., *A History of Prophecy in Israel* (Philadelphia: Fortress Press, 1983).
Bloom, Harold, *The Book of J* (New York: Vintage Books, 1990).
Boling, Robert G., 'In Those Days There Was No King in Israel', in his *A Light Unto my Path* (Philadelphia: Temple University Press, 1974), pp. 33-48.
Bostock, D. Gerald, 'Jesus as the New Elisha', *ExpTim* 92 (1980), pp. 39-41.
Boyarin, Daniel, 'The Politics of Biblical Narratology', *Diacritics* 20.4 (1991), pp. 31-42.
Brams, Stephen J., *Biblical Games: A Strategic Analysis of Stories in the Old Testament* (Cambridge, MA: MIT Press, 1980).

Brichto, Herbert C., *Toward a Grammar of Biblical Poetics: Tales of the Prophets* (New York: Oxford University Press, 1992).
O'Brien, Mark, *The Deuteronomistic History Hypothesis: A Reassessment* (Göttingen: Vandenhoeck & Ruprecht, 1989).
Bright, John, *A History of Israel* (Philadelphia: Westminster Press, 2nd edn, 1972).
Brodie, Thomas Louis, 'Jesus as the New?? Elisha: Cracking the Code', *ExpTim* 93 (1981), pp. 39-42.
Bronner, Leah, *The Stories of Elijah and Elisha* (Leiden: E.J. Brill, 1968).
Brooks, Peter, *Reading for the Plot* (New York: Alfred A. Knopf, 1983).
Brown, Raymond E., 'Jesus and Elisha', *Perspective* 12 (1971), pp. 85-104.
Brueggemann, Walter, *2 Kings* (Knox Preaching Guides; Atlanta: John Knox Press, 1982).
—'The Embarrassing Footnote', *TTod* 44 (1987), pp. 5-14.
—'The Kerygma of the Deuteronomistic Historian', *Int* 22 (1968), pp. 387-402.
—'The Prophet as Destabilizing Presence', in E. Shelp and R. Sunderland (eds.), *The Pastor as Prophet* (New York: Pilgrim, 1985), pp. 49-77.
—'Trajectories in Old Testament Literature and the Sociology of Ancient Israel', *JBL* 98 (1979), pp. 161-85.
Burnett, Fred W., 'Characterization and Reader Construction of Characters in the Gospels', *Semeia* 63 (1993), pp. 1-28.
—'Postmodern Biblical Exegesis: The Eve of Historical Criticism', *Semeia* 51 (1990), pp. 51-80.
Burney, C.F., *Notes on the Hebrew Text of the Book of Kings* (Oxford: Clarendon Press, 1920).
Campbell, A.F., *Of Prophets and Kings* (Washington: Catholic Biblical Association, 1986).
Carlson, R.A., 'Elisée: Le successeur d'Elie', *VT* 20 (1970), pp. 385-405.
Carroll, R.P., 'The Elijah-Elisha Sagas: Some Remarks on Prophetic Succession in Ancient Israel', *VT* 19 (1969), pp. 400-415.
—*When Prophecy Failed: Cognitive Dissonance in the Prophetic Traditions of the Old Testament* (New York: Seabury, 1979).
Chatman, Seymour, *Story and Discourse: Narrative Structure in Fiction and Film* (Ithaca, NY: Cornell University Press, 1978).
Childs, Brevard S., 'On Reading the Elijah Narratives', *Int* 34 (1980), pp. 128-37.
Clements, R.E., 'The Deuteronomistic Interpretation of the Founding of the Monarchy in 1 Samuel VIII', *VT* 24 (1974), pp. 378-410.
—*Isaiah and the Deliverance of Jerusalem: A Study in the Interpretation of Prophecy in the Old Testament* (Sheffield: JSOT Press, 1980).
—*Prophecy and Tradition* (Atlanta: John Knox Press, 1975).
Clevenot, Michel, *Materialist Approaches to the Bible* (trans. William J. Nottingham; Maryknoll, NY: Orbis Books, 1985).
Clines, David J.A., 'The Story of Michal, Wife of David, in its Sequential Unfolding' (paper read at the 1988 Annual Meeting of the Society of Biblical Literature, Chicago).
Coats, G.W., 'The Wilderness Itinerary', *CBQ* 34 (1972), pp. 135-52.
Cogan, Mordechai, 'Israel in Exile: The View of the Josianic Historian', *JBL* 97 (1978), pp. 40-44.
Cogan, Mordechai, and Hayim Tadmor, *II Kings* (AB, 11; Garden City, NY: Doubleday, 1988).
Cohn, Robert L., 'Form and Perspective in 2 Kings V', *VT* 31 (1983), pp. 171-84.

—'The Literary Logic of I Kings 17-19', *JBL* 101 (1982), pp. 333-50.
Conroy, Charles, *1–2 Samuel, 1–2 Kings* (Wilmington, DE: Michael Glazier, 1983).
Coote, Robert B., *Early Israel: A New Horizon* (Minneapolis: Fortress Press, 1990).
Coote, Robert B., and Mary P. Coote, *Power, Politics and the Making of the Bible* (Minneapolis: Fortress Press, 1990).
Coulot, Claude, 'L'investiture d'Elisée par Elie (1 R 19:19-21)', *RSR* 57 (1983), pp. 81-92.
Crenshaw, James L., *Prophetic Conflict: Its Effects upon Israelite Religion* (BZAW, 24; Berlin: W. de Gruyter, 1971).
Cross, F.M., *Canaanite Myth and Hebrew Epic* (Cambridge, MA: Harvard University Press, 1973).
Crossan, John Dominic, *The Historical Jesus* (San Francisco: HarperCollins, 1992).
Culler, Jonathan, *On Deconstruction* (Ithaca, NY: Cornell University Press, 1983).
Culley, Robert C., 'Oral Tradition and the Old Testament: Some Recent Discussions', *Semeia* 5 (1976), pp. 1-33.
—'Punishment Stories in the Legends of the Prophets: Orientation by Disorientation', in *idem, Studies in Literary Criticism* (Pittsburgh: Pickwick Press, 1980), pp. 167-81.
—'Structural Analysis: Is It Done with Mirrors?', *Int* 28 (1974), pp. 165-81.
—*Studies in the Structure of Hebrew Narrative* (Missoula, MT: Scholars Press, 1976).
—*Themes and Variations* (Semeia Studies; Atlanta: Scholars Press, 1992).
Davies, Philip R., *In Search of 'Ancient Israel'* (JSOTSup, 148; Sheffield: Sheffield Academic Press, 2nd edn, 1992).
Davis, D.R., 'The Kingdom of God in Transition: Interpreting 2 Kings 2', *WTJ* 46 (1984), pp. 384-95.
Deist, F., 'Two Miracle Stories in the Elijah and Elisha Cycles and the Function of Legend in Literature', in W. Wyk (ed.), *Studies in Isaiah* (Pretoria: University of Pretoria, 1979), pp. 79-90.
Dietrich, Walter, *Prophetie und Geschichte* (Göttingen: Vandenhoeck & Ruprecht, 1972).
Domeris, William R., 'The Office of the Holy One', *JTSA* 54 (1986), pp. 35-38.
Donaldson, Mara E., *Holy Places Are Dark Places* (Lanham, MD: University Press of America, 1988).
Donner, Herbert, 'The Separate States of Israel and Judah', in J.H. Hayes and J.M. Miller (eds.), *Israelite and Judean History* (Philadelphia: Westminster Press, 1977), pp. 381-434.
Eagleton, Terry, *Literary Theory* (Minneapolis: University of Minnesota Press, 1983).
Eissfeldt, Otto, 'Die Komposition von I Reg. 16,29 - II Reg. 13,25', in F. Maas (ed.), *Das ferne und nahe Wort* (Berlin: Alfred Töpelmann, 1967), pp. 49-58.
Elliott-Binns, Leonard, *From Moses to Elisha* (Oxford: Clarendon Press, 1929).
Ellul, Jacques, *The Politics of God and the Politics of Man* (trans. Geoffrey W. Bromiley; Grand Rapids: Eerdmans, 1972).
Eskenazi, Tamara C., 'Ezra–Nehemiah: From Text to Actuality', in J.C. Exum (ed.), *Signs and Wonders* (Atlanta: Scholars Press, 1992), pp. 165-97.
Eslinger, Lyle, *Into the Hands of the Living God* (JSOTSup, 84; Sheffield: JSOT Press, 1989).
—*Kingship of God in Crisis* (Bible and Literature, 10; Sheffield: Almond Press, 1985).
Exum, J. Cheryl, *Fragmented Women: Feminist (Sub)versions of Biblical Narratives* (JSOTSup, 163; Sheffield: JSOT Press, 1993).
—'Murder They Wrote: Ideology and the Manipulation of the Female Presence in Biblical

Narrative', in Alice Bach (ed.), *The Pleasure of her Text* (Philadelphia: Trinity Press International, 1990), pp. 45-67.
—*Tragedy and Biblical Narrative* (Cambridge: Cambridge University Press, 1992).
—'Whom Will He Teach Knowledge: A Literary Approach to Isaiah 28', in D.J.A. Clines, David M. Gunn and Alan J. Hauser (eds.), *Art and Meaning: Rhetoric in Biblical Literature* (JSOTSup, 19; Sheffield: JSOT Press, 1982), pp. 108-39.
Fewell, Danna Nolan, *Circle of Sovereignty* (JSOTSup, 72; Sheffield: Almond Press, 1988).
—'Introduction: Reading, Writing and Relating', in *idem* (ed.), *Reading between Texts: Intertextuality and the Hebrew Bible* (Louisville, KY: Westminster/John Knox Press, 1992), pp. 11-20.
—'Joshua', in C.A. Newsom and S.H. Ringe (eds.), *The Women's Bible Commentary* (Louisville, KY: Westminster/John Knox Press, 1992), pp. 63-66.
Fewell, Danna Nolan, and David M. Gunn, *Compromising Redemption* (Louisville, KY: Westminster/John Knox Press, 1990).
—*Gender, Power and Promise* (Nashville: Abingdon Press, 1993).
—'Tipping the Balance', *JBL* 101 (1991), pp. 193-211.
Flanagan, James W., *David's Social Drama: A Hologram of Israel's Early Iron Age* (JSOTSup, 73; Sheffield: Almond Press, 1988).
—'The Deuteronomic Meaning of the Phrase "kol yisra'el"', *SR* 6.2 (1976–77), pp. 159-68.
—'Judah in All Israel', in *idem*, *No Famine in the Land* (Missoula, MT: Scholars Press, 1975), pp. 101-16.
Fohrer, Georg, *Die Propheten des Alten Testaments* (Gütersloh: Gerd Mohn, 1977).
Fokkelman, J.P., *Narrative Art in Genesis* (Assen: Van Gorcum, 1975).
—*Narrative Art and Poetry in the Book of Samuel*. I. *King David* (Assen: Van Gorcum, 1981).
—*Narrative Art and Poetry in the Book of Samuel*. II. *The Crossing Fates* (Assen: Van Gorcum, 1985).
Foucault, Michel, *The Archaeology of Knowledge* (trans. A.M. Sheridan Smith; San Francisco: Harper Torchbooks, 1972).
—*Power/Knowledge* (ed. Colin Gordon; New York: Pantheon Books, 1980).
Fowl, Stephen, 'Texts Don't Have Ideologies' (paper read at the SBL Annual Meeting, San Francisco, November 1992).
Fowler, Roger (ed.), *A Dictionary of Modern Critical Terms* (New York: Routledge & Kegan Paul, 1987).
Frei, Hans, *The Eclipse of Biblical Narrative* (New Haven: Yale University Press, 1974).
Fretheim, Terrence E., *The Deuteronomic History*, (Nashville: Abingdon Press, 1983).
Fricke, K. D., *Das zweite Buch von der Könige* (Stuttgart: Calwer Verlag, 1972).
Friedman, Richard E., *The Exile and Biblical Narrative* (Chico, CA: Scholars Press, 1981).
Frye, Northrop, *The Great Code* (New York: Harcourt Brace Jovanovich, 1982).
—*Words with Power* (New York: Viking, 1990).
Fuchs, Esther, 'The Literary Characterizations of Mothers and Sexual Politics in the Hebrew Bible', in A.Y. Collins (ed.), *Feminist Perspectives on Biblical Scholarship* (Chico, CA: Scholars Press, 1985), pp. 117-36.
—'Status and Role of Female Heroines in the Biblical Narrative', *Mankind Quarterly* 23 (1982), pp. 149-60.
—'Who Is Hiding the Truth', in A.Y. Collins (ed.), *Feminist Perspectives on Biblical Scholarship* (Chico, CA: Scholars Press, 1985), pp. 137-44.

Fussel, Kuno, 'Materialist Readings of the Bible', in W. Schottroff and W. Stegemann (eds.), *God of the Lowly* (Maryknoll, NY: Orbis Books, 1984), pp. 13-26.

Galling, Kurt, 'Der Ehrenname Elisas und die Entrueckung Elias', *ZTK* 53 (1956), pp. 129-48.

Geller, Stephen A., 'Through Windows and Mirrors into the Bible', in *idem*, *A Sense of the Text: The Art of Language in the Study of Biblical Literature* (Winona Lake, IN: Eisenbrauns, 1983), pp. 3-40.

Genette, Gerard, *Narrative Discourse: An Essay in Method* (trans. Jane E. Lewin; Ithaca, NY: Cornell University Press, 1980).

Gerbrandt, Gerald E., *Kingship According to the Deuteronomistic History* (SBLDS, 87; Atlanta: Scholars Press, 1986).

Gesenius' Hebrew Grammar (ed. E. Kautzsch; rev. A.E. Cowley; Oxford: Clarendon Press, 1910).

Glueck, N., *The Other Side of the Jordan* (Cambridge, MA: American Schools of Oriental Research, 1940).

Gottwald, Norman K., *All the Kingdoms of the Earth: Israelite Prophecy and International Relations in the Ancient Near East* (New York: Harper and Row, 1964).

—*The Hebrew Bible: A Socio-Literary Introduction* (Philadelphia: Fortress Press, 1985).

—*The Tribes of Yahweh* (Maryknoll, NY: Orbis Books, 1979).

Graves, Robert, *My Head! My Head!* (New York: A.A. Knopf, 1925).

Gray, John, *I and II Kings* (OTL; Philadelphia: Westminster Press, 2nd edn, 1970).

Greenstein, Edward L., 'Biblical Narratology', *Prooftexts* 1 (1981), pp. 201-208.

Gressmann, Hugo, *Die älteste Geschichtsschreibung und Prophetie Israels* (Göttingen: Vandenhoeck & Ruprecht, 2nd edn, 1921).

Gros Louis, Kenneth R.R., 'Elijah and Elisha', in *idem* (ed.), *Literary Interpretations of Biblical Narratives* (Nashville: Abingdon Press, 1974), pp. 177-90.

Grottanelli, Cristiano, 'Healers and Saviors of the Eastern Mediteranean in Pre-Classical Times', in U. Bianchi and M. Vermaseren (eds.), *La soteriologia dei culti* (Leiden: E.J. Brill, 1982), pp. 649-70.

Gunkel, Hermann, *Elias, Jahve und Baal* (Religionsgeschichtliche Volksbücher, 2.2; Tübingen: Mohr Siebeck, 1906).

—'Elisha: The Successor to Elijah (2 Kings ii.1-18)', *ExpTim* 41 (1929), pp. 182-86.

—*Geschichten von Elisa* (Meisterwerke hebräischen Erzählungskunst, 1; Berlin: Karl Curtius, 1925).

—'Ziele und Methoden der Erklärung des Alten Testaments', in *idem*, *Reden und Aufsätze* (Göttingen: Vandenhoeck & Ruprecht, 1913), pp. 10-36.

Gunn, David M., 'Reading Right: Reliable and Omniscient Narrator, Omniscient God, and Foolproof Composition in the Hebrew Bible', in D.J.A. Clines, S.E. Fowl and S.E. Porter (eds.), *The Bible in Three Dimensions: Essays in Celebration of Forty Years of Biblical Studies in the University of Sheffield* (JSOTSup, 87; Sheffield: JSOT Press, 1990), pp. 53-64.

—'Samson of Sorrows: An Isaianic Gloss on Judges 13-16', in D. N. Fewell (ed.), *Reading between Texts: Intertextuality and the Hebrew Bible* (Louisville, KY: Westminster/ John Knox Press, 1992), pp. 225-56.

Gunn, David M., and Danna Nolan Fewell, *Narrative in the Hebrew Bible* (Oxford: Oxford University Press, 1993).

Haag, E., 'Die Himmelfahrt des Elias nach 2 Kg 2, 1-15', *TTZ* 78 (1969), pp. 18-32.

Habel, Norman C., *Yahweh Versus Baal* (New York: Twayne, 1964).

Hagan, G. Michael, 'First and Second Kings', in L. Ryken and T. Longman, III (eds.), *A Complete Literary Guide to the Bible* (Grand Rapids: Zondervan, 1993), pp. 182-92.
Hallevy, Raphael, 'Man of God', *JNES* 17 (1958), pp. 237-44.
Halpern, Baruch, 'Doctrine by Misadventure: Between the Israelite Source and the Biblical Historian', in R.E. Friedman (ed.), *The Poet and the Historian* (Chico, CA: Scholars Press, 1983), pp. 41-74.
—*The First Historians: The Hebrew Bible and History* (San Francisco: Harper and Row, 1988).
Haran, Menahem, 'From Early to Classical Prophecy: Continuity and Change', *VT* 27 (1977), pp. 385-97.
Hayes, John H., and Paul K. Hooker, *A New Chronology for the Kings of Israel and Judah* (Atlanta: John Knox Press, 1988).
Heller, Jan, 'Drei Wundertaten Elisas', *Communio Viatorum* 2 (1959), pp. 83-85.
Hentschel, G., 'Die Propheten Elija, Micha und Elischa', in G. Wallis (ed.), *Von Bileam bis Jesaja* (Berlin: Evangelische Verlagsanstalt, 1984), pp. 64-83.
Herzog, C., and M. Gichon, *Battles of the Bible* (Hindhead, Surrey: Soncino, 1978).
Hill, Scott D., 'The Local Hero in Palestine in Comparative Perspective', in R.B. Coote (ed.), *Elijah and Elisha in Socioliterary Perspective* (Semeia Studies; Atlanta: Scholars Press, 1992), pp. 37-74.
Hobbs, T.R., *2 Kings* (WBC; Waco, TX: Word Books, 1985).
—'2 Kings 1 and 2: Their Unity and Purpose', *SR* 13 (1984), pp. 327-34.
Hoffmann, H.-D., *Reform und Reformen: Untersuchung zu einem Grundthema der deuteronomistischen Geschichtsschreibung* (Zürich: Theologischer Verlag, 1980).
House, Paul R., *1 2 Kings* (Nashville: Broadman and Holman, 1995).
Huizinga, J., 'A Definition of the Concept of History', in R. Klibansky (ed.), *Philosophy and History: Essays Presented to Ernst Castiver* (New York: Harper & Row, 1963), pp. 1-10.
Jacobus, Mary, *Reading Women* (New York: Columbia University Press, 1986).
Jameson, Fredric, *The Political Unconscious* (Ithaca, NY: Cornell University Press, 1981).
Jenks, Alan W., *The Elohist and Northern Israelite Traditions* (Missoula, MT: Scholars Press, 1977).
Jepsen, Alfred, 'Gottesmann und Prophet', in idem, *Probleme Biblischer Theologie* (Munich: Chr. Kaiser Verlag, 1971), pp. 171-82.
—*Die Quellen des Königsbuches* (Halle: Max Niemeyer, 1956).
Jeremias, J., *Kultprophetie und Gerichtsverkundigung in der späten Königzeit Israels* (WMANT, 35; Neukirchen–Vluyn: Neukirchener Verlag, 1970).
Jirku, Anton, *Von Jerusalem nach Ugarit: Gesammelte Schriften* (Graz: Akademische Druck- und Verlagsanstalt, 1966).
Jobling, David, 'Deconstruction and the Political Reading of Biblical Texts', *Semeia* 59 (1992), pp. 95-128.
—'Feminism and "Mode of Production" in Ancient Israel', in D. Jobling, P.L. Day and G.T. Sheppard (eds.), *The Bible and the Politics of Exegesis* (Cleveland: Pilgrim Press, 1991), pp. 239-52.
—'Forced Labor: Solomon's Golden Age and the Question of Literary Representation', *Semeia* 54 (1991), pp. 57-76.
—'Hannah's Desire', *Bulletin of the Canadian Society of Biblical Studies* 53 (1994), pp. 19-32.
—'Mieke Bal on Biblical Narrative', *Religious Studies Review* 17.1 (1991), pp. 1-10.

—*The Sense of Biblical Narrative* (JSOTSup, 7; Sheffield: JSOT, 1986).
—*The Sense of Biblical Narrative II: Structural Analysis in the Hebrew Bible* (JSOTSup, 39; Sheffield: JSOT Press, 1986).
—'Writing the Wrongs of the World', *Semeia* 51 (1990), pp. 81-118.
Johnson, Barbara, *The Critical Difference: Essays in the Contemporary Rhetoric of Reading* (Baltimore: The Johns Hopkins University Press, 1980).
Jones, Gwilym H., *1 and 2 Kings* (NCBC; Grand Rapids: Eerdmans, 1984).
Josipovici, Gabriel, *The Book of God: A Response to the Bible* (New Haven: Yale University Press, 1988).
Kilian, R., 'Die Toterweckungen Elias und Elisas—eine Motivwanderung?', *BZ* 10 (1966), pp. 44-56.
Koch, Klaus, *The Growth of the Biblical Tradition* (trans. S.M. Cupitt; New York: Charles Scribner's Sons, 1969).
—'Das Prophetenschweigen des deuteronomistischen Geschichtswerks', in *idem*, *Die Botschaft und die Boten* (Neukirchen–Vluyn: Neukirchener Verlag, 1981), pp. 115-28.
Kort, Wesley, *Story, Text and Scripture* (University Park, PA: Pennsylvania State University Press, 1988).
Krummacher, Fredrich Wilhelm, *Elisha* (London: Warren, n.d.).
Kuenen, Abraham, *Historisch-Kritische Einleitung in die Bücher des Alten Testaments* (trans. T. Weber; Leipzig: Otto Schulze, 1887).
LaBarbera, Robert, 'The Man of War and the Man of God: Social satire in 2 Kings 6:8-7:20', *CBQ* 46 (1984), pp. 637-51.
Lang, Bernard, 'The Social Organization of Peasant Poverty in Biblical Israel', in *idem*, *Anthropological Approaches to the Old Testament* (Philadelphia: Fortress Press, 1985), pp. 83-99.
Lasine, Stuart, 'Jehoram and the Cannibal Mothers (2 Kings 6:24-33): Solomon's Judgment in an Inverted World', *JSOT* 50 (1991), pp. 27-53.
Lategan, Bernard C., and Willem S. Vorster, *Text and Reality: Aspects of Reference in Biblical Texts* (Philadelphia: Fortress Press, 1985).
Lelchuk, Alan, 'II Kings', in D. Rosenberg (ed.), *Congregation* (New York: Harcourt Brace Jovanovich, 1987), pp. 135-43.
Lemaire, Andre, 'Gehazi et les "Hauts Faits D'Elisée": Remarques sur l'histoire de la redaction des cycles d'Elie et d'Elisée', in J.J. Alder (ed.), *Haim M.I. Gevaryahu Memorial Volume* (Jerusalem: World Jewish Bible Centre, 1990), pp. 41-52.
—'Joas, roi d'Israel et la première redaction du cycle d'Elisée', in C. Brekelmans (ed.), *Pentateuchal and Deuteronomistic Studies* (Leuven: Leuven University Press, 1990), pp. 245-54.
Lemke, Werner, 'The Way of Obedience: 1 Kings 13 and the Structure of the Deuteronomistic Historian', in F.M. Cross *et al.* (eds.), *Magnalia Dei* (Garden City, NY: Doubleday, 1976), pp. 301-26.
Licht, J., *Storytelling in the Bible* (Jerusalem: Magnes Press, 1978).
Lindars, Barnabas, 'Elijah, Elisha and the Gospel Miracles', in C.F.D. Moule (ed.), *Miracles* (London: Mowbrays, 1965), pp. 63-79.
Liver, J., 'The Wars of Mesha, King of Moab', *PEQ* 99 (1967), pp. 14-31.
Long, Burke O., 'The 'New' Biblical Poetics of Alter and Sternberg', *JSOT* 51 (1991), pp. 71-84.

—'2 Kings', in J.L. Mayes (ed.), *Harper's Bible Commentary* (San Francisco: Harper & Row, 1988), pp. 323-41.
—*2 Kings* (FOTL, 10; Grand Rapids: Eerdmans, 1991).
—'2 Kings 3 and the Genres of Prophetic Narrative', *VT* 23 (1973), pp. 337-48.
—'Artistry in Hebrew Historical Narrative: Observations on 1–2 Kings', in *Proceedings of the Eighth World Congress of Jewish Studies* (Jerusalem: World Union of Jewish Studies, 1982), pp. 29-34.
—'A Figure at the Gate: Readers, Readings and Biblical Theologians', in G. Tucker *et al.* (eds.), *Canon, Theology and Old Testament* (Philadelphia: Fortress Press, 1988), pp. 166-86.
—'Historical Narrative and the Fictionalizing Imagination', *VT* 35 (1985), pp. 405-16.
—'II Kings 3: An Oracular Fulfillment Narrative', in *Society of Biblical Literature Seminar Papers* (Missoula, MT: Scholars Press, 1971), pp. 183-205.
—'Prophetic Authority as Social Reality', in G.W. Coats and B.O. Long (eds.), *Canon and Authority: Essays in Old Testament Religion and Theology* (Philadelphia: Fortress Press, 1977), pp. 3-20.
—'The Shunammite Woman: In the Shadow of the Prophet?', *BR* 7 (1991), pp. 12-19, 42.
—'The Social Setting for Prophetic Miracle Stories', *Semeia* 3 (1975), pp. 46-63.
—'The Social World of Ancient Israel', *Int* 37 (1982), pp. 243-55.
Lundbom, J.R., 'Elijah's Chariot Ride', *JJS* 24 (1973), pp. 39-50.
Mayes, A.D.H., *The Story of Israel between Settlement and Exile* (London: SCM Press, 1983).
Marcus, David, *From Balaam to Jonah: Anti-Prophetic Satire in the Hebrew Bible* (BJS, 301; Atlanta: Scholars Press, 1995).
McCarthy, D.J., 'II Samuel 7 and the Structure of the Deuteronomistic History', *JBL* 84 (1965), pp. 131-38.
—'The Wrath of Yahweh and the Structural Unity of the Deuteronomistic History', in J.L. Crenshaw (ed.), *Essays in Old Testament Ethics* (New York: Ktav, 1974), pp. 97-110.
McConville, J.G., 'Narrative and Meaning in the Books of Kings', *Bib* 70 (1983), pp. 31-49.
McCracken, David, 'Character in the Boundary: Bakhtin's Interdividuality in Biblical Narratives', *Semeia* 63 (1993), pp. 29-42.
McKenzie, Steven L., 'The Prophetic History and the Redaction of Kings', *Hebrew Annual Review* 9 (1985), pp. 203-20.
Miller, J. Maxwell, 'The Elisha Cycle and the Accounts of the Omride Wars', *JBL* 85 (1966), pp. 441-54.
Miller, J. Maxwell and John H. Hayes, *A History of Ancient Israel and Judah* (Philadelphia: Westminster Press, 2nd rev. edn, 1986).
Miller, Patrick D., 'The Divine Council and the Prophetic Call to War', *VT* 18 (1968), pp. 105-106.
Miscall, Peter D., *1 Samuel* (Bloomington: Indiana University Press, 1986).
—'Elijah, Ahab and Jehu: A Prophecy Fulfilled', *Prooftexts* 9 (1989), pp. 73-83.
—*Isaiah* (Readings: A New Biblical Commentary; Sheffield: JSOT Press, 1993).
—*The Workings of Old Testament Narrative* (Philadelphia: Fortress Press, 1983).
Montgomery, J.A., 'Archival Data in the Book of Kings', *JBL* 53 (1934), pp. 46-52.
—*A Critical and Exegetical Commentary on the Books of Kings* (ICC; Edinburgh: T. & T. Clark, 1951).

Bibliography

Moore, Rick Dale, *God Saves: Lessons from the Elisha Stories* (JSOTSup, 95; Sheffield: JSOT Press, 1990).
Moore, Stephen D., *Literary Criticism and the Gospels* (New Haven: Yale University Press, 1989).
Mosala, Itumeleng, *Biblical Hermeneutics and Black Theology in South Africa* (Grand Rapids: Eerdmans, 1989).
Mullahy, Patrick, 'A Theory of Interpersonal Relations and the Evolution of Personality', in Harry S. Sullivan, *Conceptions of Modern Psychiatry* (New York: W.W. Norton & Co., 1940), pp. 493-94.
Mullen, E.T., *Narrative History and Ethnic Boundaries* (Semeia Studies; Atlanta: Scholars Press, 1993).
—'The Royal Dynastic Grant to Jehu and the Structure of the Book of Kings', *JBL* 107 (1988), pp. 193-206.
Nelson, Richard D., 'The Anatomy of the Book of Kings', *JSOT* 40 (1988), pp. 39-48.
—*The Double Redaction of the Deuteronomistic History* (JSOTSup, 18; Sheffield: JSOT Press, 1981).
—*First and Second Kings* (Interpretation; Atlanta: John Knox Press, 1987).
—'God and the Heroic Prophet', *Quarterly Review* 9 (1989), pp. 93-105.
Nicholson, E.W., *Preaching to the Exiles* (Oxford: Basil Blackwell, 1970).
Noth, Martin, *The Deuteronomistic History* (JSOTSup, 15; Sheffield: JSOT Press, 1981).
Overholt, Thomas W., *Channels of Prophecy: The Social Dynamic of Prophetic Activity* (Minneapolis: Fortress Press, 1989).
—'Seeing Is Believing: The Social Setting of Prophetic Acts of Power', *JSOT* 23 (1982), pp. 3-31.
Parzen, Herbert, 'The Prophets and the Omri Dynasty', *HTR* 30 (1940), pp. 69-96.
Patte, Daniel, and Aline Patte, *Structuralist Exegesis* (Philadelphia: Fortress Press, 1978).
Peckham, Brian, *The Composition of the Deuteronomistic History* (HSM, 35; Atlanta: Scholars Press, 1985).
—*History and Prophecy* (New York: Doubleday, 1993).
Petersen, David L., *The Roles of Israel's Prophets* (JSOTSup, 17; Sheffield: JSOT Press, 1981).
Phillips, Gary A., 'Exegesis as Critical Praxis: Reclaiming History and Text from a Postmodern Perspective', *Semeia* 51 (1990), pp. 7-50.
Polzin, Robert, *David and the Deuteronomist* (Bloomington: Indiana University Press, 1992).
—*Moses and the Deuteronomist* (New York: Seabury, 1980).
—*Samuel and the Deuteronomist* (San Francisco: Harper & Row, 1989).
Porter, J. Roy., 'The Succession of Joshua', in J.I. Durham and J.R. Porter (eds.), *Proclamation and Presence* (Atlanta: John Knox Press, 1970), pp. 102-32.
Porter, Joshua R., 'Bene-Hanabi'im', *JTS* 32 (1981), pp. 423-29.
—'The Origins of Prophecy in Israel', in R. Coggins, A. Phillips and M. Knibb (eds.), *Israel's Prophetic Traditions* (Cambridge: Cambridge University Press, 1982), pp. 12-31.
Prince, Gerald, *Narratology: The Form and Function of Narrative* (The Hague: Mouton, 1983).
Provan, I.W., *Hezekiah and the Book of Kings* (Berlin: W. de Gruyter, 1988).
—*1 and 2 Kings* (NIBC; Peabody, MA: Hendrickson, 1995).

Rad, Gerhard von, 'The Deuteronomic Theology of History: 1 and 2 Kings', in *idem*, *The Problem of the Hexateuch and Other Essays* (London: Oliver & Boyd, 1966), pp. 208-12.
—*Genesis* (OTL; Philadelphia: Westminster Press, 1972).
—*God at Work in Israel* (trans. John H. Marks; Nashville: Abingdon Press, 1980).
—'Naaman: A Critical Retelling', in *idem*, *God at Work in Israel* (Nashville: Abingdon Press, 1980), pp. 47-57.
—*Old Testament Theology*, II (trans. D.M.G. Stalker; New York: Harper & Row, 1965).
Rehm, Martin, *Das zweite Buch der Könige* (Wurtzburg: Echter Verlag, 1982).
Reiser, Werner, 'Eschatologische Gottessprüche in den Elisa-Legenden', *TZ* 9 (1953), pp. 321-38.
Renteria, Tamis Hoover, 'The Elijah/Elisha Stories: A Socio-Cultural Analysis of Prophets and People in Ninth-Century B.C.E. Israel', in R.B. Coote (ed.), *Elijah and Elisha in Socioliterary Perspective* (Semeia Studies; Atlanta: Scholars Press, 1992), pp. 75-126.
Richter, Wolfgang, *Die Bearbeitungen des 'Retterbuches' in der deuteronomischen Epoche* (BBB, 21; Bonn: Peter Hanstein, 1964).
Ricoeur, Paul, *Essays on Biblical Interpretation* (ed. Lewis S. Mudge; Philadelphia: Fortress Press, 1985).
—*Interpretation Theory* (Fort Worth, TX: Texas Christian University Press, 1976).
—'Interpretive Narrative', in R. Schwartz (ed.), *The Book and the Text* (Oxford: Basil Blackwell, 1990), pp. 237-57.
—'The Narrative Function', *Semeia* 13 (1978), pp. 177-202.
Robertson, D., 'Micaiah ben Imlah: A Literary View', in R. Polzin and E. Rothman (eds.), *The Biblical Mosaic* (Chico, CA: Scholars Press, 1982), pp. 139-46.
Robinson, J., *The Second Book of Kings* (Cambridge: Cambridge University Press, 1976).
Rofé, A., 'Classes in the Prophetical Stories', in G.W. Anderson (ed.), *Studies on Prophecy* (Leiden: E.J. Brill, 1974), pp. 143-64.
—'The Classification of the Prophetical Stories', *JBL* 89 (1970), pp. 427-40.
—*The Prophetical Stories* (Jerusalem: Magnes Press, 1982).
Rosenbaum, Jonathan, 'Hezekiah's Reform and the Deuteronomistic Tradition', *HTR* 72 (1979), pp. 23-44.
Rowley, H.H., *The Growth of the Old Testament* (London: Hutchinson's University Library, 1950).
Ruprecht, Eberhard, 'Entstehung und zeitgeschichtlicher Bezug der Erzählung von der Designation Hasaels durch Elisa', *VT* 29 (1979), pp. 73-82.
Sanda, A., *Die Bücher der Könige* (Münster: Aschendorffscher Verlag, 1911).
Savran, G., 'The Character as Narrator in Biblical Narrative', *Prooftexts* 5 (1985), pp. 1-17.
Schaefer-Lichtenberger, Christa, '"Josua" und "Elischa": Eine biblische Argumentation zur Begründung der Autorität und Legitimatät des Nachfolgers', *ZAW* 101 (1989), pp. 198-222.
—'Joschua und Elischa: Ideal-Typen von Führerschaft in Israel', in M. Augustin (ed.), *Wünschet Jerusalem Frieden* (New York: Peter Lang, 1988), pp. 273-80.
Schmitt, A., 'Die Toterweckung in 2 Kon 4:8-37', *BZ* 19 (1975), pp. 1-25.
Schmitt, Hans C., *Elisa: Traditionsgeschichtliche Untersuchung zur vorklassischen nordisraelitischen Prophetie* (Gütersloh: Gerd Mohn, 1972).
Schwartz, Regina, 'Introduction: On Biblical Criticism', in *idem* (ed.), *The Book and the Text* (Cambridge, MA: Basil Blackwell, 1990), pp. 1-15.

Schweizer, Harald, *Elischa in den Kriegen: Literaturwissenschaftliche Untersuchung von 2 Kön 3;6,8-6,24-7,20* (SANT, 37; Munich: Kösel, 1974).
Sekine, M., 'Lituratursoziologische Beobachtungen zu den Elisaerzählungen', *AJBI* 1 (1975), 39-62.
Shapiro, Susan E., 'Failing Speech: Post-Holocaust Writing and the Discourse of Postmodernism', *Semeia* 40 (1987), pp. 65-92.
Shields, Mary E., 'Subverting a Man of God', *JSOT* 58 (1993), pp. 59-69.
Skinner, J., *I and II Kings* (Century Bible; Edinburgh: T.C. & E.C. Jack, n.d.).
Slotki, I.W., *Kings* (Hindhead, Surrey: Soncino, 1950).
Smend, Rudolf, 'Der biblische und der historische Elia', in L. Alonso Schökel (ed.), *Congress Volume: Edinburgh 1974* (VTSup, 28.1; Leiden: E.J. Brill, 1975), pp. 167-84.
—'Das Gesetz und die Völker: Ein Beitrag zur deuteronomischen Redaktionsgeschichte', in H.-W. Wolff (ed.), *Probleme biblischer Theologie* (Munich: Chr. Kaiser Verlag, 1971), pp. 494-509.
Smith, Morton, *Palestinian Parties and Politics that Shaped the Old Testament* (New York: Columbia University Press, 1971).
Soggin, J.A., 'Der Entstehungsort des deuteronomischen Geschichtswerkes', *TLZ* 100 (1975), pp. 3-8.
Sternberg, Meir, *The Poetics of Biblical Narrative* (Bloomington: Indiana University Press, 1985).
Stipp, H.-J., *Elischa–Propheten–Gottesmänner?* (St Ottilien: EOS Verlag, 1987).
Sullivan, Harry S., *Conceptions of Modern Psychiatry* (New York: W.W. Norton, 1940).
Thiel, Winfried, 'Sprachliche und thematische Gemeinsamkeiten nordisraelitischer Propheten-Überlieferungen', in J. Zmijewski (ed.), *Die alttestamentliche Botschaft als Wegweisung* (Stuttgart: Verlag Katholischer Bibelwerk, 1990), pp. 359-76.
Timm, Stefan, *Die Dynastie Omri: Quellen und Untersuchung zur Geschichte Israels im 9. Jahrhundert vor Christus* (FRLANT, 124; Göttingen: Vandenhoeck & Ruprecht, 1982).
Todd, Judith A., 'The Pre-Deuteronomistic Elijah Cycle', in R.B. Coote (ed.), *Elijah and Elisha in Socioliterary Perspective* (Semeia Studies; Atlanta: Scholars Press, 1992), pp. 1-36.
Trible, Phyllis, *God and the Rhetoric of Sexuality* (Philadelphia: Fortress Press, 1978).
—*Texts of Terror* (Philadelphia: Fortress Press, 1984).
Tucker, Gene, *Form Criticism and the Old Testament* (Philadelphia: Fortress Press, 1971).
Uspensky, Boris, *A Poetics of Composition* (Berkeley: University of California Press, 1973).
Van Seters, John, *In Search of History: Historiography in the Ancient World and the Origins of Biblical History* (New Haven: Yale University Press, 1983).
Vaux, Roland de, *Ancient Israel: Social Institutions* (New York: McGraw–Hill, 1965).
Veijola, Timo, *Das Königtum in der Beurteilung der deuteronomischen Historiographie* (Helsinki: Suomalainen Tiedeakatemia, 1977).
Voloshinov, V.N., *Marxism and the Philosophy of Language* (New York: Seminar Press, 1973).
De Vries, S.J., *Prophet against Prophet* (Grand Rapids: Eerdmans, 1975).
—*Yesterday, Today and Tomorrow: Time and History in the Old Testament* (Grand Rapids: Eerdmans, 1975).
Wallace, Ronald S., *Elijah and Elisha: Expositions from the Book of Kings* (Edinburgh: Oliver & Boyd, 1957).

—*Readings in 2 Kings* (Edinburgh: Scottish Academic Press, 1996).
Weber, Max, *Ancient Judaism* (trans. Hans H. Gerth and Don Martindale; New York: The Free Press, 1952).
Weinfeld, M., 'Divine Intervention in War in Ancient Israel and in the Ancient Near East', in H. Tadmor and M. Weinfeld (eds.), *History, Historiography and Interpretation* (Jerusalem: Magnes Press, 1983), pp. 121-47.
Weippert, Helga, 'Die "deuteronomitischen" Beurteilungen der Könige von Israel und Juda und das Problem der Redaktion der Königsbucher', *Biblica* 53 (1972), pp. 301-39.
Wellek, R., and A. Warren, *Theory of Literature* (London: Peregrine Books, 3rd edn, 1963).
Westermann, Claus, 'Die Arten der Erzählung in der Genesis', in *Forschung am Alten Testament* (Munich: Chr. Kaiser Verlag, 1964).
White, Hayden, *The Content of the Form* (Baltimore: The Johns Hopkins University Press, 1987).
White, Hugh C., *Narrative and Discourse in the Book of Genesis* (Cambridge: Cambridge University Press, 1991).
—'The Value of Speech Act Theory for Old Testament Hermeneutics', *Semeia* 41 (1988), pp. 41-64.
Whitley, C.F., 'The Deuteronomic Presentation of the House of Omri', *VT* 2 (1952), pp. 137-52.
Wifall, W., *The Court History of Israel* (St Louis: Clayton, 1975).
Williams, James G., *The Bible, Violence and the Sacred* (San Francisco: HarperCollins, 1991).
—'The Prophetic Father', *JBL* 85 (1966), pp. 344-48.
Wilson, Robert R., *Geneology and History in the Biblical World* (New Haven: Yale University Press, 1977).
—'Prophecy and Ecstacy: A Reexamination', *JBL* 98 (1979), pp. 321-37.
—*Prophecy and Society in Ancient Israel* (Philadelphia: Fortress Press, 1980).
—*Sociological Approaches to the Old Testament* (Philadelphia: Fortress Press, 1984).
Wiseman, Donald J., *1 and 2 Kings* (Leicester: Inter-Varsity Press, 1993).
Wolff, Hans-Walter, 'The Kerygma of the Deuteronomic Historical Work', in W. Brueggemann and H.-W. Wolff (eds.), *The Vitality of Old Testament Traditions* (Atlanta: John Knox Press, 1975), pp. 83-100.
—'The Understanding of History in the Prophets', in C. Westermann (ed.), *Essays in Old Testament Hermeneutics* (Atlanta: John Knox Press, 1963), pp. 236-56.
Würthwein, Ernst, *Die Bücher der Könige* (Das Alte Testament Deutsch, 11/2; Göttingen: Vandenhoeck & Ruprecht, 1984).
Yannai, Y., 'Elisha and the Shunammite (II Kings 4:8-37): A Case of Homoeoteleuton, or a Text Emendation by Ancient Masoretes?', in E. Fernandez Tejero (ed.), *Estudios masoreticos* (Madrid: Instituto 'Arias Montano', 1983), pp. 123-35.
Zevit, Ziony, 'Deuteronomistic Historiography in 1 Kings 12–2 Kings 17 and the Reinvestiture of the Israelian Cult', *JSOT* 32 (1985), pp. 57-73.

INDEXES

INDEX OF REFERENCES

BIBLE

Old Testament

Genesis
11.30	20
12.11-13	21
18	21, 98
18.1	55
18.9-15	97
18.23	21
20	21
20.11-13	21
21.2	98
22.1	55, 56
23.19	169
25.19-25	97
25.19	169
25.21	20
26	150
26.2	150
26.3	150
26.5	150
27.37	85
29.31	20
35.27	169
35.29	169
38	24
41	150
41.28-36	150

Exodus
2.22	130
4.1-4	100
4.6	123
7.1	116
8	131
8.1-4	131
8.9	130
8.27	130
9.3	13
11.3	90
12.35	131
15.23-25	107
17.8-13	100
19.15	61
21.2-6	84
21.2	149
22.22	84
23.16	109
23.19	109
27.41	47
29.7	47
29.36	47
32.11	64
32.28	131
34.22	109
34.26	109

Leviticus
2.14	109
10.7	131
13	112
13.44-45	112
19.15	90
21.10	90
23.17	109
23.20	109
25.23-38	38
25.23-25	151
25.23	151

Numbers
5.2	112
10.10	99
11.23	13
12.10	123
18.13	109
20.1	169
27	53
27.18-23	52, 53
27.18	62
28.2	109
28.11	99
28.26	109

Deuteronomy
1.1	38
2.15	13
10.6	169
10.18	84
12	119
12.14	52
15.1-18	149
16–18	53
16.1-8	52
18.10	82
18.15-22	49
18.15	49
18.16	49
18.21-22	49
18.22	49, 75, 174
21.17	62
26.12-15	84
28.47	138

28.52-57	138	13.12	97	*1 Kings*	
31.1	38	15	43	1.3-4	89
		15.1	47	3.13	172
Joshua		15.27-28	50	3.16-28	137
1.12-14	29	16.3	47	4.29-31	50
1.14	29	19	172	9.14	48
2	92	20	99	9.19	50
2.4	92	20.7-8	84	12.24	67
2.5	92	21.10-15	150	13	69, 173
2.9	92	24	50	13.2	173
4.24	13	24.4	50	13.3	173
6	92	24.6	135	13.26	67
7.6-15	64	24.21	50	14.5	100
8	145	25.2	90	14.15-16	171
8.8	67	25.3	90	14.18	67
8.27	67	25.26	101	15.29	67
		26.18	51	16.5-10	55
Judges		27–31	150	16.12	67
2.15	13	28.6	172	16.25-30	55
3.7-11	67	28.15	172	16.25-27	72
3.15-30	79	29.8	51	16.29-30	72
7.15-22	79	30	112	16.31-33	149
9	145			16.34	67
13	97	*2 Samuel*		17–18	43
13.2	20	2.1	135	17	86, 163
19.23	97	3.1	91	17.1	115, 149
		3.38	90	17.2-3	89
1 Samuel		5.10	90	17.5	67
1	97	6.6-8	71	17.8-24	83
1.2	20	7.5	76	17.8-9	89
1.20	100	7.8	76	17.10-11	84
1.27	100	7.9	90	17.12	86, 101
5.6	13	8.1	135	17.14	93
5.9	13	10.1	135	17.15	67
7.13	13	10.5	90	17.16	67, 131
8.5	56	12	43	17.17-24	103
8.14-17	122	12.7	76	17.20	103
8.14	151	12.11	76	17.21	103
8.20	177	13.35	131	17.22	103
9.7-8	117	15.5	91	17.24	103
9.9	117	18.19	91	18	172
9.16	47	19.28	150, 151	18.1	89
10	92, 172	19.33	90	18.12	62
10.5-13	57	21.3	85	18.17-19	89
10.5	75	21.18	135	18.18	149
10.12	75	24.19	131	18.19	48, 172
10.19-20	57	31.1	135	18.24	115
12.15	13			18.36-39	171

Index of References   195

18.36	115		159, 172,	2.13	50
18.37	115, 178		174	2.14-15	50
18.39	48, 115	22.4	73	2.14	13, 49,
18.40	48	22.5-28	73		50, 61,
18.46	13, 89	22.6	74, 145		62, 64, 65
19	47, 53,	22.7	74	2.15	57, 65,
	56, 85,	22.15	75		176
	111, 124,	22.20-23	160	2.16-18	65
	156, 163,	22.38	67	2.16	65
	172	22.51-53	72	2.17	65, 115
19.3	89, 175			2.18	66
19.7-8	89	*2 Kings*		2.19-25	111, 176
19.10	163	1–18	55	2.19-22	66, 108
19.11	49, 62	1	163	2.19	66, 68,
19.14	48, 163	1.2-3	146		177
19.15-18	155, 158,	1.2	156	2.20-21	67
	161	1.3	115	2.21-22	68
19.15-16	49, 111	1.5	115	2.21	67, 68,
19.15	89, 157	1.10	70		175, 177
19.16-18	54	1.12	70	2.22	67, 130,
19.16	47, 52,	1.16	115		175, 177
	163, 175,	1.17-18	55	2.23-25	11, 68
	178	1.17	67	2.23	57, 66,
19.17-18	179	2–9	12, 116		69, 70,
19.17	47, 135,	2	42, 50,		114
	164, 166		51, 55-57,	2.24	13, 70,
19.18	47, 165,		71, 101,		71, 159,
	169, 175		176		175, 177
19.19	49, 94	2.1-18	111, 176	2.25	57, 72,
19.20	50, 51	2.1	56, 57,		124
19.21	50-53, 87,		65, 104	2.42	177
	101	2.2-3	69	3	44, 72,
19.22	53	2.2	57		78, 81,
20	57, 138	2.3	60		83, 162,
20.31	138	2.4-5	61		164, 174,
20.35	42, 57	2.4	57, 101		176
20.38	57	2.5	61, 65	3.1-27	66
20.41	57	2.6-14	57	3.1-3	72, 161
21	138, 151,	2.6	61	3.1	55, 136,
	154	2.7	61		162
21.17-24	151	2.8	50, 61, 65	3.2-3	73, 74
21.17-19	154	2.9-10	62	3.2	45, 72
21.22	178	2.9	61	3.3	45, 72,
21.27-29	138	2.10	63		149
21.27	154	2.11-12	63	3.4–9.24	73
21.28-29	154	2.11	49, 63, 65	3.4-27	111
21.52-53	45	2.12	63, 167	3.4	73
22	73, 78,	2.13-14	64	3.6	72, 177

2 Kings (cont.)

Ref	Pages	Ref	Pages	Ref	Pages
3.8	73, 78, 177	4.9	92	4.42	110
3.9	73, 78	4.10	93	4.43	130, 133, 175, 177
3.10	74	4.11-16	177	4.44	67, 110, 175
3.11	74, 78	4.11	93	5	44, 111
3.13	74, 172, 175	4.12-16	19	5.1-27	66
3.14	153	4.12-15	96	5.1-18	176
3.15	13, 75, 178	4.12-13	94	5.1-7	113
3.16-20	13, 177	4.12	93, 94	5.1	90, 95, 111-13, 115
3.16-19	146	4.13	85, 93, 95, 96, 98, 113, 177, 178	5.2	112, 113, 134, 156
3.16-17	77	4.14	20, 86, 96, 130	5.3	111, 113, 114, 124
3.16	76, 77, 175	4.15-16	94	5.4	114
3.17	76-79	4.15	94	5.5	113, 122, 157
3.18	78	4.16	86, 96-98, 103, 177	5.6	177
3.20	78-80	4.17	97, 98	5.7-8	177
3.21-27	79	4.18-25	99	5.7	103, 113, 114
3.21-26	80	4.20	101	5.8-14	113
3.21-24	79	4.22-23	99	5.8-9	140
3.21	78, 80	4.23	99	5.8	113-16, 120, 156, 157, 178
3.22	78, 80	4.25	99	5.9-19	113
3.23	79, 80	4.27	100, 141	5.9	111
3.24	79, 80	4.28-30	100	5.10	95, 102, 115, 116, 120, 156, 157, 178
3.25	79, 80	4.28	13, 101		
3.26	79-81	4.29	101	5.11	95, 102, 115-17, 152, 178
3.27	13, 78, 80-82, 87, 178	4.30	100, 101		
		4.31	130	5.13	114
4	86, 106, 108, 176	4.32-35	102, 177	5.14	13, 115
		4.33	103, 130, 177	5.15-19	117
4.1-7	66, 83, 111, 176	4.35	13, 103	5.15	115, 118, 119, 128, 152
4.1	84, 86	4.36	103		
4.2	84, 176	4.37	104	5.16	117
4.3	99	4.38-41	60, 66, 104, 111, 176	5.17	118, 119
4.7	84, 86, 110			5.18	119, 120, 143
4.8-37	66, 85, 87, 111, 148, 176	4.38	105, 106, 176		
		4.39	105, 106		
4.8	84, 86, 90, 91, 93, 112, 123, 154	4.40	106, 107, 176		
		4.41	106, 107		
		4.42-44	53, 66, 108, 111, 118, 176		
4.9-10	92				

Index of References

5.19-27	113, 130, 176		133	8.4	149, 152
5.19	113, 120, 121	6.21	132, 133	8.5	148, 149, 152, 153
		6.22	133		
		6.23-24	13, 178	8.6	153
5.20	115, 120, 122	6.23	133-36, 140, 177	8.7-15	155, 176
				8.7	66, 119, 149
5.21	123	6.24–7.20	123, 134, 136	8.8	156
5.22	121, 122				
5.25-27	123	6.24	134-36, 140	8.9	156-58
5.25	122			8.10	157-59, 175, 178
5.26	122, 123	6.25	136, 142, 143	8.11	65, 157, 158
5.27	13, 123, 152	6.26	136, 137, 139, 177	8.12	158, 159, 166
6.1-7	66, 124, 129, 176	6.27	139, 143, 144, 146	8.13	158, 159, 175
6.1	105, 124				
6.3-4	144	6.30	138, 139		
6.3	126, 145, 176	6.31	139, 143, 153	8.14	160
				8.15	160
6.5	144, 176	6.32	124, 140-42	8.16-29	161
6.6-7	13			8.16-24	167
6.6	125, 127, 144, 145, 176	6.33	141, 143, 144, 146	8.16	72, 136, 161, 162
		7.1-20	134	8.17	160
6.7	144	7.1	142-44, 175, 177, 178	8.18	161
6.8–7.20	176			8.19-23	160
6.8-23	123, 127			8.20-22	162
6.8-9	177	7.2	142, 144, 147, 168	8.21	162
6.8	124, 135, 144, 145			8.25-27	162
		7.3	144, 153	8.25	161
6.9-10	144	7.6-7	136, 146	8.26	162
6.9	128, 133, 145, 156	7.6	144, 145, 147	8.27	161
				8.28	161, 162
6.10	156	7.12	177	8.29	161, 162
6.11-13	128	7.16	67, 146, 147	9–13	162
6.12	123, 128, 133, 145, 152, 177		147	9	14, 161, 164, 175
		7.17-20	147		
		7.17	147	9.1-3	162, 177
6.13	124	7.18	147	9.1	35, 161-64, 178
6.14	130	7.20	148		
6.15	130, 145	8	42	9.2	164
6.16	130	8.1-7	176	9.3	175
6.17	63, 130, 145, 167	8.1-6	105, 148	9.7-10	164
		8.1	148, 149, 153, 154, 175	9.7	72, 164, 165
6.18	67, 130, 131, 133			9.11	163, 164
			148-50	9.16	162
6.19-22	132	8.2	148, 150	9.25-26	179
6.20	130, 132,	8.3			

2 Kings (cont.)		14–25	169, 170	22.16-20	173
9.25	165	14	12	22.18	170
9.26	67, 165	14.25	46, 67, 170	22.19	145
9.36	165			22.29	46
10	48	14.26-27	170	23	69
10.6	90	17.6	169	23.2	170, 172, 173
10.10	165	17.7	138		
10.11	90, 179	17.13	12, 171, 172	23.15-18	173
10.17	67, 165, 166, 179	17.16	115	23.16	67, 173
				23.18	173
10.18-27	179	17.18	141, 169	23.27	173
10.18	165	17.23	12, 171, 172	23.29	46
10.21	165			24.2	67, 173
10.30	166	18.19	90		
10.32	158, 166	18.28	90	Amos	
11.17-18	158	19–20	170	7.14	58
12.17-18	166	19	136, 138		
13	155	19.2-7	46, 170	New Testament	
13.2-3	167	19.3	138	Matthew	
13.3	166, 167	19.14-34	170	14.13-21	108
13.5	167	19.15-21	12		
13.10-13	167	19.20	46	Mark	
13.13	167	20.1-11	46	6.35-44	108
13.14-21	12	20.1	170		
13.14-19	72, 169	20.2-6	170	Luke	
13.14	63, 162, 167	20.7	46	4.27	144
		20.8-11	170	5.17-26	120
13.16	168	20.15-18	170	9.12-17	108
13.17	168, 169	20.16-18	46		
13.18	168	20.17	173	John	
13.19	168	21.10-15	171	6.1-14	108
13.20-21	169	22.11-14	172		
13.22-25	166	22.13	46, 170	Talmuds	
13.22-24	169	22.14	173	b. Soṭ.	
13.25	169	22.15	46, 170	46b	69

INDEX OF AUTHORS

Ahlström, G.W. 96, 141, 164
Alter, R. 17, 23, 27, 57, 97, 164
Anderson, G.W. 113
Auld, A.G. 104

Bal, M. 15, 18, 22, 31-35, 41, 96, 128, 170
Bar-Efrat, S. 151
Baumgartner, W. 94
Beek, M.A. 63
Bergen, W.J. 72
Berlin, A. 33, 88
Binns, L.E. 90, 116, 164
Boyarin, D. 19
Brodie, T.L. 108
Brown, R. 62, 108
Brueggemann, W. 132
Burnett, F.W. 88
Burney, C.F. 68, 77

Carlson, R.A. 61, 63, 144
Carroll, R.P. 52
Cogan M. 56, 62, 64, 69, 74, 77, 81, 82, 92, 100, 101, 124, 134, 136, 141, 142, 148, 151, 152, 155, 157-60
Cohn, R.L. 51, 113, 114, 117, 121, 122
Conroy, C. 69, 102
Coulot, C. 50-52
Cowley, A.E. 105
Crossan, J.D. 84
Culler, J. 23
Culley, R.C. 25, 26, 141

Deist, F. 62, 69, 98, 103

Exum, J.C. 28, 83

Fewell, D.N. 24, 25, 29, 30
Flanagan, J.W. 48
Fohrer, G. 85, 93, 100, 105
Freeman, D.N. 81
Fretheim, T.E. 115, 116
Fuchs, E. 91, 96, 97, 102

Galling, K. 63
Genette, G. 33
Ginzberg, L. 62
Gottwald, N.K. 128, 164-66
Gray, J. 56, 58, 60, 68, 75, 81, 85, 91, 93, 95, 100-103, 105, 112, 125, 126, 128, 129, 134, 136, 139, 141-43, 147, 155, 158, 160, 163
Gunkel, H. 52, 55, 59, 63, 117, 118, 120
Gunn, D.M. 19, 24, 25

Haag, E. 55, 62
Hobbs, T.R. 55, 58, 81, 100-103, 107, 113, 122, 126, 134, 139, 142, 145, 154, 158, 160, 164
House, P.R. 11
Huizinga, J. 38

Jobling, D. 30, 56
Jones, G.H. 47, 68, 74, 77, 81, 93, 99, 101, 105, 121-23, 125, 139, 142, 148, 155, 158, 164, 167
Josipovici, G. 26, 27

Kaufmann, Y. 82
Kautzch, E. 105

LaBarbara, R. 128, 130, 131, 136, 137, 141, 143-46
Lasine, S. 137, 138, 140

Liver, J. 73
Long, B.O. 55, 77, 81, 91, 94, 95, 99, 101, 108, 124, 138, 142, 158
Lundbom, J.R. 63

Marcus, D. 11
McCracken, D. 88
Miller, J.M. 72
Miscall, P.D. 20, 22, 23, 36, 49, 54, 164
Montgomery, J.A. 81, 92, 96, 148, 158
Moore, R.D. 117
Moore, S.D. 23, 118, 122, 140, 167
Mullahy, P. 89

Nelson, R.D. 49, 55, 59, 60, 69, 81, 92, 97, 121, 125, 136, 139, 154, 158, 160, 161

Parzen, H. 48
Petersen, D.L. 58, 92
Polzin, R. 151
Porter, J.R. 52, 59
Provan, I. 11

Rad, G. von 112, 113, 118
Rehm, M. 81, 82
Reiser, W. 77
Renteria, T.H. 96, 106
Robinson, J. 93, 99, 107

Rofé, A. 59, 69, 83, 96, 102, 103, 113, 118, 119, 148
Ruprecht, E. 58, 158

Schaefer-Lichtenberger, C. 50, 53
Schmitt, H.-C. 58
Shields, M.E. 87, 96, 97, 102
Slotki, I.W. 89, 102
Smith, M. 59, 60
Sternberg, M. 18, 19, 22, 71, 95, 129
Sullivan, H.S. 89

Tadmor, H. 56, 62, 64, 69, 74, 77, 81, 82, 92, 100, 101, 124, 134, 136, 141, 142, 148, 151, 152, 155, 157-60

Van Seters, J. 38, 88, 164

Wallace, R.S. 11
Weisman, Z. 62
Westermann, C. 91
Wifall, W. 59
Williams, J.G. 58, 60
Würthwein, E. 59, 63, 70, 74, 81, 92, 96, 97, 112, 115, 127, 129, 134, 149
Wyk, W. 62

Yannai, Y. 94